ENGINE SWAPPING
TIPS AND TECHNIQUES

Reprinted by permission of Petersens Publishing Company,
8490 Sunset Boulevard, Los Angeles, California U.S.A.
Reproduction in any manner, in any language,
in whole or in part without prior written permission of
Petersen Publishing Company is expressly prohibited.

ISBN 1 85520 0171

Published by
Brooklands Books with the permission of Petersen Publishing Company

BROOKLANDS BOOKS LTD.
P.O. BOX 146, COBHAM,
SURREY, KT11 1LG. UK
sales@brooklands-books.com

INTRODUCTION

This book has been compiled from various editions of Petersens 'Complete Book of Engine Swapping'. The engine swapping series ran for well over 10 years and is now sadly missed by hot rodders. We are fortunate that Lee Kelley and others in the Petersen publishing team understand our motives and generously allow us to make this information available again for todays enthusiasts. The following introduction by Spence Murray appeared in one of the editions and is as relevant today as when it was written.

R.M. Clarke

If you think that the very root of hot rodding - engine swapping - died out after the advent of the musclecar era, then you haven't looked under some hoods lately. Engine swapping is back, and in a big way. But where motor transplants were formerly in the interests of brute power, swaps today are more often after fuel economy with improved performance only second in the scheme of things.

The bulk of today's swaps are in the interests of practicality: to restore lost performance to older cars (and trucks) and to at least bring to newer cars the power they would have had if things like high fuel prices and the environmentalists hadn't forced Detroit to cut back on cubic inches.

Regulations in some states prohibit engine swaps, or at least limit what you can and can't do in the way of emissions equipment, so would-be swappers had best check their local rules through the department of motor vehicles, the highway patrol, or the Environmental Protection Agency (EPA). But if the bureaucrats give the nod, then get those tools out and plan on a couple of weekends of work.

On the pages that follow are some very interesting swaps, including a few that should warm the hearts of diesel enthusiasts. One noteworthy swap we've tossed in just to show you it can be done, is the installation of a big V6 in place of the little transverse V6 in a GM X-car. Swaps of this nature will become increasingly popular as more and more of the domestic front-drives take to the roads, so we thought we'd break the ice for you.

But there's a lot more to an engine swap than merely replacing one engine with another, and that's why we've tailored chapters to include the why's and wherefore's of cooling systems, brakes, drivelines, transmissions, and, yes, even suspension, exhaust, fuel systems, and more. Almost every conceivable question you might have on a practical swap lies between these covers, so there's no time like the present to roll up your sleeves and get to work.

Spence Murray

DISTRIBUTED BY

Brooklands Books Ltd., P.O. Box 146, Cobham, Surrey, KT11 1LG, England
Phone: 01932 865051 Fax: 01932 868803
Brooklands Books Ltd., 1/81 Darley St., P.O. Box 199, Mona Vale, NSW 2103,
Australia Phone: 2 9997 8428 Fax: 2 9979 5799
CarTech, 39966 Grand Avenue, North Branch, MN 55056, USA
Phone: 800 551 4754 & 651 277 1200 Fax: 651 277 1203
Motorbooks International, P.O. Box 1, Osceola, Wisconsin 54020, USA
Phone: 800 826 6600 & 715 294 3345 Fax: 715 294 4448

CONTENTS

Swapping Strategy

There was a time when engine swapping was considered a passé trend in hot rodding. This was the heyday of the Detroit muscle cars and super cars, and fewer people were doing engine swaps at home or building hot rods because it was easier to just go down to the local dealer and sign for "low down payment and easy monthly terms" on a pre-built hot rod. They were quick, reasonably trouble-free—compared to backyard projects—and could be easily licensed, insured, financed and even warrantied.

But as we all know now, the factory muscle car is dead. The Detroit high-performance car was killed off long ago by the amalgamated forces of the safety "experts," insurance companies, inflation, and federal anti-smog regulations. It used to be that every year cars got faster, with improved engines, but sadly, today's offerings are skyrocketing in price while losing power and driveability with every passing new-car introduction period. We won't belabor the point that new cars don't have the excitement they once did, but it does offer a reason for the current interest in one of the oldest facets of hot rodding, the engine swap. When you can't buy a high-performance car ready-made anymore, the only way to have one is to build it yourself. You'll not only save money, have more performance—and in some cases better fuel economy—but you'll have that sense of personal satisfaction that just can't be purchased at any price.

Economics of Swapping

Time costs money, and as the old performance adage goes, "Speed costs money . . . how fast do you want to go?" An engine swap can cost $300 or $3000 with the placement of the decimal point depending on how difficult the swap is, what engine you select, how much professional time (welders, machinists, etc.) is involved and many other factors. Proper planning beforehand can save you headaches, time, and money if you just envisage the results and foresee the inevitable problems which are attendant upon every swap.

The majority of engine swap-related mail received at HOT ROD Magazine is concerned with replacing a stock 6-cylinder engine, either an in-line or a V, with a later/better V8. Although queries are on the increase on swapping late-model 4's with ditto V6's.

Taking first things first, let's consider the 6-for-an-8 trade. Say the subject is an Anymake '74. The owner may have bought it new or, more likely, picked it up used a couple of years ago. Either way it's probably not too far from the 100,000-mile mark and definitely tired. What should he do? Junk it, or spend some money to rebuild the engine? The car has depreciated to the point that after the first 6 years of ownership, the monthly cost of operation has gone as low as it will ever go. Unfortunately, with a sick engine and a century mark showing on the odometer, the resale or trade-in value of a car is also down about as low as it can go. If the owner we're talking about is really the average person, he'll probably sell the car, trade it in or junk it. But if he wants to continue with low-cost transportation, he'll keep it. It's entirely possible to keep a vehicle

Before running out to buy or otherwise acquire an engine to swap into your car, check the car itself first. A tape measure can save you many a headache. Elsewhere in this book we give most major exterior dimensions of the more popularly-swapped engines.

running indefinitely by continually rebuilding components, but the amount of time spent in repair shops will eventually become a drag, and the owner's ego will have to enter the picture at some point. He's going to get tired of driving in that right-hand lane with his eyes glued to the oil pressure light.

If he is determined to keep the car for inexpensive transportation but would like a little more performance, he still has two choices left. He can rebuild the original engine and add some speed equipment to it, or he can swap in a later V8. Even if he *did sell* the car, the second owner (which could be *you*) would be faced with these same choices.

Rebuilding the 6 and adding a few aftermarket speed shop pieces could bring the cost of the engine to $500-$600 very easily—a lot of money, but it would accomplish what he wanted. Now here's where the economics of swapping comes in. He could easily shop the local wrecking yards and come up with a low-mileage '73 or '74 V8 for the car for around $300-$400, with money left over (compared to the 6 rebuild) for a new transmission, or other parts updating, to go along with the new engine. Now he would not only have reliable motive power for transportation, but much better performance. His ego and his pocketbook would feel a lot better, and he could finally get out of that slow lane. These are the economic considerations of many swaps.

Even in cases where the original engine was in good shape (maybe even a V8 to start with) and the owner just wanted more performance, swapping in a later and more powerful engine is often still cheaper in the long run than modifying the original engine. While the old engine might have lost some reliability and longevity if modified, the new engine

can remain in reliable form because it puts out more power even in stock configuration. This is the beauty of a well-planned swap.

V6's for 4's

As noted, transplants of V6's for late-model 4's are growing (we're speaking here of "conventional" rear-wheel driven cars). Many newer 4-cylinder cars are available with a V6 as an option, so the car is designed to accommodate the beefier engine which makes the swap a snap. But even in the case of models where a V6 is not available from the factory, they'll swallow a V6 without much strain since the engine lengths are generally the same, and under-hood space always has sufficient width for two banks of cylinders.

In such a case, we're not dealing with a worn-out car; many such swaps see '78's and '79's giving up their 4-in-a-row's simply because the owner previously felt the surge of a good power/weight ratio in his older car a few years ago, and wants it back in his downsized-mobile. The tack to take here is to shop the wrecking yards for a low-mileage V6, haul it home, then look around for someone whose same-make 4-banger is on the ragged edge and come to an equitable price agreement for your healthy, near-new motor. While the newer 4's have a pretty good reputation for liveability, there's always *someone* with an out-of-warranty 4 with a serious problem. Whatever he'll give you for your engine will go a long way toward you recouping your investment in the V6.

What to Swap

Of course, not every swap has been done for economic reasons. It's probably safe to say that more rodders make swaps in search of more power and acceleration than for any other factor. Swapping in the past had always been a question of stuffing the largest behemoth possible into your car. But, with the wide variety of efficient, modern V8's Detroit has produced in the last decade and the new V6's of the present decade, an en-

Despite the spelling error, reconditioned engines such as these will usually carry a guarantee, but find out what is guaranteed and for how long. You won't find any odd-engine bargains at a reconditioner; they usually service only the most popular engines on virtually an assembly line basis.

Strategy

You're in luck if you find the engine you want at a wrecking yard and still in its original chassis. If you can hear it run, you'll have a fair idea of what you're buying. Try to be there when the engine is pulled to make sure you get all the little extras to save hassles later on. This engine, being readied for a customer, comes complete with water hoses.

gine swapper can now pack a lot more horsepower into an engine compartment without resorting to the bulk and weight of a Chrysler Hemi. The design progress in passenger-car engines in the past 10 years pays a number of dividends to the engine swapper today.

With the recent advances in thin-wall casting techniques for blocks and heads, to say nothing of lopping two cylinders worth of weight from a V8 to make a V6, engines now weigh a lot less than they used to. This means that the total car weight of the swapped vehicle is lighter, which promotes better handling, performance and economy; and less suspension reworking is necessary to compensate for any extra weight on the front end compared to the original engine.

The "new breed" of Detroit engines also has a whole new image when it comes to their performance in stock form. Despite the years of un-racing and un-sponsorship, a lot of finely honed pieces whose development heritage shows "off-the-road" breeding wind up today in passenger-car engines and dealer parts books.

This high-performance influence isn't felt only by those manufacturers whose engines are used in race cars, either. Efficiency coupled with potency can be found in almost any manufacturer's line of engines, which is good news for the engine swapper today. Formerly, whatever year, make or model of car was the object of an engine swap, the new engine installed was almost always a small-block Chevy V8. Everything from antique cars to Volkswagens and Ferraris have felt the throb of one of Ed

Cole's "mouse" motors, and perhaps rightly so. This engine has been around for 25 years now in various sizes, all with the same characteristically lightweight valvetrain, quick rpm, and over-square design that have made this series of engines famous on and off the road.

Additionally, an incredible array of aftermarket speed equipment is produced for this engine to give you as much horsepower as you could ever want. But what is new to the swapper's dreams is that he no longer has to restrict himself to the Chevy for a good street engine. Just before the cubic-inch downsizing program began, Ford, Chrysler, American Motors, and others had good engines with some of the desirable characteristics of the Chevy engine.

"Family" Swaps

Whatever the make of car you're swapping into, you don't have to make a hybrid out of it by swapping in something from another manufacturer. You can keep your Ford all Ford, your MoPar all MoPar, etc. Such "all in the family" swaps are among the most practical you can undertake, for several reasons. The main thing in your favor with a swap of this type is that everything usually fits much easier when the engine, trans and chassis are all of the same make. This isn't to say that just because the 426 Hemi and the Dodge Colt are made by the same company that they will go together easily. You can put anything into anything if you really want to, but we're assuming that your street machine project doesn't have a Pro Stock budget. Detroit engineers often have to take the future into consideration when they design a vehicle, making accommodations for engines which may not be available in that car for a few years. This is why the early Mavericks and Vegas take a V8 so easily; the possibility of the manufacturer doing this at some point was in the back of the engineers' minds.

Even if a V8 swap wasn't foreseen by the designers, in-the-family swaps are made easier because so many of the components within a particular line are interchangeable. Take Fords, for instance. In various years and models of Fords, the engine's oil

The choice of a car for your swap fodder is as important as the engine. Some uni-body cars like this will be severely weakened if important structural areas have to be cut to give engine space, and heavy restructuring is in store for you.

pan sump is in a different location than on most other cars, which creates a problem either when swapping a Ford into another chassis, or swapping another engine make into a Ford chassis designed for a front-sump engine. Why not just swap a good late Ford engine into your Ford chassis? The two are compatible. The same goes for swapping a MoPar into a MoPar or an Olds into an Olds. Why hassle with expensive oil pan or steering gear modifications if you don't have to?

The family swap also takes advantage of compatible motor mounts, radiator-to-water pump hookups, engine, clutch and transmission matching, and simplicity in the myriad of electrical and linkage connection problems that are usually the main hassle with an engine swap.

Resale value, while not always a concern of the average engine swapper, should be an important factor in planning your swap—and the family swap has advantages in this area also. Let's say you swap a 327 Chevy into an early Maverick, drive it for a year or so and then decide to sell it. Who's going to buy it? You might be able to sell it to someone who's going to race it, but for the street you may have more problems finding a buyer. Since the basic car is a Ford, most Chevy fans wouldn't be interested, and the Ford fans wouldn't be interested because it has a Chevy engine. By the same token, if you had swapped in a late Boss 302, you'd find a ready market among the Ford fans for this "all-Ford" Ford product. Of course, if the swap you're planning involves an older car like a '53 Studebaker, or a car whose manufacturer doesn't make a readily swapable engine, then you're stuck and you'll have to cross breeds.

"Them Furriners"

Don't consider transplanting a foreign gasoline engine (diesels are another matter, and are discussed later) in a domestic chassis; not even if your car needs *any* old engine to get it back up on all fours, and your neighbor has a clapped-out Jaguar, or whatever, with a sound powerplant that he'll *give* you. Not that the folks overseas haven't built some mighty fine engines, they have. But foreign engines are notoriously fussy, temperamental things, requiring imported (read expensive) parts, high-priced servicing and tuning—*if* you can find an agency to service it—and they're just not compatible with our generally heavier cars and long, straight roads where our engines must buzz for hours without letup. An American engine in a foreign chassis, yes; and many are the happy swappers who've dropped Ford and Chevy V8's into Jaguars, Mercedes, *et al.*, V6's into Japanese-built mini-trucks, and the like. But the other way around—don't even consider it, even if the electrics are compatible (or dependable), which most aren't.

Diesel Swaps

There is a small but growing segment of the engine swapping fraternity interested in the improved mpg offered by diesels over gas engines. It cannot be denied that such a swap is on

No matter how badly you want to combine a specific engine with a specific car, don't overlook your resale potential. This 454 Chevy in a Ford Torino makes a great street sleeper, but who would be interested in it and for how much. It wouldn't necessarily appeal to a Ford fan or a Chevy enthusiast.

the expensive side, but with most diesels needing virtually no service for many thousands of miles, and with only a light overhaul at perhaps 100,000 miles, these swaps have merit if you plan on keeping the car for an extended period; providing, too, the chassis and rest of the car will last that far.

But even in the case of a "family swap," an Olds diesel into a formerly gas-powered Olds, for example, your work is cut out for you even though the block bellhousing will bolt to most late Hydramatics. It's with the after-the-engine-is-in work that the real problems begin. Diesels require two 12-volt batteries, so a second one with attendant wiring has to be shoehorned in somewhere. There's a little custom-tailoring of vacuum lines, too; vacuum is supplied by an auxiliary pump since a diesel has no manifold to tap into. Also, the Olds diesel can be up to several hundred pounds heavier than the gas V8 it might be replacing, so front suspension beefing is involved. Yet, such swaps are relatively popular in light of the current fuel picture, so we'll detail a few diesel-into's later in the book.

Proper Planning

When you come right down to it, it really doesn't take too long to swap an engine. The act of dropping it into the chassis once you have the mounts set up is pretty straightforward. So what's the big deal about an engine swap? If you've ever done one, you know that the real hassles have only begun at that point. It's the hooking up of all the accessories, radiator, clutch linkage, shifter, throttle, etc., that really takes the time and ingenuity. Some swaps take weeks and weeks to finish and never turn out the way the swapper intended; and yet there are other swaps that can be

Strategy

An ideal swap for the newer 4-cylinder cars is the aluminum 215-inch V8 used in the Olds F-85 in 1961, '62 and '63, and also in Buick Specials and Pontiac Tempests. Believe it or not, it outweighs the Vega 4 shown here by only 20 pounds!

done in a week that turn out great with a minimum of problems. The difference in many cases is proper planning before the swap is consummated. Usually the choice of car is a foregone conclusion because the car is on hand; so once you have settled on the engine choice, it's time to use a tape measure.

Don't just worry about the mounts and assume you'll figure the rest of the details out later. A lot of measuring and cardboard mockup work must take place before you ever lower the engine into the chassis—even for a trial fit. Try to plan all the facets of the swap first; it may turn out that the swap just isn't going to be as practical as you thought. It's good to find this out before you have the engine in the car and you're committed.

Try to plan for all the expenses involved, with an eye to your own budget, and then add at least 20 percent on general principles. If you figure by all rights that the swap will cost $400, then it'll probably top out close to $500 or $600 when you're done. Murphy's Law ("if something *can* go wrong, it *will* go wrong") must have been written by a hot rodder, because this law always seems to apply to engine swaps. If you can remember the rule that "there is no such thing as a bolt-in engine swap," you'll keep yourself aware of the many irritating little problems that can crop up. A typical situation would be swapping an engine with a tight compartment and an equally tight budget. You have everything (you think) painted, detailed and hooked up; it's ready to fire when you realize that you've left no room for an oil filter, and all your money is spent so you can't afford a custom remote oil filter setup. Planning!

Engine Shopping

Naturally, before you can complete your well-planned engine swap, you've got to obtain said engine. Judging by the number of letters

we get on this subject, the procedure isn't known to all hot rodders. Unless you're lucky enough to have a well-padded wallet or a relative who owns a car agency, you'll wind up buying a used engine like the rest of us. A new engine right out of the crate would be ideal, of course, but many dealers don't like to handle unusual orders, and brand new motors cost anywhere from $1000 to well over $1500—usually *without* such expensive accessories as carburetor, alternator, starter, fan or air cleaner.

It would be safe to say that nine out of ten engines used in swaps come from wrecking yards. The others come from stolen cars, and unless you think a steel suite at the "Hotel Greybar" is a comfortable place to spend a few years, we'd advise strongly against buying any engines from the "midnight auto supply" sources. Not only do law enforcement agencies have a number of tricks for identifying stolen engines and parts, but you're helping to protect yourself and other automotive enthusiasts when you either actively or passively do what you can to help stop "Otto Ripoff."

It's possible to purchase an engine as a rebuilt or overhauled unit, either complete or as a short-block, from a shop or engine rebuilding company. Find one listed in your Yellow Pages and check out the prices. It may be a good deal in your area. Usually, though, buying a rebuilt or overhauled engine outright without turning in an old engine as a core means that you have to pay a core charge, and the price of the rebuild plus the core charge might be more than you're willing to pay. There's a big difference, too, between a "rebuilt" and an "overhauled" engine. A rebuilt or "remanufactured" engine is usually done by a factory-authorized rebuilder, and all the parts are remachined or replaced with new ones. In an overhauled engine, only obvious steps like rings, valve grind and bearings are taken, so the truly rebuilt engine is going to be more thoroughly done and also more expensive.

There are, however, definite advantages to buy-

Ford's Pintos will swallow anything within reason, though some firewall massaging and, depending on the transmission used, the floor may have to be twiddled with.

ing an engine from a wrecking yard that should not be overlooked, especially since most of you will purchase your swap material from such a source. First of all, you may be searching for an engine that isn't widely available in rebuilding houses, but at the local "auto dismantling establishment" (they don't appreciate the appellation "junkyard"), you could have better luck.

It takes a few years before a new engine will show up in the rebuilding houses, but what with our high accident rate in this country, new engines show up in wrecking yards almost as soon as the new cars come out each fall. In addition, most rebuilding houses deal only in the most popular engines in general service; you'd be hard-pressed to find a Boss 302 or 350 horsepower or 327 Chevy there. Not only is there a better chance of finding an unusual or high-performance engine in a wrecking yard, but most yards in a given geographical area are linked by a teletype system. If the yard you visit doesn't have what you're looking for, the counterman can put your request on the teletype to many other yards to locate your engine.

While it varies from state to state and yard to yard, you can almost always get a guarantee on a used engine from a wrecking yard, if it is a reputable operation. Check with your local Better Business Bureau to see if there have been any complaints against the place, and ask your buddies for recommendations on where to go. Guarantees from wrecking yards vary from the vague to the positive, money-back type. Sometimes it's just a verbal arrangement—but we'd suggest not buying an engine unless there is something in writing on your bill of sale. In some yards, all they will guarantee is that the engine runs, doesn't use oil excessively and doesn't knock. On the other hand, many wrecking yards will give you a 90-day guarantee on all but the most minor of parts like plugs, points, air cleaner, and oil filter. We've purchased engines this way and have always been completely satisfied. Usually the yards that give the best guarantee have good prices, too, because they have a lot of satisfied customers and deal in volume.

When shopping for an engine, beware of the steam-cleaned engine sitting inside the shop or office. It may be no better than the greasy ones out in the yard.

Some yard operators realize that customers want to hear an engine run before closing the deal, so they leave popular engines in the cars until the engines are sold. Check the serial numbers of the engine against a *Motor Manual* or dealer shop manual to be certain that it is indeed the horsepower-model you're looking for. And don't rely on the car's emblems or medallions, the engine you're looking at may itself have been swapped-in. All small-block Chevys from 265-400 cubic inches look pretty much alike on the outside, for instance. Only by checking the block number and a few other telltale signs, as listed in the manual, can you be sure of what vehicle the engine came out of and what version it is.

If the engine is in the chassis and you can hear it run, take a compression check if you're not sure how sound it is. Or even bring along a friend who's a mechanic; he might be able to spot a potential

If you want gobs of torque, don't overlook the late Ford 428. This Cobra-Jet will bring almost anything to life, and it goes especially easy into earlier Ford pickup trucks.

trouble noise, which could save you some grief as you'll have found it before you part with your hard-earned, inflated dollars. Even guaranteed engines can have problems, since the yard operator can't take the time to check out every engine he's got with the proverbial fine-tooth comb. So even if the engine is guaranteed, it's wise to check it carefully before you buy; this will save you an unfortunate hassle if you find out only after installing the engine in your chassis that something's wrong and you have to bring it back to the yard for an exchange.

When you buy an engine from a wrecking yard, try to get them to include as many of the accessories as possible. Things like regulators, wiring, coil, mounts, bolts, and other little goodies can get expensive when you have to buy them separately at a dealership to complete a swap. In many swaps, you'll also be using the transmission that came with the engine, so be sure to get everything that's part of the hookup. The transmission may have a different spline than the one in your car, so get the driveshaft or front yoke when you buy the engine/trans setup. If possible, save the shifter, linkage, cooling lines (if an automatic), flex plate and flywheel bolts, and any vacuum or electrical links to the engine. In fact, if your swap is of the type where you are changing the whole driveline of a car, with new engine, transmission, and rearend, then there's another route you might consider. Just buy a whole *car*.

This may sound a bit extreme, but it can turn out much cheaper when the swap involves more than just an engine change. Let's say you've got a cherry '49 Ford coupe that you'd like to restore and update to modern performance levels. It would make a fine street machine, but if you just dropped in a late engine, you'd have to adapt it to the Ford transmission, and there's no certainty that the original transmission and rearend could take the power of the new engine. And there's also the matter of the switch from 6-volt to 12-volt electrics. Let's further assume that you buy a 327 Chevy engine from a friend for $200. A local wrecking yard furnishes you

Strategy

Transmissions have their reconditioning houses, too. Here's a typical array on a rebuilder's shelves, all freshened up and ready to go, and identified as to their source.

with a 350 Turbo Hydra-matic trans for $175 and a 10-bolt Chevelle rearend for $50, drum-to-drum. Not bad so far; you've only got $425 in the project. But what you *haven't* got are all the little goodies you'll need to make the swap complete—like electrics, mounts, driveshaft, bolts, etc.

Now, assume that instead of buying everything piecemeal, you went to an insurance company auction and bought a wrecked '67 Camaro. Not only do you now wind up with the engine, trans and rearend for less money, but you also get the bucket seats, floor shift, wiring harness, 12-volt battery, 12-volt horn, wipers, headlights, heater motor, radio, bolts, wheels, radiator and more. You could even adapt the Camaro power steering and power brakes if you wanted.

Of course, you'd have a stripped Camaro hulk in your yard when it was all over; but with the price of scrap metal as high as it is today, you might even make some money on the hulk by cutting it up with a torch and truckin' the pieces down to the local scrap yard! In swaps where the vehicle is an older model that needs changing in more than one department, buying a complete car to swap drivelines with can be to your advantage in saving money, hassles and time spent chasing down small parts.

Legal Hassles

One of the less pleasurable legacies of the VW-powered dune buggy fad are some very strict laws concerning engines and engine numbers. Because hot VW motors have wound up in a lot of dune buggies, the result we now face is

that insurance companies and state inspectors cast a scrutinizing eye on *any* kind of engine swap. First of all, be absolutely certain that you get a legal bill of sale for any engine or drivetrain part that you buy for your swap; and this applies to parts that you buy from friends, too. If the parts in question aren't hot, the seller shouldn't have any objections to signing a bill of sale. A final touch of authority on any bills of sale you sign would be to have them notarized at a local notary public.

In some states, a car's engine number as well as the car identification number is on the registration papers. If this is the case in your state, then you should go about getting this number changed when you do an engine swap, to keep everything legal. Also, your insurance company may have records that include the engine number, so contact them and tell them the number of your new engine. If you think that telling them about your engine swap may up your rates, you could keep the fact to yourself; but if there were an accident, they might find out you had a different engine and hassle you about it—or even claim that this contributed to the accident.

Emissions equipment is another hassle to be reckoned with in legalizing an engine swap. In some states, emissions requirements are based on the year of the car, in which case you can swap in any year engine you want and only have the smog equipment required for your year car. For example, maybe your '55 Chevy is only required to have a PCV system; in this case, you could swap in a '73 LT-1 motor and not have to run a smog pump or TCS—or any other system beyond the PCV. In many other states, however, the requirements are based on the year of the engine, which means that your LT-1-powered '55 would have to have all the emissions equipment required on the '73 car that your

Older passenger cars make neat swap material; they usually have more than sufficient engine space for even the biggest V8's, and add years of fun/use to the car in question. This '56 Ford is undergoing a 302 Ford transplant.

Those older Chevy pickups, and most later ones, too, offer maximum under-hood space. Even this tall Edelbrock manifold on a whopping 454 Chevy rat motor has hood clearance, and getting at the spark plugs is a snap.

engine came from. If you've done a particularly nice job on the swap, you can take your chances that the inspector won't know you've swapped engines, but this is risky. Our best advice to you on the legal aspects of swapping, just as with any other aspect, is to take everything into consideration before you swap—and *always* plan ahead.

And, in Closing

Before we leave the engine swapping strategy story there are a few words to be said about our new front-drive cars. As we all know, they're coming out of Detroit like there's no tomorrow, and there probably wouldn't be an automotive tomorrow if the manufacturers weren't bowing to government mandates for fuel-efficiency through downsizing. Most major car builders now offer the little front-drives, and even more are coming. It isn't improbable, then, that some enterprising hot rodder will engineer a fore/aft-mounted engine driving the rear wheels in "conventional" car style. But early examples will undoubtedly be strictly for the quarter-mile. We wouldn't advise you or anyone else who wants to build a street machine out of a GM X-Car, a Chrysler K-Car, or whatever, by substituting a big V6 or even bigger V8 to power the car conventionally. The front-drives just aren't engineered for this. To convert one will be a major challenge, far beyond the definition of an engine swap.

In the not-too-distant future, there'll be enough of a diversity of front-drive cars running around that engine swapping (which in many cases will include transaxle and drive components swapping) will be realistic. For the time being, though, if you bought, say, a 4-cylinder Pontiac Phoenix for the economy it promised but now you wish you had a little more spunk, you could substitute the optional V6 since the hardware is interchangeably compatible. But for now, you'd be money ahead to simply trade in your present car for either a used or new one with the V6 already factory installed.

Engine Mounts and Adapters

Outside of starting your swapped engine for the first time, the excitement comes after you've made the engine and transmission mounts, and you're lowering your engine into its new home for the final time.

Although it may seem like a gargantuan task to the novice, construction of new engine and transmission mounts for an engine swap is really one of the easiest jobs in the whole conversion, but not one to be taken lightly. The success of the swap may very well depend on how strong and practical you make these mounts.

Among the factors you have to consider are the weight of the new engine compared to the old one, how the new mounts will handle the torque reactions of the engine, and how to construct them so as not to interfere with other critical parts such as steering linkage. After your initial measurements and trial-fittings, the engine and transmission mounts are the first hurdles of your swap; in some cases it will be an easy hurdle and in others a challenge to your abilities.

According to the type of swap you're doing and its degree of difficulty, you have four choices for mounts: you can build them yourself, have them built at a professional swap shop or welding shop, utilize pre-made mounts available from a number of firms for popular swaps, or use factory mounts for the same engine but a different application. Trying to determine exactly what kind of mount to use is the bane of all swappers, professional and amateur alike. The professional will approach the problem from a slightly different angle, usually.

First, the stock motor mount registered with (bolted to) the engine should be used if at all possible, since these mounts contain insulation properties felt necessary by the manufacturer for that engine. They may be stiff to control excessive engine vibrations, or soft to allow absorption of engine torque. Whatever the construction, they will bolt directly to the engine block and should be the beginning point in all considerations.

The mount from the engine insulator to the frame is where the special fabrication may be necessary. As an example, take the swap which puts an Oldsmobile engine into a Thunderbird. The T-Bird has a front single-point mount ahead of the engine, while the Olds engine has central mounts on either side of the block. A front mount could be made, of course, but then it would not include the original Olds insulators. Instead, short mounts are fabricated to come off the frame rails on either side, and the engine never knows what kind of chassis it's in.

It's often quite possible to find more suitable insulators in the parts book—items that are made for the engine but not utilized on a specific installation or car. A good example of this is the mounts for the Slant-6 Chrysler engine. It's possible to use V8 engine mounts for some unusual applications, and the stock mounts can be turned upside down and swapped side for side; or two right or two left-side mounts may be used. It takes some searching through the parts catalogs to find what may work, but the time spent there will often save many hours of special mount fabrication.

Another example of the special motor mount are the items generally listed as "industrial." Practically every engine maker has an industrial section, creating powerplants for stationary applications. These engines usually are mounted in very narrow confines and normally keep the mounts tucked as tight-

Most quality swapping kits will include well-engineered mounts; these are for a 350 Chevy V8/Jaguar combination. These have been bolted in place, but they will be solidly welded.

ly to the engine as possible. Often, the side mounts are not used and a special saddle mount is created for the front. If side mounts are involved, they are usually small in size and attached directly to the narrow framework surrounding the engine.

Specialty Mounts

After all stock mounts have been eliminated as possibilities, the professional will search the speed catalogs for specialty mounts. If the engine and chassis involved are quite popular, chances are that some kind of mounts will be available. Even if there are no specific mounts, something will probably work. A prime example of this is the Chevy V8-to-Ford mounts sold through practically every speed shop. Simple little platforms that bolt to the engine front corners, these mounts can be mated with Ford insulator biscuits and made to fit practically any frame in existence.

Rising in popularity and availability are swap kits for the newer V6's, especially for transplanting these engines into mini-trucks. Earlier, small-block Chevys were the hot setups for giving the little pickups the power they deserve, and while kits are available, they almost all require some heavy firewall revamping, radiator replacing plus relocating, and so forth. But the V6's are generally no longer than the Japanese 4's to be replaced and the stock radiators can handle coolant requirements, so swappers are going this route, and so are the major kit manufacturers. Hooker Industries, for example, has kits to drop Buick V6's into Vegas as well as LUV, Datsun and Toyota pickups. Andy Herbert Automotive has kits for the same combinations excepting Toyota.

Of these potential swaps, the Datsun pickup is probably the least desirable. Even with the short overall length of the Buick V6, severe firewall massaging is required. The Hooker kit includes a

formed fiberglass insert to replace that portion of the firewall which must be cut out, so Datsun truck owners should take this as a warning.

While on the subject of the Buick V6, the physical dimensions of the engine have changed very little since its introduction in 1962. However, a major change for 1964 was the revising of the bellhousing bolt pattern to make it the same as other GM engines (except Chevys) so transmissions are a plain bolt-up. The '62-'63 pattern is unique, so these early models are to be avoided when shopping the wrecking yards.

If there are no engine mounts available—that is, the part of the mount bolting directly to the engine and holding the insulator—that can be successfully used with the new chassis, then new ones must be made up. It is seldom necessary to do this, however, unless there is steering linkage interference. The drag link may run inside the frame to a pivot arm on the front crossmember. If the engine selected has very low exhaust manifolds, it is possible for the motor mounts to be shoved into the drag link area. In such a situation, the stock mounts can no longer be utilized and must be replaced by a set of special mounts.

Assuming the engine mounts can be used as normal, it then becomes a matter of making frame mounts that will work. As a rule, the average swapper will need to have available at this time several specific items—including an arc welder, gas torch, large drill, and engine hoist. It's possible to create mounts without the torch and arc welder, but figure on consuming a lot more time.

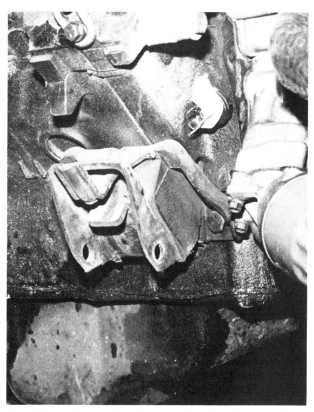

If at all possible, use the stock insulator since it was made for that engine's weight and torque. This is the Buick V6 insulator. Should the rubberized compound tear or separate from its bonding, the engine still won't shift out of alignment.

Mounts

There are two points of interest here. Note the custom but neatly fabricated engine mount that comes straight inboard from the frame rail to tie to the block's insulator. With an under-hood space problem, this swapper has mounted his alternator down low on the engine, then protected it with splash guards (arrows).

Trying it for Size

Remove the exhaust manifolds if there is even the remotest chance they will interfere with anything. With the manifolds off, nearly every V8 and V6 will drop into any chassis. Once in a great while the steering shaft will still interfere with the left-side headpipe at the extreme rear corner. This interference is limited to very old cars with narrow frames, or very wide engines, such as the Chrysler Hemi. If the steering does touch the head and the engine cannot be mounted high enough or far enough ahead to clear, the steering should be removed temporarily. Now is the time to judge whether and how much the steering should be moved. Because of this particular interference some swaps turn out to be very bad, since steering geometry should never be changed if at all possible.

A slight relocation of the steering box from 1 to 2 inches is not all bad, depending upon the direction. Dropping the gearbox straight down slightly usually won't modify steering, but moving a cross-link steering box to one side definitely does change steering. Moving a side drag-link box to the side won't hurt matters, but moving it up or down will change the relationship of drag link to spring/wishbone and have an effect on steering. Keep all steer-

ing relocation or modification to a minimum.

With the engine in approximate position, find the final location by raising and lowering in slight increments. Chances are the back of the engine must be raised or lowered since it won't hang true on the hoist. If bolting to a transmission adapter, go ahead and install several bolts between the engine and transmission. This will help locate the crankshaft centerline.

While engines may be of the same general height, it's possible for the crankshafts to be at different centerlines relative to this height. The idea is to approximate the original engine centerline, which means the engine will usually be set into the car as low as possible. All this is done to eliminate any severe U-joint angles.

If a new transmission is being used, locate the rear U-joint flange in approximately the original position, then level the engine from there. By using some kind of leveling device, you can get the engine level in both the fore-aft and side-to-side planes. This may require some trimming of the front crossmembers, which can be done to a minor extent. If a major modification of the front crossmember is necessary, it may be better to raise the rear of the engine slightly and make a compromise at both ends.

With the engine in location, some lack of steering clearance may still be experienced. Now is the time to determine if it is feasible to offset the engine slightly to the right side. Such an offset can be accomplished, and is often part of factory design for clearance. If the engine can be moved to the right an inch or so to eliminate steering relocation, by all means move the engine!

Mount Location

After all this, cardboard patterns for the frame mounts can be made. A little inspection will show where the engine mounts should best be located. Again this will prove easier if the exhaust manifolds are out of the way. Always try to keep the frame mounts as short as possible, connecting to the frame at a downward angle. If the

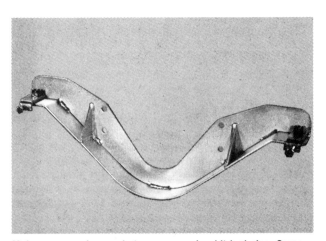

Make sure you know what your swapping kit includes. Some are complete even down to throttle hookup and exhaust headers. Others, as this Hurst item, is just a universal crossmember for use with big-block Chevys and whose ends can be trimmed to fit between almost any pair of frame rails.

mounts are horizontal off the frame, the leverage will cause some frame twisting, which can be eliminated by making extra gussets off the frame mounts. If the mounts intersect the inner top frame edge at a downward angle, the force is spread through the frame rail and twisting is not so prevalent.

The frame mounts should be attached at a strong section of the frame. A good example of bad mount location is when a center side-mount is located on the frame mounts of a pre-1948 Ford. The area between the front crossmember and the center crossmember (or X-member) is strong enough to take a straight up-down force, but the frame mounts will twist the frame in a weak spot. For such cars, it's always wise to make up a set of mounts which work off the front crossmember. As most modern cars have much stronger frames in this particular area this problem is usually found only in older cars.

After the general location of the frame mounts has been determined, make up a full cardboard mount, cut from small pieces and taped together. If an arc welder is available, this mount can be made out of steel to weld directly to the frame. If no welder is available, the mount should be made to bolt to the frame. Make the perch pad for the frame mount that will bolt directly to the rubber insulator portion of the engine mount, and slot the connection hole slightly. This will be very important if the insulator mount is at an angle, since the mounting bolt will relocate as engine weight depresses the insulator. If you're not quite sure of clearance measurements around the firewall or steering box, a slotted frame mount will also allow slight adjustment both fore-aft and side-to-side after the engine is installed.

Using the cardboard as a template, make up the

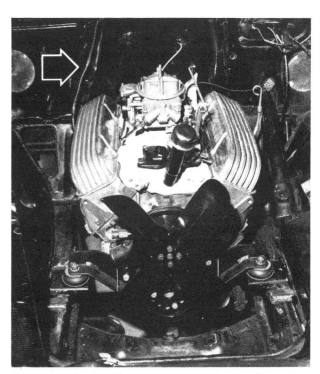

But on the other hand, there may be slight engine/firewall interference that can be cured with deft touches of the hammer. Here the sheetmetal flange (arrow) needed a little "convincing" to provide for valve cover removal.

new frame mounts from a minimum ¼-inch steel plate or .125-inch wall tubing. If you have the gas torch, the parts can be cut out and arc-welded together. Otherwise, go to the local welding shop and have the pieces made up. Cost for a pair will be quite reasonable if you furnish a good pattern. If the frame mounts are to be bolted to the frame, drill both mount and frame holes to the exact size and install with at least Grade 5, high-strength bolts, using a minimum of four bolts at each mount where there is a good deal of leverage on the mount.

The quickest way to determine just how well an engine swap was performed is to look at the mounts. If the job was a "hatchet quickie," the mounts will be ragged and sloppy, usually with very little thought as to what is the best design. The simpler the mount, the better!

Trans Mounts

Once the front mounts are made the transmission mount can be started. The engine is bolted to the front mounts and allowed to settle the half-inch or so that the insulator compresses. It's then re-leveled by raising or lowering the rearend and locating it sideways. If the engine used a mount(s) in the area of the bellhousing—such as in Hydramatic-equipped Olds and Cad engines—these same mounts should be installed in the new chassis. If the mount was at the rear of the transmission, use that point for new mounting. It is in the realm of transmission mounting that many amateurs make their greatest mistake.

The transmission mount must be very strong and it must be attached to the frame securely. Just any old piece of angle iron hung between the frame rails

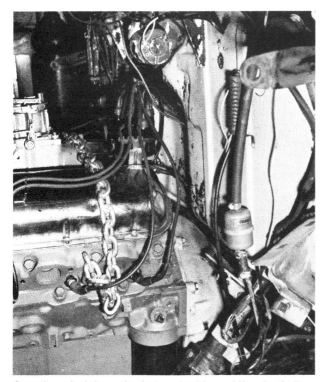

Sometimes luck is on the swapper's side, and there's plenty of firewall clearance, as shown by this big-block Chevy with Turbohydro in a '55 Ford pickup.

Mounts

Most radical is this instance of squeezing a 289 Ford into a Datsun pickup where a large portion of the firewall had to be removed. A custom cover will be welded in place inside the driver's compartment.

will not do the job. If the engine has been mounted at the front end, the trans mount takes on the added importance of holding a great deal of engine weight.

As a guide, always use a stock mount whenever possible. In the case of Hydramatic transmissions, find the mount member for stock Hydros and adapt it to the new frame, making it a bolt-in attachment. If the stock trans mount cannot be used, at least use the stock transmission insulator and attach this insulator to either a piece of tubing or channel.

It is best to provide for bolting the transmission crossmember/mount to the frame side rails, rather than welding it in permanently. This may seem unnecessary at the time of initial installation, since, if you're using the same transmission that came with the engine, you'll likely shove the whole assembly down through the engine bay. But at some future date it may become necessary to remove the trans for overhaul and it'll have to come out from the underside of the car unless you want to go through the hassle of removing the engine again, too. Here again, planning ahead is important.

Tubing makes an excellent transmission mount, since it can be bent into shape so easily. If the mount is made of channel, this channel should be of ¼ X 3-inch section if the engine weight is supported on it. If the engine is supported by center or bellhousing mounts and very little weight is held on the transmission tailshaft, then anything down to 16-gauge metal can be fabricated to do the job.

Other Mounts

It is interesting to note that motor and transmission mounts are not the only mounts necessary with a typical swap. There is often the problem of the emergency brake cable mount that may connect directly below the original transmission mount. Sometimes there is the problem of relocating the generator mount, making up a new mount for an air conditioner or power steering pump, and new mounts for the radiator. Even rear suspension mounts may be needed.

The size and structure of a mount should be dictated by the work it must do. As a rule, nothing less than ¼-inch steel plate should be used for mounts. Generator and air-conditioner mounts must be extremely rigid, suspension mounts must take and transfer tremendous force to the frame, and even mounts for throttle linkage must be rigid enough to eliminate any flexing. It is easier to make the mounts from heavy material to begin with than to have to rebuild them later on. Steel should be used for mounts where there will be strength demanded. Aluminum plate is fine, but few people know how to weld it so it should be limited to low-stress applications, such as throttle connections, etc.

To make mounts appear more custom-made (and impress all the other enthusiasts with your talents), it's possible to drill lightening holes. These holes should be located well to the inside of all mounting plates and will not normally detract from the strength. It's better to drill two or three large holes than a jillion tiny ones. Always bevel the edges of lightening holes.

The "Downsizers"

Today's econo-cars are of unitized construction; that is, they don't have the beefy frame side rails as did cars of the past. Some mid-sized models, like Camaros and Firebirds, have just half a frame; the front sub-frame is indeed a separate, hefty unit, but it extends back under the floor-

Once you have the engine properly placed in a fore and aft position, use a level to make sure it sits true horizontally.

pan behind the firewall only far enough to reach its mounting points. Others have no true frame at all. It's not enough to weld a super-duty engine or trans mount to what amounts to folded-over sheetmetal. Where there is no choice but to use an area of light substructure for mount welding, make sure you consider all the stresses of engine weight, torque, and so forth, then gusset everything in sight. Often such an area can be "plated"; a length of steel strap or plate, say 3/16 or ¼-inch thick and maybe up to a foot long if there's room for it, can be heavily welded right over the lightweight sub-structure "tin." Then the mount(s) are welded or bolted to this plate and the weight and/or torque stresses involved are transferred to something really solid.

Transmission Adapters

The only proper way to start out this section of the mount/adapter story is by warning you that the best swap is one in which there are *no* adapters, either homemade or commercial. You're always in better shape when you can utilize stock components, because you *know* they are compatible. It's best to use the transmission that came with your engine. This means buying a new transmission when you buy the new engine for your swap. In most instances, the new transmission can be adapted to the car's chassis with no more hassle than mating the new engine to the original transmission would be with no attendant problems such as pilot bearing adapters, starter modifications and misaligned mainshafts. For foreign and small cars not designed to take the torque of the motor you plan to shoehorn in, this is definitely the way to go.

However, there may be several reasons why you might want to retain the original transmission, pro-

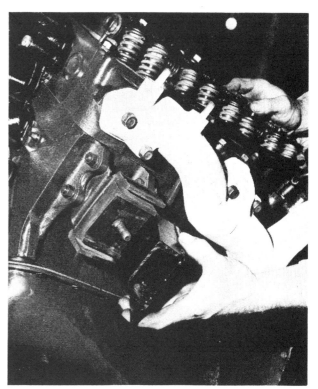

This mount turned out to be simplicity itself. It was welded up from pieces of steel plate and doesn't need machining.

viding it is strong enough to do the job. The car's original transmission may have an unusual shift linkage setup that would be hard to adapt to another transmission; it may be an earlier overdrive transmission which you want to retain for its fuel economy; or it may be a simple matter of economics. Think twice about the economic end, though. You may think that retaining the original transmission will save a satchel of cash, but remember that the new engine probably has more torque, and although it may not tear up the transmission immediately, repairs may still be more frequent. And the money you save on the transmission may be offset by having to buy an adapter to hook the new engine to your old transmission. Of course it does save you the trouble of cutting up the floorboards and making a crossmember or mount for the new transmission, and this is one of the reasons why so many engine-to-transmission adapters are sold today.

It would be impossible to list here all of the adapters currently being sold, even by just one company, but each company has its own informative catalog and its addresses are all in our suppliers' directory. There are so many different adapters available that the chances are good there is one for the swap you contemplate, assuming your contemplations are a little more practical than putting an Allison into a Honda Civic!

There are, of course, occasions when a commercial adapter isn't available for a particular swap (from time to time we all get a little daring) and for space or other reasons you must retain the original transmission rather than switch to the transmission that belongs with the new engine. Your only out in such an instance is to forget the swap or build your own adapter. Many handy swappers have chosen

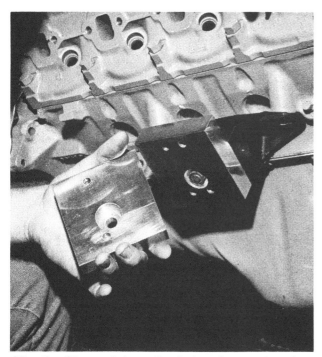

Often, the difference between the stock engine mounts and the mounts on your chassis is small and will mean only some shimming and possibly new bolt holes. Here's a neat set of homemade spacers.

Mounts

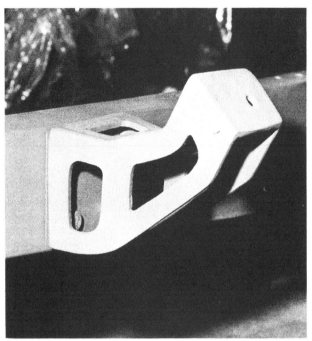

This mount had to be sizeable, but the swapper made it neat-looking by cutting holes and grinding down the welds. If you're faced with something like this, be sure to leave plenty of metal for strength.

the latter way rather than admit defeat at the hands of a mechanical challenge; and if you have access to the proper tools and some materials it wouldn't hurt you to take a crack at it. After making your own transmission adapter, the little details like alternator mounts, linkages and wiring will seem anticlimactic in terms of the challenge they offer.

Homemade Trans Adapters

Your first step in engineering your own adapter is to check for any peculiarity that may need to be included along with the basic adapter. For instance, when an American engine is installed in an Austin-Healey, any adapter plate between Yankee bellhousing and Healey trans must accommodate some form of oil transfer gallery. It pays dividends to think ahead when you make an adapter.

It is not necessary to have the transmission and/or engine out of the car, but, at least, a spare block and transmission case or bellhousing must be available. A block is easy to locate, since most garages have several of the more popular makes waiting for the junkman. To use the engine you have, tilt it forward and brace it well so there is plenty of working room around the flywheel area.

There are two types of transmission adapters: one between the bellhousing and engine block, and one between bellhousing and transmission. As a rule, the former is for automatic transmissions with integral bellhousings, while the latter is for standard transmissions. A third type of adapter is the full bellhousing, similar to the scattershield housings used in drag racing cars, but this one is more difficult to

fabricate and not at all popular with home craftsmen.

In addition to the basic adapter, there is often a requirement for a crankshaft flange adapter, a starter adapter, throwout lever adapter, and torque converter flex driveplate. These are incidentals that will be discussed at length later.

If the only requirement is an adapter plate between transmission and engine bellhousing, some study might show that no adapter at all is necessary. Such is the case between many Ford transmissions and the Chevrolet bellhousing. Often, the bearing retainer on the face of the transmission is the exact diameter as the register hole in the engine bellhousing. If the hole is slightly small, it may be machined larger to fit the transmission, and a hole which is too large may have a shim ring added.

This register hole is very important, because it must be *dead center* with the crankshaft no matter what engine or transmission combination is involved. Often, one or more of the transmission bolt holes will align, as in the case of the Chrysler manual transmission to the Chevy engine. Since the bearing register is the critical spot, the transmission may be aligned at this area, and center punches used to locate holes in the bellhousing. If there is a depression in the bellhousing where the new holes are drilled, spacers should be used to pull the housing and transmission together tightly. In any case, it is essential to check alignment between the transmission and the crankshaft flange with a dial indicator.

If you're making your own mounts at home, make the job easy on yourself. If two plates have to be bolted together, drill the holes through them at the same time for a sure fit.

The indicator base is attached to the crankshaft flange, with the indicator plunger on the hole in the front of the transmission case. As the crank is rotated, the dial indicator will show any runout between the two parts. Theoretically, you should be able to get the front hole in the transmission case lined up perfectly, but if you can get the runout down to less than .002 inch, it will be okay. Of course, the lining-up must be done before the transmission mounting holes are drilled. Misalignment between transmission and bellhousing will cause the bearings and gears to bind, leading to early failure.

To determine if a spacer-adapter block is necessary between manual transmission and bellhousing, measure from the transmission face to the extreme tip of the input shaft. Compare this measurement to that of a transmission intended for the engine. If the transmission to be used has a slightly shorter input shaft, there will still be enough contact (a minimum of ½ inch) between shaft and pilot bearing. A second pilot bearing that extends behind the crankshaft flange slightly can be turned on a lathe, but the problem is having enough spline length on the input shaft to ensure clutch operation. It is also possible to machine both mounting faces of the bellhousing, but be careful. If the mounting faces are cut too much, the housing can flex and ultimately break.

If the input shaft is too long, it may be cut off or a spacer block made from steel or aluminum plate. Aluminum is much easier to work with, but must be grade 6061 T6. Use this grade material for any kind of adapter. Using the bearing register as a guide, machine the aluminum block, then mark the bolt holes as explained in the section on bellhousing-to-block adapters. After the block is made, it is imperative to have the mounting surfaces checked. They must be exactly parallel! The secret is to make the adapter from a plate slightly thicker than the desired

At first glance it looks like this swapper really did his homework and fabricated a nice transmission mount. But notice that all the weight is on the weld. He'd be better off adding gussets as shown by the dotted lines.

If, for a driveline problem, you have to retain your car's present transmission, there are all kinds of adapter plates available, covering most swap combinations. This one, from Trans-Dapt, fits a Chevy bellhousing to a Jeep transmission.

size, then have the plate machined to correct thickness.

Making up an adapter plate to fit between engine and bellhousing is more difficult, since there will be no register to work from. Instead, this type of plate must rely on precision measurements from the crankshaft flange. Fortunately, dowel pins in either block or adapter will help.

To begin an adapter plate, it is necessary to know how thick the plate must be. In most cases, since this type of adapter is most common with automatic transmissions, it will be less than 1 inch thick. Measurement of distance from the crankshaft flange to the back of the installed torque converter will indicate how much difference there is in length between the stock and replacement transmissions. If the two transmissions are quite similar in this measurement, which would mean the adapter would be too thin for strength, the adapter is made thicker, and a spacer the same as the added thickness is made for the crankshaft flange.

When making up the adapter, whether of steel or aluminum plate, first rough-cut the outside shape. This can be done with a saber saw but is much faster with a good metal bandsaw. Once the rough shape is cut, the piece will be easier to handle.

Mounts

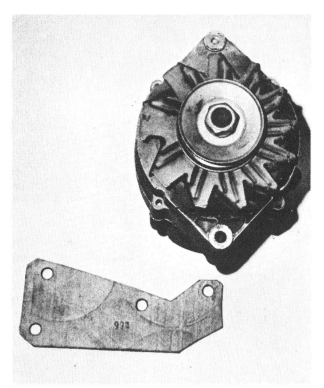

Other things need mounts besides the engine and transmission. Fitting an alternator when space is at a premium may mean a custom bracket. Once you've found where the alternator will fit, cut an attaching bracket from cardboard before transferring the shape to a metal plate.

The plate may be held against either cylinder block or transmission to locate the critical dowel pin holes. Use C-clamps or vise grips to keep the plate in place and center punch the dowel pin holes. These must be perfect. Remove the plate and drill the pin holes on a drill press (to get straight holes) using a bit exactly the same size as the pattern hole. If the dowel pins are in the engine block, which is usually the case, use the original transmission bellhousing as a guide for the pin holes. Once the holes have been drilled, the plate can be set on the block and the approximate center located from the crankshaft. Using this center, cut the large hole in the adapter. This must be at least the size of the torque converter, and must give clearance for the starter ring gear.

To locate the bolt holes from the block, it is necessary to fabricate a special center punch. A quality-grade bolt is cut off to leave about ½ inch of threaded end. Using a lathe, turn a sharp point on one end of this threaded length. Two flat spots can be filed on either side so it can be turned with a small wrench. The stud is turned into a block hole until the sharp tip barely protrudes, then the adapter plate is positioned on the dowel pins. A light hammer blow on the plate above the center punch will mark the hole center. Continue until all the block holes have been marked. Remove the plate and use an ordinary center punch to enlarge the marks; then drill the holes.

If there is to be an overlap of the block bolt circle and the new transmission bellhousing, it will be necessary to countersink the block bolt holes and install the adapter plate with countersunk Allen-head bolts.

With the adapter in place on the block, the transmission must be centered to mark dowel pin holes and bolt circle. This is where maximum precision is required. Locate a dial indicator on the crankshaft flange, free to move around the flange diameter. The torque converter should be removed for this operation so the dial indicator tip can run on the front pump housing. By juggling the transmission on the adapter plate, the exact centerline between pump housing and crankshaft can be found. Maximum tolerance is .002 inch.

Once the crankshaft and transmission are aligned, clamp the transmission housing to the adapter and center punch the bellhousing dowel pin holes. If there are dowel pins in the bellhousing, these should be punched out and replaced later. If a duplicating center punch is not available, a piece of rod the exact diameter of the pin hole can be sharpened on a lathe. Mark the adapter plate through the dowel pin holes, then check crankshaft-to-transmission alignment again to be sure it hasn't moved. If everything is still okay, drill the pin holes in the adapter plate.

The pin guide holes should be just a fraction larger than the dowel pins, but not enough to allow the slightest bit of movement. Countersink the pin hole edges to remove any chance for a bind. In the event the dowel pin must be in the adapter (no pin in the transmission.housing), always drive the pin through the bellhousing hole into the adapter to keep it straight. When a dowel pin must be inserted in the

It may look odd, but it's o.k. as long as it works—and this one does. Room was so limited after this Chevy V8 went into a Jaguar XKE, the alternator was mounted backwards so it extends ahead of the engine and mounts to a support from the block.

adapter, drill the adapter hole for an interference press fit.

With the bellhousing dowel pins in place, mark the remaining bolt holes and drill. The adapter plate may be drilled and the holes threaded if the plate is thick enough. A thin plate will require capscrews, with the nuts on the bellhousing side. If there are any bolts covered that hold the adapter to the engine block, the adapter must always be threaded for bellhousing bolts. Like the standard transmission, the adapter must be ground perfectly parallel on both surfaces, since the slightest misalignment will cause bearing and front pump failure. To check a plate adapter, use a micrometer to measure its thickness, which should be the same no matter where you take the measurement. If the thickness varies, then the two sides are not flat, not parallel, or both.

While it is possible to make an adapter plate up to several inches thick from a single piece of material, this can become expensive in the case of aluminum and heavy with steel. The alternative becomes the bellhousing, or pseudo-bellhousing, type of adapter, usually with a thickness that exceeds 3 inches. By far the easiest method of constructing such a housing is to create two different adapter plates—one to fit the engine, another for the transmission. The two plates are then connected by a cylinder of the proper length. When such a bellhousing adapter is made, a dial indicator is used to position the transmission for alignment; then the three adapter pieces are tack-welded in several places. It is seldom necessary to make a full weld on an adapter, a number of 1 to 2-inch strips being just as effective. This method also reduces warpage

Starter motors can be the swapper's biggest problem and are often responsible for fore-aft engine location. If there is minor interference between the starter housing and some immovable object, clearance can often be gained by grinding some of the relatively soft cast iron away.

of the adapter surfaces, which will always occur.

Once the adapter is tack-welded together, check alignment again and then make the final welds. If possible, leave the adapter bolted to both engine block and transmission to reduce warpage. Have the surfaces ground parallel after welding.

Another type of modified bellhousing adapter may be necessary in special cases. It consists of using part of an existing bellhousing and part of another. With the correct depth measurement between new transmission and engine, both bellhousings are cut in half, so that you end up with half of one bellhousing on the engine and half of the other bellhousing on the transmission. Then the two halves are welded together in order to make a new bellhousing.

A dial indicator is used to get crankshaft-transmission alignment. An alternative is to use part of one bellhousing and weld on a flat adapter plate to match either engine or transmission. In all cases, the adapter must be machined to have parallel mounting surfaces.

And that's all there is to spinning up your very own transmission adapter. But, as we mentioned earlier, always make sure the transmission you use is up to the job. As a rule, a transmission designed for use behind the new engine will be far better than the one that came in the car, particularly if the replacement engine has considerably more horsepower or torque than the original. Cost of the homemade adapter will be quite low if you do most of the labor, usually below $30 which makes it quite a bargain. Time involved will be anywhere from 4 hours to 2 days, depending upon how fast you work and how complicated the design.

What seemed a dilemma at first blush, wasn't, after some thought. Alternator alignment was solved by merely using a few washers as shims to bring alternator into alignment with water pump and crank pulleys.

Driveline and Suspension

The friendly wrecking yard will have stacks of alternate springs for your car. Unless you already have the heavy-duty units, find a pair from an air-conditioned and/or station wagon model of your year and make.

Will I have to replace the front springs? Will the stock front end stand up under the heavier engine? Are the heavier springs from a station wagon or air conditioned model better? What other kind of suspension can I put under my car to compensate for the bigger engine? Practically every letter written to an automotive magazine inquiring about an engine swap will include questions about the suspension. It's always easy to figure out how to squeeze a different engine into the chassis. Not so simple is how the change will affect vehicle handling.

Any time there is a change in the relative location of vehicle weight, there will be a change in vehicle response. An engine moved just 3 inches aft may have a tremendous effect on steering characteristics. An increase in weight on the front end may induce understeer or excessive front-end bottoming. An engine placed lower in the chassis will lower the' overall center of gravity, which affects cornering response. The assurance that the engine swap increases vehicle chassis performance, or at least doesn't change it, is the object of the professional engine swapper.

The first requirement of any suspension system is to keep all of the wheels on the ground all of the time. This isn't possible, of course, but the more closely the requirement is met, the better a vehicle will handle. At the same time, the suspension must give the vehicle good road holding qualities, which means keeping the vehicle under driver control at all speeds. Ride, or passenger comfort, is a direct result of suspension design, and because comfort is invariably the opposite of handling, some sort of compromise is necessary in passenger car suspension design.

In race car design, everything is aimed at keeping the wheels on the road, particularly those to the outside of a turn. The desire is to keep the tires upright (vertical) for maximum tire contact. Up until the late 1950s, stiff springs were considered the way to get maximum handling, but race car builders have now found that soft springing with good shock absorbers is more effective.

Vehicle stability is paramount to the performance engineer, while comfort is the byword of the salesman. To have a car that rides nicely, and still handles like a Ferrari, is well-nigh impossible. But the dream can be approached. Several factors influence vehicle stability, including ratio of sprung to unsprung weight, height of center of gravity, roll center heights in relation to front and rear suspension, wheelbase and tread width (track), suspension geometry, steering, tires and wheels, and load in the vehicle. Obviously, the Detroit engineer faces an awesome task in creating a car that will meet all the requirements of the buying public. But when cars are subject to an engine swap, the balance can be upset. The slightest change in a stock automobile will invariably have an effect on its handling.

Road Holding

The average American driver is concerned about four aspects of automobile performance: how fast the car will get up to speed,

The same yard will offer all types of brakes, but make sure those chosen have a compatible stud pattern for the wheels you already have. This choice drum is aluminum with cooling fins, originated on a mid-'60s Pontiac.

how comfortably it rides, how the car stops, and how good the gasoline mileage is. In a nation of expressways, quality road holding is not stressed. It is still important, however.

Road holding can be described as how well the car will handle through turns. Maximum road holding for any particular car is how fast the car can be driven through corners.

A passenger car may go through a turn nearly as fast as a well designed sports car, but the driver has his hands full all the way. His car is on the verge of breaking loose and spinning, while the car with better road holding can go several miles an hour faster through the same turn with less fuss.

Weight Factors

Weight is the most important factor in road holding and is especially important in an engine swap. In the early days, a heavy car was considered better handling than a light car, but this theory has been refuted by race car development during the last two decades. A heavy car requires a heavy suspension, particularly springs, and thus requires a more powerful engine to attain a desirable power-to-weight ratio. The importance of p/w ratios is illustrated by the fact that drag racing classifications are developed around them. No attention is given to the car make or engine, since a particular p/w ratio grouping will invariably produce similar results.

How the vehicle weight is distributed on the suspension is also very important. The typical passenger car will have roughly 60 percent of the weight on the front wheels and 40 percent on the rear, while a racing car will have about 45 percent front and 55 percent rear. Obviously, an engine swap that increases front-end weight by 200 pounds is taking the ideal weight ratio in the wrong direction.

As cars have become lighter in weight, they have also become lower in height. While this decrease in height is generally a consequence of styling, it has the side effect of reducing the center of gravity (CG), which will, in turn, improve handling. If a car

were to have a perfect suspension system, then the CG would be the limiting factor in handling. If the CG were at ground level, there would be no weight transfer to the outside tires, and handling would be superb. The CG cannot be at ground level, however. Also, the CG will always try to counteract any deviation in vehicle path; it wants to make the car go straight ahead instead of turning.

Centrifugal force, acting through the center of

If you've been using a mock-up engine to plan your swap, remember to account for the effect of the engine's full weight on the suspension. Unless the new engine is the same weight as the old one, some suspension work must be done to compensate for it.

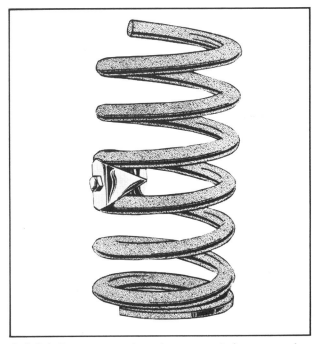

Definitely the wrong way to go to compensate for more engine weight is the traditional spring spacer. It'll only make your suspension bottom out sooner. Use the proper springs.

Driveline

It's not a bad idea to replace as many front-end parts as possible with heavy-duty items, like this idler arm fitted with ball bearings.

gravity, results in weight transfer. During a turn, the outside wheels actually record more weight than they would if the car were traveling straight ahead. On acceleration, weight transfers toward the rear, and on braking toward the front. Location of an engine during a swap will have a direct bearing upon weight transfer.

Sprung and unsprung weight is something most swappers never consider, but it can be influenced by a change in wheels, brakes, engine, or transmission. Unsprung weight is that part of the suspension not being supported by the springs. This includes the tires and wheels, spindles, hubs, and even part of the suspension linkage. In the case of the rearend, it includes the entire axle assembly and part of the driveshaft. Reduction of rearend unsprung weight, and the chance to control tire contact with the road are the reasons that the independent rearend is so popular in race car design.

This sprung-unsprung weight ratio is very important to the serious engine swapper, since he can actually increase or decrease the ratio during the swap. For example, a heavier-than-stock engine and transmission will increase the ratio of sprung weight, while a lighter engine will do the opposite. If the sprung weight is lessened considerably, a mass of unsprung weight will show as poor jounce-rebound tendencies of the suspension. To reduce the unsprung weight of the rearend it might be possible to install a lighter, yet stronger, rear axle assembly.

Roll center is practically unknown to most automotive enthusiasts, yet it has a direct influence on how a vehicle will handle. There are really two roll centers, one for the front and one for the rear. If the suspension components are unmodified, the roll centers will not be changed. High and low roll centers both have disadvantages, so the average car is a compromise. Most production cars have a lower roll center at the front, which is a built-in way to induce understeer. The ideal combination is a front roll center only slightly lower than the rear. If

the rear center is too high it causes excessive understeer, or diving in a turn, which will tend to lift the inside front wheel.

Suspension frequency is another generally unconsidered part of performance. Most cars have a low frequency, or less than 100 cycles per minute in free oscillation. The front and rear springs will have different frequencies, to avoid harmonics, which means that the swapper who changes front springs may be installing incorrect units relative to frequency, which will affect handling. The only way to be sure is to check the specifications on the units involved and keep the same relationship if possible.

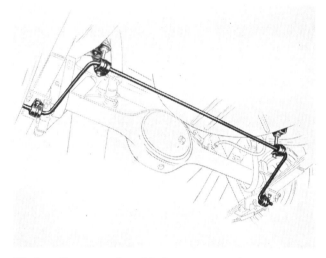

Whatever the year and model of your swap project, you ought to have improved handling to match your new performance. After beefing the front suspension, one of your best moves would be to install a rear sway bar.

Even if you have a coil-sprung rearend, sway bars from Detroit and the aftermarket are available which bolt to lower control arms.

Obviously this question of frequency cannot always be observed with a swap; it then becomes necessary to make the change and live with the results.

Suspension Types

There are a number of different suspension types. At the front can be a trailing link, wishbone (A-arm), strut, swing axle or sliding pillar. Volkswagen is a prime example of trailing link and some Ford pickups are examples of the swing axle. Most American cars rely on the A-arm independent front suspension. Older cars and pickups used a solid axle.

At the present time, the only American car offering anything but a live rearend is the Corvette, that is, a car of conventional design: front-engined and rear-wheel driven. The Vette (and of course the earlier Corvair, '65-'69, which, due to its rarity and popularity with restorers, makes an engine swap for this model out of the question) has a true independent *driving* rear suspension. Some front-drives offer an independently sprung, *non*-driving rearend, but we categorize these differently and they are not relevant to this discussion.

Working with the problems of roll center, A-arm front ends have undergone every form of evolution. Most American cars use the unequal-length configuration, which reduces the effect of body roll on wheel camber. Unparallel, unequal-length A-arms keep the wheels virtually upright under body roll, which is one reason this type of suspension is so popular with road racing machinery. If a change in the relationship of the A-arms to each other will affect wheel camber during a turn, then any extension of the spindle length (as with the raising blocks common to drag racing) will have an effect on how the car handles.

Most engine swappers want to increase the pow-

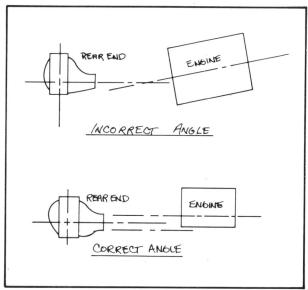

Proper driveline angles are more important to a trouble-free swap than many rodders realize. The centerline of the engine can be higher or lower than the rearend centerline, but the centerlines must be parallel.

Here's an example of poor angle on the rearend installation in this Chevy-powered Datsun. Shims should be put under the spring pads (arrow) to bring the pinion nose up.

er of their vehicle and couldn't care less about making any other changes. This is an unwise course. A faster car will need better brakes. It will need better linkage between rearend and chassis to control torque and axle windup. It may need different springs at the front to control increased or decreased engine weight. The really complete engine swap does not stop in the engine compartment.

Since the frame of a vehicle—and this would include the body—is nothing but a connection between front and rear suspension, the frame and body will have little to do with performance. A change of the engine does not mean much in the way of making a modern frame stronger, or the body tighter. Therefore, it is possible to consider the suspension and the engine as a single package.

If the car is a Falcon, for example, and the original

A good addition for any car with coils in back is a panhard rod from the frame to the rearend (arrow).

Driveline

Driveline angles can be checked easily with one of these hardware store level/angle finders.

engine is replaced with a high-performance Boss 302, then the front and rear suspensions should be made to coincide closely to those of a late-model Ford which uses a 302 as stock power. Of course, body weight will be a contributing factor, but it is minor. Check the later Falcons and try to duplicate the changes that have been made to accommodate the V8. Better yet, check the high-performance cars and duplicate their suspension systems.

Suspension Help

Generally speaking, the suspension members of a modern front end are adequate as far as structure is concerned. However, if the car is to see lots of high-speed work, it is good to go over the suspension parts and beef them in obvious areas. This might be a plate added to the bottom of a pressed lower control arm, or additional welding of the mating edges of the metal panels on a unit-construction chassis. It certainly includes the possibility of replacing the stock ball joints with a quality joint. Experience has proven that quality products, such as the Moog joint, are better than most factory parts if high performance is desired. At the rear, it might be replacement of the springs with units of a different rate, or beefing up the spring attachment points on the frame or body. In all cases, it will mean installation of better shock absorbers.

The best advice to any engine swapper is to install a set of heavy-duty, adjustable shock absorbers. Remember the part about racing cars going to soft springs and firm shocks? Most production cars have the soft springing, but the shock absorbers are not firm enough.

A good set of anti-roll bars could be included. The front bars on most cars can be increased in diameter slightly to control body roll. This will help handling, but be careful not to include a bar too stiff or the car will be too uncomfortable to ride in. A bar installed at the rear can be a delicate subject, but it is worth the effort with a more powerful engine. Take time to make adjustments to the rear bar and you'll get premium handling in return.

It is possible to replace the front springs if the engine is too light or too heavy, but always select a re-

placement that is the same overall diameter and height. Thicker wire usually means a stiffer spring, thinner wire a softer spring. Don't cut a coil spring just to make it fit, since the way coils are wound determines the ratio, and a cut spring may end up worse than the stock unit.

Rather than install spacers between the coils to reduce front-end sag, change coils. If this isn't pos-

Some of the problems in matching driveline parts can be alleviated by swapping different companion flanges on the front of the rearend pinion.

At the other end of a driveshaft, swapping U-joints and front yokes can also solve problems in matching the driveshaft to your new transmission.

sible, a set of good front load levelers can be included. Monroe makes an excellent version, with small-diameter flat-wound coil springs adjacent to the heavy-duty shock absorber.

As a rule, substitution of one of the larger-displacement engines for a small-block V8 or inline 6 will add about 200 pounds to the front end. This extra weight is about the same as a hefty man sitting on the hood, and will lower the profile about 1½ inches. This isn't enough to worry about normally, and good shocks will control the difference. If you need to, you can get new springs for your car from an air-conditioned model or station wagon of the same make to handle the additional weight. Installation of a Hemi, or one of the early Cadillac or Olds-

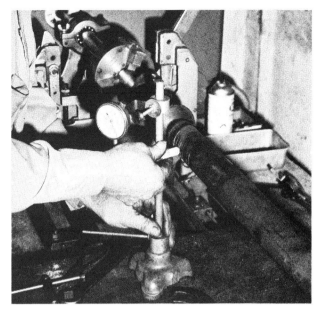

Before a driveshaft can be balanced, it must be straightened. You start by putting it in the lathe at a slow spin. Carefully push a piece of chalk up to it until it just makes a mark. This indicates a high spot.

The only right way to modify a driveshaft's length is in the lathe, where you can precisely cut the old weld off, shorten the tube, press the yoke back in, and reweld it. There's little chance of misalignment when this method is employed.

mobile anchors with heavy automatic will often increase front-end weight 400 pounds or more. That is too much of a change and will affect vehicle handling—especially cornering and stopping.

Making changes in the suspension is not difficult, but they should be included as part of the overall engine swap planning process. Trying to make a perfect engineering switch may not be possible, but at least use similar vehicle combinations as a reliable guide.

Driveline Modifications

Most engine swaps in which a new transmission is swapped in along with the new engine will involve some kind of modification to the driveshaft, U-joints or rearend. Besides the common problem of differing length, there may also be a difference in front yoke size or spline, or the rearend may have been swapped also and there's a difference in rear U-joint size. Many of these problems can be easily solved by a simple exchange of rearend yoke or front driveshaft yoke to complete the match-up.

In previous editions of this book there was some discussion of modifications that applied to closed-driveshaft or torque-tube drive systems, which haven't been used since the mid-1950s. In this book, we'll forego such discussion and concentrate on current systems in keeping with our goal of making things up-to-date and practical.

Those torque-tube setups were under pre-'49 Fords, pre-'55 Chevys, and '50s Buicks, but any swap involving one of these cars today would include a driveline swap to a Hotchkiss or Salisbury rearend and open driveshaft anyway. With the power and torque of today's engines, there's no reason to go through a lot of mechanical hassles to retain an obsolete drivetrain; the open driveshaft is definitely the only way to go.

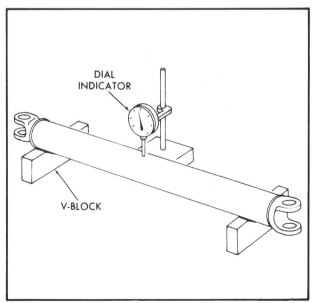

Preliminary straightness checks on a driveshaft can be made with a simple pair of V-blocks and a dial indicator to check runout.

DIAL INDICATOR

V-BLOCK

Driveline

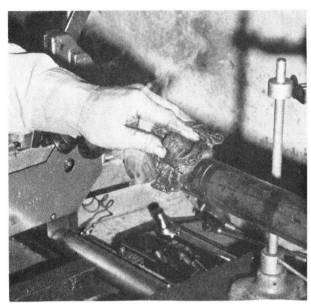

When the marks have established the high spots, they must be shrunk by heating them cherry red and then quickly quenching with a wet rag.

In nine out of ten engine swaps, the only problem with the driveshaft is either that it needs to be shortened or lengthened, or two different-make driveshafts (one that mates with the new transmission and the other being the car's original driveshaft) must be mated together. Perhaps both operations are necessary, but they amount to the same thing when the modification is done, so both can be "killed" at one fell swoop of the local machinist's lathe.

Cutting down an open driveshaft is really quite easy, but the operation does have several special requirements peculiar to the design. To get the length for an open driveshaft is easier than for the closed version because the rearend can be mounted permanently in the vehicle. With the vehicle resting on the wheels to get static spring deflection, measure from the centerline of the rear universal joint to the centerline of the front U-joint. At the front, slide the slip-yoke into the transmission tailshaft housing until it bottoms, then pull it back out at least 1½ inches. This will allow for the sliding action caused by the rearend swinging through an arc during suspension travel, and is especially important. Too little clearance of the slip-yoke can cause serious damage to the transmission, especially if it happens to be an automatic.

Make a mark on the slip-yoke when it's positioned, for handy reference during the shaft measurement process. The centerline of the U-joint is usually indicated by the ends of the joint, with the U-joint bearings being held in place by small U-bolts.

There are several ways to cut, align and reweld a driveshaft, but only one method is suggested here for accurate, vibration-free results. After you have your center-to-center measurement, take the complete driveshaft, or the two pieces to be mated, to a machine shop. With the driveshaft chucked up in the lathe, the machinist should carefully machine away the original factory weld at the yoke end of the shaft—just enough to cut the weld and not the yoke (which is pressed into the tube). Then the driveshaft tube can be heated and the yoke slipped out. The tube is then cut down (still in the lathe for accuracy) to the desired length and the yoke is pressed back in. Because the yoke self-aligns when it is pressed back into the driveshaft tube, there is almost no chance of misalignment in the finished shaft.

All that's left to do is tack-weld around the juncture, cool it off, then finish-weld all the way around. If you have carefully marked the yoke and tube before you cut them apart, and lined the marks up

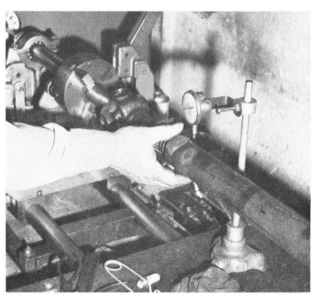

After shrinking the high spots, use a dial indicator to check runout; then apply clay where the balancer says weight should be added.

After playing with the clay, you should have an idea of where to add any balancing weights. Weigh the piece of clay you wound up with and weld on an equivalent-weight piece of steel. All balancing should be done in a machine like this Stewart-Warner unit.

again when the yoke was pressed back into the shortened tube, your new shaft will be as true as it was originally. In most cases, a driveshaft shortened by this method will not even need to be balanced. We've done it this way many times and have never had a problem, though we've often seen driveline problems resulting from a shaft that was simply cut in the middle and gas-welded back together. That kind of shortening method invariably requires straightening and balancing. Nothing can ruin an otherwise good engine swap easier than a simple thing like a badly made driveshaft that loosens your dental work at road speed.

On some open driveshafts there will be balancing washers added at some location. If these balancing washers are apparent, it's probable the shaft will need to be rebalanced once it is cut. This is not an expensive operation and is often included in the overall cost of $25 to $35 by most modern machine shops. If the driveshaft is not balanced and there is an unusual vibration in the car at speed, chances are it will prove to be the shaft which is at fault.

When a different rearend is being installed in the car—or when there is a difference between transmission and rearend—there will be different types of U-joints involved. This is of little concern, but it may mean that the front part of one shaft must be mated to the rear part of another shaft. Often, one shaft will have a greater diameter than the other. If so, the larger shaft can be heated at the joint and beveled down to fit. Generally speaking, a double-ended shaft with different joints will be common to many swaps.

Performance Brakes

An important facet of an engine swap that is sometimes forgotten is the braking capability of the vehicle. Assuming that you've added considerably to the ability of the car to accelerate,

No need to take your driveshaft U-joint replacement to the machine shop if you have an ordinary vise. Use a large and small socket to push the old bearing cups out and a small one to push the new cups in.

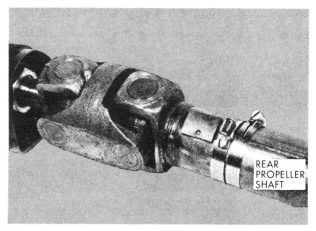

Minor driveshaft imbalance can sometimes be solved with hose clamps. Experiment with different positions of the heavier clamp heads until you take care of the balance problem.

New stopping power would be an obvious suspension update to match your new go-power. Here's a Maverick fitted with '70 Mustang disc brakes. Spindles were a bolt-on swap.

what have you done to improve its *stopping* power by a corresponding amount?

It used to be that hot rodders spent all their time worrying about how fast their car would go, but driving faster brings a responsibility to be able to stop just as quickly. Hot rodders today have become increasingly aware of the performance of their chassis as well as what's under the hood, and of all the aspects of a chassis, brakes are the most important. This applies not only to the guy with a hot street machine with 400 horsepower, but also to the weekend pickup driver saddled with a heavy

Driveline

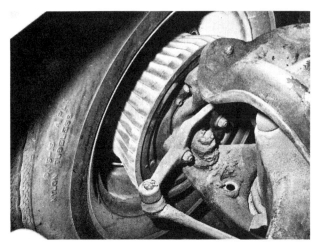

Here's another easy, bolt-on brake swap. This Chevelle readily accepted larger, finned GTO drums.

most popular of such linings is the Velvetouch Metalik brand distributed by Lakewood and available in speed shops everywhere. An average, full-size car was tested by a popular magazine and a first stop from 70 mph took 230 ft. with succeeding stops from the same speed of 288, 321, 360 and 380 feet. After that the brakes were completely gone! While you may never have to stop in repeated fashion from 70 mph, have you ever felt your brakes fade on

Realizing that he would be using more pedal pressure with his disc brakes, this wise rodder braced the firewall near the pedal setup.

camper.

It's interesting to learn that doubling the weight of a vehicle requires double the stopping power, but what most drivers don't realize is that doubling the speed requires *four* times the stopping power! Unfortunately, lessons learned in this area sometimes come with tragic penalties. How many times have you wished you had brakes that really stopped?

In the case of an engine swap with an older vehicle, you're going to have to do something about the outdated braking system. At the rear, your problem may have been solved by the simple substitution of a late-model rearend. You may have installed it just to handle the extra power of your new engine, but a side benefit not to be overlooked is the late-model brakes it brings with it. Then your only problem is the front brakes. On older vehicles this means swapping the front brakes for something better. There are a number of ways to go, depending on your wallet's health. You can go either to late-model drum brakes or to discs.

Shopping around in a wrecking yard may turn up something that will adapt very easily to your spindles, and your time will be well spent at a parts house looking over the books on bearings to see if there isn't a stock bearing that fits the inside diameter of your new hubs and has the correct inside diameter to fit snugly on your old spindle. Check the Hollander manuals at the wrecking yard also, to see what is available that directly interchanges with your car. There are a number of commercial kits to adapt stock Detroit or European discs to your spindle—and most of these kits are bolt-on propositions with only minimal machine work necessary. Check with your local speed shop.

If your swap project is a later model with drums, and you just can't afford the discs right now, you can have an excellent performance braking system by adding a power booster to the system and using metallic brake linings in your drums. They not only stop quicker and last longer, but they won't fade after repeated stops on the drag strip or going down a long grade in your camper/pickup. One of the

In most swaps, it's an easy job to swap in a late-model power brake master cylinder and booster to make stopping easier with swapped disc brakes or metallic linings.

a long downgrade or counted the number of stops you make from 35 mph in stop-and-go traffic? Just to show you what a difference true high-performance brakes can make, the same car was tested after installing the Metalik linings. From the same speed of 70 mph, the driver made 13 stops one after the other, and with stopping distances ranging from 195 to 225 feet—all stops were shorter than the

Power steering pump provides pressure for Hydro-Boost with no effect on the power steering. Unit requires three hydraulic lines; from power steering pump to Hydro-Boost, then to the power steering unit, then back to the pump. The third line is for oil bleed from the unit's piston back to the reservoir when the brakes are released. Conventional steering pump reservoir must have its tube brazed on for line attachment.

If you do swap to disc brakes up front, but still have drums at the rear, you'll need a proportioning valve (arrow) in line to rear brakes.

Disc brakes require a lot of line pressure, so Bendix developed its Hydro-Boost unit for cars with four-wheel discs. Used on '76 Thunderbird, Lincoln and Granada, and on diesel-engined GM cars (because of severe engine weight), the Hydro-Boost gives added muscle to the brake pedal.

stock lining's *first* stop.

The Velvetouch Metalik is a soft metal; if you scratch its surface, graphite-like particles will come loose. Under severe braking conditions at higher speeds, ordinary lining material crystallizes and glazes, acting as a lubricant and lowering the coefficient of friction between lining and drum to practically zero. But when used under identical conditions, the molecules of the Metalik lining expand, improving the frictional grip between the two surfaces, and even more important, this grip does not fade under repeated high-speed stops. The lining dissipates heat because it's segmented.

The Metalik lining has other distinct advantages, especially for the driver who's hard on his brakes. A changeover to Velvetouch will increase lining life to roughly double that of ordinary linings. They do require more pedal pressure, as do disc brakes, so if you can't get used to the hard pedal, just install a power brake master cylinder and booster from another car. You won't worry about switching over to disc brakes after you've made this conversion; in some ways the Metaliks are better than discs, and they really seem like the answer for campers and street machines.

The thing to keep in mind with braking, as with all other aspects of suspension and driveline for engine-swapped cars and trucks, is to match all your components and capabilities to the extra power and speed of the new engine. You'll wind up with a balanced package and many, many miles of pleasurable performance.

The Rearend

A freshened-up Capri V6 swapped into a '72 Pinto was too ambitious for the stock rearend, so one from a '75 Mustang II was slipped into place. Later unit has beefier axles, better ratio choice, yet retains Pinto's four-bolt wheel pattern so wheel-swapping isn't necessary.

Will the rearend stand up to the new engine? So goes at least one question in the majority of engine swap inquiries. This question cannot be answered for each and every car, because there are so very many variables, such as the condition of the new engine, how much power it will produce, will it be hopped-up, how will the owner drive, and will the car be raced. As a rule, most older rearends are very strong, because 6-cylinder engines give a great deal of torque and that is what will twist off an axle. But a better rule to follow is to match the rearend to the engine if at all possible, assuming a different transmission is being used. If the stock transmission is involved, then keep the stock rearend and live with it, unless a better rearend of the same make can be found.

If a new rearend is to be installed, chances are good it will not bolt right in place. One car will use semi-elliptic rear springs, another will use coils. One will use a certain type of dual torque rods, another will have none. For a guide, try first to select a rearend that has the same type of springing as the vehicle with which it is to be mated.

Springing

In some instances, it will be necessary to adapt the entire springing system to the vehicle. This is perhaps easier than trying to adapt the rearend to stock springs. Remember, if new springs are installed, spring rates will vary considerably and will have a direct effect on both riding comfort and handling characteristics. For instance, the complete rearend, with springs, from an Olds 4-4-2 put under a Chevy Nova will give a much harsher ride, because the Nova is far lighter. It then becomes a matter of trying to use the 4-4-2 rearend with light-duty springs. Obviously, things can get very complicated, very quickly.

The "Unbreakables"

In the majority of swaps with pre-1960 cars, there is usually no problem in mounting up a good late-model rearend, as the tread widths on many cars are very close. There are a number of "unbreakable" late rearends to choose from, too. First on the list, by virtue of its strength combined with low cost and super availability, would be the '57-'64 Pontiac and Oldsmobile rear. This is an inexpensive rearend, readily available in wrecking yards, and features a nodular iron carrier and bearing caps. It's a Hotchkiss type with removable carrier, and can be identified by the perfectly round shape of the housing at the rear, with a bulge where the ring gear is. The best third members to use are those with three ribs cast into the side, which make them more rigid than the 2-rib models.

About the strongest available rearend is the Spicer 60 (Dana), which can be found in wrecking yards in some late high-performance MoPars and in medium-duty pickup trucks. The Spicer 60 is one of the few suitable rearends which has *four* pinion gears. Drag racers often call it the "King Dana." The passenger car units, found in late MoPars equipped with Hemis, 440's or Six-Paks, can be identified by

Early Chevy ('55-'64) carriers equipped with Positraction can be easily identified by the large "P" cast into the third member (left).

the front of the housing, which has bolt holes for the factory pinion snubber. With a Salisbury-type rear, modified Spicers have become extremely popular in drag racing, seeing use in classes all the way from modified production up to Pro Stocker and Funny Car.

If you're running a Ford, we suggest staying with the high-performance factory rearend. This one is found in station wagons, Galaxies, and the performance versions of midsize and pony car Fords. It features a strong 9-inch ring gear and a removable carrier. The 8-inch ring gear unit found in the other cars looks identical, but the good carrier has a 4-pinion differential, and the cheap one has only two pinions. The strongest third members are those with a large "N" cast into the top front, which means it's made of nodular iron. The bearing caps (also marked with an "N") are nodular iron also. Unfortunately, Ford has stopped making these housings from nodular iron, but the standard housing can be modified to take just about anything you can dish out. You may have heard a lot about the Detroit Locker rearend, but we don't recommend it for the street. It's too noisy, it's treacherous in ice and snow, and it operates in an in-it, out-of-it situation. The engagement of the lock-up device isn't smooth as with other posi's.

For the MoPar fans, there is the 8.75-inch diameter ring gear rearend used from 1957 on, which is a Hotchkiss type. The basic rearend has been offered at various times with three different pinion diameters: 1.625, 1.75 and 1.875 inches. Those with the smallest pinion are less suitable for high-performance use, and are identified by an "X" cast into the third member. The middle-sized is the most common, being used from '57-'68, and has a straight pinion. The largest one is also the latest one, '69-'72, and is easily distinguished from the early one because the late one has a tapered pinion instead of a straight one. The carriers to look for are those with casting numbers that end in "42" or "85"; these are made of stronger steel.

Chevy Rears

Chevy builders are not left out of the high-performance rearend scene either. There are three basic rearends used under Chevys.

The '55-'64s used a Hotchkiss rearend (removable carrier) which can be modified to take more horsepower; but you'd be dollars ahead in any swap where there is a lot of torque involved (such as with a rat motor in an early Chevy) to switch to one of the later ones: either a 10-bolt or 12-bolt. The number of bolts actually refers to how many bolts are used to fasten the ring gear to the carrier flange, but rodders more commonly count the number of bolts holding the rear cover on, for quicker identification. It's easy to spot the differences in the two rearends, because the number of bolts on the rear cover do correspond to the number on the ring gear. A 12-bolt rearend has 12 bolts holding the rear cover on. The 12-bolt Chevy rear uses an 8.75-inch diameter ring gear and is the stronger, preferred unit, although the 10-bolt can be used for high-performance work if modified and set up properly. The 12-bolt is found in late-model, high-performance Chevys and rat-motored cars, while the 10-bolt is the most common, and is used under everything else.

Junkyard Shopping

Now that you know what rearends to look for and how to identify them, here are a few tips on shopping for one of these units in your local wrecking yard. First, you should try to determine whether it's an open rearend or a limited-slip unit. If there's someone with you, try to turn both wheels or drums independently, one forward and one reverse. If they won't turn independently, but the pinion flange rotates, then it is probably a limited-slip unit.

Once you've determined whether it's an open or a limited-slip, then you'll want to know what the gear ratio is. If it *is* a limited-slip, then you can tell

The best of the beefy big Fords is the type with the nodular iron case and rear caps; unfortunately, this type is no longer in production. The spanner nut is a steel type that is custom made and better than the stock one (below).

Rearend

REAR AXLE WIDTHS		
Model	Width In Inches	Type
1966 Olds	63½	coil
1967 Cougar	60	leaf
1968 Chevy	64	coil
1963 Cadillac	63	coil
1963 Dodge	59	leaf
1969 Firebird	61	leaf
1968 Chevelle	61	coil
1955 Pontiac	61	leaf
1967 Dart	57¼	leaf
1967 Fairlane	63¼	coil
1972 Ford Van ¾-ton	68½	leaf
1964 Riviera	59	coil
1964 Falcon	58	leaf
1962 Skylark	58½	coil

the ratio by simply counting the number of turns the pinion makes for *one* turn of the wheel, drum, or axle. However, this will give you an inaccurate reading on an open rearend, for which you should cut the number of pinion turns in half. For example, on a limited-slip rearend, if the pinion turns almost four times for one turn of the wheel, then the ratio is approximately 3.90:1. On an open unit, hold one wheel still, turn the other wheel, and if the pinion turns seven times for one turn of the free wheel, then the ratio is 3.50:1. Simple, right?

These methods would be used if the rearend was still in a car and you didn't want to take it apart. If it was apart already, or the rear cover was off (in the case of a Salisbury type), then you can just count the teeth on the pinion and divide this into the number of teeth on the ring gear.

If you plan on buying the rearend, then you ought to take the cover off or take the third member out to inspect the gears. First of all, look for extreme looseness in the gears. This probably indicates that the rearend needs all new bearings. Inspect the ring and pinion gears and spiders for signs of galling or discoloration due to lack of lubricant or poor lubricant. A good clue to how well the rearend may have been originally set up and run is the tooth contact pattern on the ring gear. Look for an even wear pattern on *both* sides of the teeth.

Switch 'n' Swap

If you're still open-minded about what type rearend to use, here's a tip right in line with these times of high fuel prices. Since with a Hotchkiss type rearend the ring and pinion gears are set up in a carrier removable from the axle assembly, you can exchange one pre-set carrier for another in a very short time. Why not, then, settle for *one* Hotchkiss assembly and *two* carriers with different ratios. By merely dropping your driveshaft and unwinding a few bolts, you can choose between, say, your 3.9:1 for street cruising or city driving, and your other 2.54:1 for an economical long-haul vacation or

sightseeing trip. No problems here setting up the ring and pinion each time; just remove/replace the carriers as desired.

High-Performance Mods

If you intend any serious hard driving with your swap project, and certainly if you plan any weekend side trips to the 1320, you should think about making the rearend more suitable for high-performance work. Of course, the spring pads on the axle housings should be reinforced with extra weld, and you would do well to check the alignment of the pinion with the rear of the transmission. Many factory-built cars come with as much as 5 degrees too high an angle on the rearend, which is a major cause of rearend failure under extreme conditions.

This can be corrected in cars where the rearend is already mounted by using tapered shims under the spring pads on leaf-sprung cars, and shimming the upper and lower control arms on cars with coil springs.

Traction bars will benefit most engine-swapped street machines, but not all so-called traction bars or lift bars are suitable for street machines. Generally, the type that is welded to the rearend should be left to the dragstrip-only vehicles. For street use, stick to the type that bolt under the spring plates and go no further forward than the front end of the leaf springs; these won't increase your ride harshness too much if you leave the front clamp off the spring. With the clamps that normally come on such traction bars in place the ride is stiff, and when cor-

Easiest way to install most rearends with leaf springs is to remount the pads. First drill out the spot welds on the pads, move the pads to the correct spacing for your springs and then reweld the pads in place.

If yours is a high-horsepower car, now that you've swapped engines and you're putting a new rearend in, it's a good time also to brace the pads with steel straps (arrow).

nering, the rearend of the car will have a tendency to "hop" around the curve.

There have been numerous articles in automotive magazines (plus auto repair and shop manuals) on how to set up rearend gears, so there's no need to repeat that kind of information here. However, after assembling thousands of units for race cars and street machines, some experts have certain recommendations for setting up rearends for high-performance use. Of particular importance is the tooth contact pattern on the ring gear. Not only is the proper pattern important, but it must be right on both drive and coast sides of the teeth for long life. Adjusting the side and pinion bearings will shift the pattern; use white lead or machinist's blue dye to show up the contact pattern.

Backlash in the ring gear is measured with a dial indicator on one of the teeth and should never be more than .006-inch. You should check every tooth to avoid a bind condition at any point on the gear. As blueprinting has as much value in a rearend assembly as in an engine, your carrier flange and journals should be held to .001-inch variation, or else have them trued. Pinion bearing preload should be 15 in.-lbs. with new bearings, and use Loctite's Stud-Loc (red liquid) to retain front pinion bearings instead of the stock crush sleeves. Always clean parts with acetone before treating them with Loctite. Another place to use red Loctite is on the side bearings in the Dana posi, which are a loose fit and may spin if not treated. An additional caution is not to always blindly obey the gear-setting numbers stamped on new gears since incorrectly marked ones have been found.

Most of the modifications we'll discuss here relate to limited-slip (generally called "posi") carriers, since this is what you should really have for serious performance use, because of superior traction and power transfer capabilities. First of all, remove and discard any springs or other "preload" devices from your posi unit. These are really just for ice and snow driving, and unless you drive your street machine under these conditions you don't really need them. These parts can even cause galling in the tapered side clutch or cone area if left in.

Most of the driving force and torque reaction is concentrated on the left side of a rearend, whether an open or a posi. And because the carrier tries to "walk" away from the housing under torque, you

After you've hung the new rearend on the springs, take your time to figure out the details like the shock mounts, new brake lines, and hookup of the emergency brake.

If you plan to use rear discs like one of the Airheart kits on your new rearend, you'll probably have to weld on Olds or Pontiac ends to your Dana or 12-bolt because the kit discs are designed for them.

have to strengthen that left side to keep something from breaking. One of the modifications the racers perform on rearends that don't feature nodular iron bearing caps is to have a leftside cap machined out of billet steel. This really isn't necessary for normal street use, but you should replace the bearing cap bolts with hardened Allen bolts. With the "walking" force mostly on the left-side bearing cap, you really only need the super bolts for just that side.

After dealing with the problems of trying to make rearend parts live under the strains of blown fuel dragsters and funny cars, the values of proper metal treatment have been learned and a few tricks developed that you can do yourself. Your ring gear, pinion, and spider gears should be magnafluxed before any assembly work to check for possible flaws. If there's someone in your area with a glass-bead blaster, then this is also a good treatment for gears. Not only does it clean them thoroughly of any oxidation and provide a better wear surface, but it also shows up minute cracks—like a poor man's magnaflux.

Once this is done, then it's time for some backyard heat treating. Put the gears in an ordinary oven for 2 to 8 hours at 400-450 degrees. Handling them with gloves or pads, of course, remove and immediately quench them in warm water. This removes some of the inherent brittleness of mass-produced gears.

Another treatment, this time for any steel castings such as posi cases, axles or pinion yokes, is to freeze them. Find a container which will just hold these pieces (a cardboard box will do) and pack them in dry ice, which you should be able to order from a drug store or ice cream shop. Keep the parts in the dry ice for 2 days, then remove them and let them thaw out again as slowly as possible. Even such crude metal treatments as these can result in doubling rearend life.

Decide on what gear ratios you want to run before you select a carrier, because certain carriers are designed for certain gear ratios. Cases come in different "series." For instance, in the Eaton cases, the standard unit is the 3-Series, which accepts gear ratios up to 3.70. The 4-Series cases accept ratios from 3.90 up to 6.14, and these are the cases you'll want for high-performance work. Everyone's seen those aluminum ring gear spacers hanging on the wall at the local speed emporium, but these are

Rearend

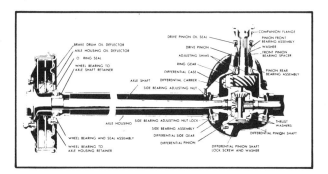

not recommended. They place too much load on the ring gear bolts and weaken the assembly. The only rear that can use them is the King Dana, and only because it uses ½-inch ring gear bolts. Some cases can be machined to accept ratios other than those they were designed for, but this is work best left up to a specialist.

The vital links in any limited-slip unit are the reaction mechanisms, the plates or cones that lock up to provide equal traction to each wheel. Since they are so important, they figure importantly in performance modifications, too. In some posi units such as the Dana, there are flat plates with slightly dished plates between them. Use only the flat plates, since the dished ones are only necessary for ice and snow driving; but even for those situations use only one dished plate per side. Also have the posi plates Tufftrided, a metal treatment licensed in the U.S. by the Kolene Corp. Tufftriding forms a wear-resistant layer of iron nitrides and iron carbide which curtails corrosion, adds toughness, and greatly improves anti-galling and non-seizing qualities. Racers have long utilized this protection on cams, cranks, rockers, clutch plates and other parts. If you live near any major city, you should be able to find a Kolene Corp. licensee who can do your Tufftriding.

Also, on some rearends, the posi unit uses plates lined with a friction material, like that on automatic transmission clutches. Remove these linings and have the plates Tufftrided. By removing the friction material, there's more room inside the posi unit and you can carry more of the unlined plates. For instance, on late Ford Traction-Lok posi's, replace the stock 8 lined plates with 13 unlined, Tufftrided ones for much better power transfer and longer life.

Experts use and recommend only 140-weight gear oil for use in a rearend or standard transmission, not the normal 90 weight sold at the corner gas station. Two oils that are highly recommended are Valvoline 140 and Torco 140. This type of lubricant should be used in any rearend including stock ones, but in the case of a rearend set up for high-performance use, it's a must. Horsepower represents heat—enough to melt or weld bearings when there's too much friction. And despite what you may have thought, the heavier 140-weight oil actually reduces the friction in a rearend. Additives are unnecessary, even harmful sometimes, and using the proper lubricant and changing it now and then is

the best thing you can do for your high-performance rearend.

Before you take to the streets or strips with your freshly assembled rearend and new gears, though, break them in by jacking the rear wheels off the ground and running the car in gear for 5 minutes at 3000 rpm. Now you can venture forth safe in the knowledge that your rearend and posi are blueprinted and "squared away" and won't leave you embarrassingly high-and-dry with unexpected broken teeth, grinding, lost traction, or other maladies. Not having to worry about whether or not it's going to break lets you concentrate on extracting from your engine the extra power that your beefed rearend can now take.

Fitting Time

Now that you've chosen the rearend you want and have it all set up to proper specs, will it fit under your car? For a time, not so long ago, cars seemed to be getting wider almost every year, then downsizing began and they began getting narrower once more. Somewhere, there's another rearend exactly tailored to your needs; and generally the right one will be an earlier model than your car (or at least than the engine you're swapping in) since pure strength (read heft) in axle assemblies began to be pared down when the car-downsizing program started. To this end, we're including a chart of commonly available (from wrecking yards) rearends, together with the type of springing used (though this isn't of paramount importance) and the width, which is important.

Now, listen carefully; if you need a rearend 60 inches wide and the wrecking yard man says they have just the thing, make *sure* you and he are talking the same language. How are you, and how is he, measuring the width; between the inner surfaces of the brake backing plates, between the outside ends of the axles, or between the outer brake drum

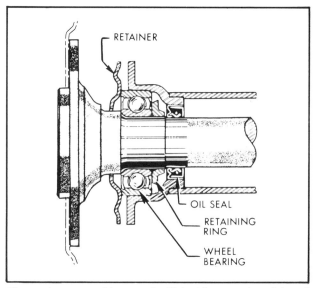

The modern rearend is rugged, efficient in power transfer, and generally requires no major service in the life of a car, other than adding a bit of lube or changing a bearing.

faces? It doesn't matter which measurement you use, just be certain you and he are talking about the same thing. Our rearend width chart is based on the outer brake drum face on one side to the outer brake drum face on the other.

Incidentally, we've known people who, when forced to measure a rearend alone and couldn't hold both ends of the tape at the same time, simply measured from the brake drum face (or axle end or inner backing plate surface) to the center of the differential housing then doubled the figure. Now, you and I know (but apparently our friend didn't know) that rarely is a housing exactly centered in an assembly. To do it correctly, measure *all* the way across.

Proper Tread Width

Don't throw your hands up if the rearend is too wide. The new rearend can be narrowed to the same tread width (the width between the tires) as your old one. It's not something you can do at home, though, you'll have to have it done at a competent machine shop. Narrowing a rearend follows the same general pattern as shortening a driveshaft, and there are two specific possibilities. To begin with, the housing must be cut off and narrowed the exact amount necessary, which may range from 1 inch on either side to 3 or 4 inches on either side.

To shorten the axle housing, it must be cut apart in a lathe, with the separation point as near the outer flange as possible. The two mating edges are beveled and rewelded, then checked for alignment.

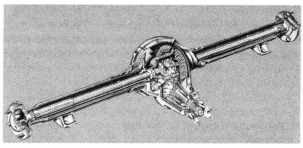

Of the two basic types of rearends, the Hotchkiss and Salisbury, the most common today is the latter. As shown here, the differential gear, bearings and all, is contained in a housing that is part of the whole rearend. The gears have to be worked on through a cover on the back. With the Hotchkiss type, the gearset is in a removable carrier and can be set up or adjusted on the bench.

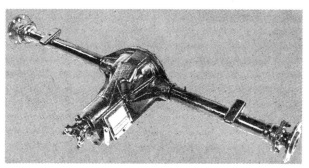

A few years ago Dana Corp. came out with this rearend for Mercury's Cougar. Rare today, it was basically a redesign of their truck 2-speed unit. It works like an overdrive, so it would be handy today for mileage.

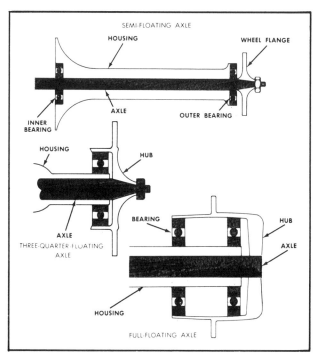

Not all axle bearings are located the same way. The three basic types of rearends are semi-floating, three-quarter floating, and full floating. The semi-floating is the most common type, while the three-quarter and full floating are used primarily in trucks, because they can handle higher bearing loads and are thus ideal for many engine swaps.

The housing is then set aside to cool.

The axles may be shortened in one of two ways, both acceptable and proven. The first way is to cut off the axle the appropriate amount and respline the ends. This can be done if the shaft diameter is constant from the splines outward, but in some instances this does not hold true. In such a case, the smaller diameter just outboard of the splines may be built up with arc weld and then splined, but this is costly. There is a quicker way. The axle can be shortened just the way the solid part of a closed driveshaft is shortened, by cutting and welding. One piece is cut off in the lathe and machined with a stub or pin sticking out the end. The other part of the axle is shortened the appropriate amount and machined with a bevel on the edges; a hole is then bored in the cut end that exactly matches the stub on the other piece of the axle.

After pressing the two axle pieces back together (with the stub going into the bored hole), the beveled edge is now at the juncture of the two pieces and is welded to permanently join the two sections. The cut should be made just inside the wheel flange where the axle is the largest. It will cost about $40 to have axles shortened in this manner (total cost for housing and axles will run to $60 or more), but it may be the only way a narrow enough tread can be achieved. It has the advantage of allowing the use of really popular rearends in the smaller cars, with the added convenience of being able to use a wider choice of differential gears.

The Cooling System

One last, but important, detail of any engine swap is the cooling system. Its capacity must be matched to the new engine to keep it operating at the right temperature.

Engine swapping automatically entails some concern about the cooling capabilities of the stock-vehicle radiator. Seldom will the new-engine-old-radiator combination be ideal, although they may be entirely compatible. It goes something like this: heat generated inside the engine combustion chamber and by working-part friction is essentially energy. This heat is transferred from the engine to the coolant and dissipated into the surrounding air by the radiator. The amount of heat thus removed by the radiator is surprisingly high. A car running at 60 mph dissipates enough heat to warm a 5-room house at 0 degrees F. outside temperature. While heat is also dissipated by the exhaust system and the block itself, 30 percent of the effort must be handled by the radiator.

Radiator Basics

A typical modern radiator consists of a core and two tanks, the tanks being at top and bottom, or on either side (crossflow). The design of radiator cores is based on the size and cooling requirements of a given engine. The cooling capacity is determined by core thickness, total area, and number of cooling passages.

Just putting a radiator of the proper size in front of an engine doesn't necessarily mean it will control the engine temperature. That is the job of a thermostat. To determine which thermostat to use, refer to the operating instructions of the original car. It *is* possible to run an engine too cold.

When a Chevy or Olds V8 is placed in an early Ford, the engine will tend to run much too cold, usually below 160 degrees. This encourages the formation of sludge and other harmful deposits, and the metallurgy of the engine is upset because the operating components never reach the temperatures they were designed for. Sometimes, the inclusion of a 190-degree thermostat will not even get the temperature up high enough, since the thermostat will begin operating before the regulated temperature is reached. This extra water flowing through the cooling system will be enough to keep the temperature from reaching the desired level.

An auto engine is a heat engine, and the hotter you can make it, within limits, the more efficiently it will run. The general rule of 180-190 degrees is a relative compromise to prevent undesirable oil-thinning, overheating due to ambient temperatures on the high side, and incompatible metals expansion. The fuel may need to be cool, but the engine must be warm.

The radiator pressure cap will have much to do with how an engine performs. The higher the pressure of the cap, and resulting internal radiator pressure, the higher the boiling point of the water. The following table illustrates the situation:

Pressure	Boiling Point of Water
0 lbs.	212°
4 lbs.	224°
7 lbs.	233°
9 lbs.	239°
15 lbs.	257°

Depending upon your hood and fender clearance you may want to use either the low-and-wide crossflow radiator (at left) or the standard top-and-bottom, which is narrower but taller.

Most modern engines work behind a high-pressure cooling system, especially those with power options or air conditioning. As a guide, the boiling point of water increases on the order of 2.5 degrees F. for each pound of cap pressure, using sea level atmospheric pressure of 14.7 pounds as the level. At 10,000 feet, it would take a 7-pound pressure cap just to keep the boiling point up at the "normal" 212 degrees.

Whether or not to put a pressure cap on older radiators depends almost entirely on the condition of the individual radiator. However, it is never wise to use more than a 7-pound cap on early radiators, and in all cases the radiator should be reworked by a competent radiator shop before *any* pressure is used.

While on the subject of radiator rework, don't put a good engine behind a dirty radiator, and vice versa. Always flush both radiator *and* engine before the swap is made and include some kind of antifreeze thereafter. This is particularly important if a late-model V6 or V8 is used, as the metal in the blocks tends to rust up much faster than with older engines. At the same time, any time an aluminum radiator (or engine) is involved, antifreeze as a coolant is imperative.

It has been found that the quicker rates of heat dissipation come with thin metal cores. Consequently, radiators are rather fragile and should be handled carefully.

Whether to use a crossflow or vertical-flow radiator depends more on available radiator space and area shape than anything, other than cost. Some of the earlier crossflow radiators tend to clog easily, but recent designs have cured this problem. A crossflow may be the best if the engine tends to heat up anyway, because such a design normally has more area.

If a radiator is being reworked for an engine swap, the inlet and outlet necks should be made the same size as the engine components, and soldered to opposite ends of their respective tanks. If these necks are placed one below the other, the water streams down one side of the radiator faster than the other and right back into the engine, and this causes a hot spot.

Radiator hoses can be a major problem, simply because it is easiest to buy a "flex" hose. These hoses aren't the neatest by any means, so try to find some kind of "smooth" hose that can be cut to fit. Any auto parts store will have many different sizes and shapes to choose from.

Crossflow radiators usually don't have side mounting brackets, so strong top and bottom brackets must be made to retain the core without crimping it.

Cooling

In order to fit the available space, you may have to come up with some unusual inlets and/or outlets fitted to your core. This lower outlet is unique, but it works.

The problem of getting the right size radiator must be approached reasonably, because indiscriminate buying of radiators gets expensive. Naturally, you'll want to try your stock-vehicle radiator first, and unless the engine absolutely refuses to stay cool, don't make a change.

Make sure the fan sits near the radiator, but not closer to the fins than 1 inch, as the blades tend to bend forward at higher speeds. If the car runs cool while it is moving but heats up at slow speeds or idle, suspect an improper flow of air through the radiator. This can sometimes be cured by placing a shroud around the fan. All stock-equipped cars have them, and some judicious searching may turn one up that will at least come close to fitting. At other times it requires a large fan, or a fan with more blades (air-conditioning type).

There are a variety of special custom fans available in speed shops and auto parts houses to suit your requirements. There are usually two kinds, the fiberglass and the aluminum or stainless steel models; stores that carry them usually have a full line of fan spacers, too. These fans are super-lightweight and take less horsepower to drive than a standard steel fan, yet provide more blades for better cooling than with the average four or five-blade stock fan. And if you're really worried about the horsepower absorbed by your fan, utilize a factory "de-clutching" mechanism. These have a viscous drive that keeps the fan working at idle and low traffic speeds, but disengages the blade (lets it free-wheel) at higher rpm, such as at highway speed.

If the car heats up at higher speeds but is cool be-

low 50-60 mph, it is possible that the air passing through the engine compartment is not being exhausted beneath the car properly. One way to test for this is to run without a hood and keep one eye on the temperature gauge. Then install the hood in such a way that its front is tight and there is a gap at the rear where air can escape, and try it again. If this cures the problem, air vents or louvers in the fender splash panels or hood will usually solve overheating.

On the other hand, overcooling can be a big problem in engine swaps. The thermostat is the best approach to an overcooling situation. Next would be to cut down the effective area of the radiator exposed to incoming air (by placing cardboard or metal over a portion of the radiator behind the grille).

Most radiator shops cannot effectively answer your question concerning what kind of radiator to use unless they have had lots of swap experience. One place to go for information is to a new car agency. Specifications of cars often include the radiator area and this can be used to determine how much radiator you might need. The radiator initially assigned to the engine should be investigated first, to see if it can be made to fit the existing room. Most will fit. There are often several different shapes and optional sizes of radiators available for a single engine. The Corvette radiator for the 327, for example, is different from the passenger car unit; the air-conditioner radiator is of greater capacity, and so forth.

Again, it is a question of trying to duplicate the original engine operation condition. Capacity of a cooling system doesn't necessarily mean how well it will cool. Once you get 50 gallons of water hot, it is just as warm as 5 gallons!

A good radiator shop can make a core the size and shape you need if you furnish all the dimensions. They lay the finned material in a rigid form before inserting the tubes.

The ultimate cooling system is one totally fabricated, and this little jewel was whipped up for a 350 Chevy/Vega swap.

When remounting the radiator, make absolutely certain it is not going to vibrate or move around on its mounts. This cannot be overstressed. If at all possible, use a mount off the frame that is not too long, and definitely secure the sides or top of the radiator to the body metal. In vehicles of the 1940-'61 era, the radiator is usually held in a rigid yoke between both fenders. Later developments in design suspend the radiator between a lower and upper set of mounts, and when a swap is involved, these mounts must be moved fore or aft. The Corvette and Vega are prime examples of this type of mounting practice.

Water Pumps

The water pump of the new engine will have a lot to do with your cooling system's efficiency, so there's more to think about than just the radiator. If there's any question as to the condition of the water pump, don't hesitate to replace it. With any car, but particularly with a tight-fitting engine swap, it can be a real hassle to change the water pump, so why not make it easy on yourself and change it before you install the engine.

This may sound a little wacky, but it is possible for the water pump to be *too* efficient. It's not uncommon for a swap to have a water pump that pumps water through the radiator so fast that the water doesn't have a chance to be cooled off. If this is the case you will have to slow down the circulation somehow.

One of the time-honored methods from the days of the flathead Ford was to put a thin washer in the radiator hoses as a restriction, but this is tricky business, and you'll be risking easy overheating. It'd be better to experiment with drilling holes in the water pump vanes, or machining down every other vane in the water pump. Drag racers have been doing this for years, both to decrease the horsepower consumed by the water pump, and to slow down the circulation of water at high rpm. There are trick aluminum and magnesium water pumps now offered

Even with the long water pump of a small-block Ford, this fan is too far back from the radiator—and with a spacer! The only solution is a custom shroud, or moving the radiator back.

Cooling

Aftermarket fiberglass or aluminum fans take less horsepower to drive, in addition to providing more cooling than stock ones.

Another Way to Go

There's yet another alternative approach to engine cooling which at the same time will help fuel economy, reduce engine noise, and give a little added power to the rear wheels. Though stated like this it sounds like a major engineering breakthrough, the device has been used on some foreign production cars for years and is now used on our front-drive cars as well.

Simply put, it's an electric fan that operates independently of the engine, controlled either by the car's driver or (better) via a heat sensor that automatically switches it on when engine temperature reaches a pre-determined level, and switches it off when the temperature falls.

One of the immediately noticeable benefits of the electric fan is that it can be placed anywhere in relation to the radiator core, dead-center of course being the most desirable location. This is often impossible, however, with an engine swap, for the stock fan may wind up being too high or too low in relation to the radiator.

Also, in the case of a V6 or V8 transplanted into a long engine bay designed for an inline 6, the stock fan winds up too far back from the radiator, so far, in extreme cases, that not even a fan spacer helps much. Ideally, a fan should spin from one to two inches behind a radiator.

Electric fans come from a number of sources, including adaptation of units from foreign cars, but two aftermarket sources that come to mind are Hayden, Inc. (1531 Pomona Road, Corona, CA 91720), and Flex-a-lite Corp., (5915 Lake Grove Ave., S.W.,

by National and Moroso, and both of them have slower pumping speeds than stock units.

Length can be a problem with water pumps, too. This is the primary bane of engine swappers desiring to use a Ford engine. You almost need the engine compartment length for a 6-cylinder to fit a small-block Ford (or AMC V8) into a vehicle without pushing the motor back into the firewall. Help is on the way for Ford fans, though, due to the trickery of hot rodder Jerry Kugel of Kugel's Komponents. He offers a specially modified small-block Ford water pump (289-302) that is 1⅜ inches shorter than a stocker. This may not sound like much of a gain, but when your back is up against the (fire)wall, you'll be happy to take any clearance you can get.

On some oddball swaps, there just may not be room for a water pump at all. While it can't be 100 percent recommended as a direct replacement for your mechanical pump, numerous rodders in the past have gotten away with blocking off the stock pump holes and adding fittings to carry engine water to and from an accessory electric water pump mounted somewhere on the chassis. Units like the Jabsco "Water Puppy" are designed for marine use, and with a good-sized automotive engine it would take a large pump to equal the cooling efforts of the stock mechanical pump; however, these marine items have been successfully utilized in some cases where nothing else was usable. You might even find a 12-volt pump that suited your needs in an aircraft surplus house.

Electric fans are a neat solution to space, or to the frequent problem of a too-low fan placement. Aftermarket units are available, as are units from the new crop of domestic, transverse engine, front-drive cars, as well as from some foreign cars. This one's from an R16 Renault, bolted right on the core.

Hayden is just one firm offering electric fans. They can be switched on and off manually, or better, automatically via a thermocouple. One beauty of the electric fan is that it can be mounted ahead of the radiator if cramped space calls for it.

Another space-saver to consider is the use of small foreign car alternators, used here in conjunction with a trimmed-down fiberglass fan.

The Honda Civic has a nifty electric fan, and if you look closely you'll see that two are used in this installation. They are mounted via special brackets on the engine.

Tacoma, Wash. 98499). Both Hayden's "Electra-Swirl" and Flex-a-lite's "Electra-Fan" bolt directly to the radiator. Both have a variety of models, differing in fan diameter and number of blades, but most take up only about three inches or less of depth behind the radiator. But the real beauty of these units is that they can be installed, and work just as well, on the *front* of the radiator. And this may mean you won't have to shift your radiator to accommodate your new engine if there's interference between it and the stock engine-driven fan. The electric motors can be wired to run in either direction, so the fan can pull or push air as desired.

Other benefits of the electric fans are numerous. Fuel savings of as much as 15 percent have been realized by independent testers. Engine-driven fans require from 5 to 17 horsepower to turn them, especially wasteful at speeds above 25 or 30 mph where the in-flow of air from car motion alone is enough to keep most engines cool without a fan at all. Even the clutch fans that slow or stop when engine temperature falls below a certain level rob horsepower through their drive belts and the not-quite free-wheeling pulley hub.

And, engine fans are noisy, too, although you probably aren't conscious of it until a fan is removed and you *don't* hear it. Electric fans make virtually no sound at all. Because the electric fans run independently, they will continue to run after the engine is stopped, either through your remembering to turn off the switch later, or automatically through its heat sensor.

Even if space after your engine swap isn't at a premium, consider the electric fan. The horsepower it "saves" (i.e. doesn't use) may mean as much in the way of adding performance as a set of headers, and the fuel-saving certainly isn't to be sneezed at.

The Oiling System

If your swap turns out to have a clearance problem between the oil pan and the steering, look for an alternate pan to fit your engine. Most engines have several factory pans if that engine is used in different car models. One of these pans may exactly suit your purpose; so give the corner wrecking yard a going-over.

Sometimes an engine swap can be a miserable experience, such as when the steering just won't cooperate and get out of the way of the exhaust system; there's no room for a fan or radiator; your project car has a weird 10-volt system and the new engine is 13-volt; the tie rods or front crossmember insists on being closer to the oil pan than propriety allows. This is when the average swapper throws a crescent wrench across the garage and storms off looking for the guy who told him it was a "bolt-in" swap.

The kind of engine swapper who succeeds, though, is the one who *thinks* a little more, and patiently finds a practical solution to each problem as it comes along. That steering problem can be avoided with a set of tubing headers, the whole electrical system can be converted to 12 volts, and the oil pan can be modified to clear both the steering and the front crossmember.

As with so many other aspects of an engine swap, modifications to the oiling system can be done either of two ways—at home by yourself or farmed out to a professional. Luckily for the average guy who doesn't have a full shop at his disposal, there are a number of professional companies involved in making special oil pans, coolers, remote filter kits, and dropped tie rods. With all of the work they do for unusual, space-at-a-premium race cars, there isn't an oiling problem that can't be solved by one of the available professional companies.

Pan Clearance

The major hurdle that focuses an engine swapper's attention on his oiling system is lack of clearance between the pan and the tie rod or front crossmember. It may be a case of the new engine sitting too low, or being much bigger all around than the original engine; or it may be that the new engine's sump is in the wrong position on the pan, or something in the steering or crossmember was changed to fit in the new motor. Most of the clearance problems can be traced to the sump location, especially with engines that have a front or center sump, such as Fords or MoPars. The central-sump usually has only a small interference problem, one that can be cured with slight massaging of the pan; but with a front-sump engine the pan sump is that much closer to the tie rods or crossmember. This definitely requires that something be done. There is rarely a clearance problem with standard rear-sump engines, but there are swaps, such as the Chevy V8 into a Chevy II, where even the rear of the pan must be trimmed for adequate clearance.

Before jumping into a pan modification scheme, it's wise to pay a visit to a new car agency and browse (if they're kind enough to let you) through their industrial and marine engine catalog. Often, special pans and oil pumps are created for an engine that never sees the light of day in a passenger car, yet they may prove to be exactly what you need. It may be a lot easier for you to special-order one of these pans, even if it takes a while to get to your local dealer, than to go through the trouble of building a custom pan and taking the chance that it will leak, or not fit, and have to be modified fur-

Some oil pans made specifically with the engine swapper in mind are available from Milodon. This one is for steering gear clearance when a Chevy V8 is installed in a Chevy II.

ther. The Chevy II swap is a perfect example. After 1964, the Chevy II could be ordered with a V8 as stock, thus a pan from any of the later Chevy II's or Novas would be a bolt-in solution to putting a V8 into an early Chevy II.

In later-models, the Buick V6 has used four different pans since the engine's introduction. Although interchangeable, they vary enough in shape, so that one or another of them could very well solve a particularly knotty swap-fitting problem. All of them are available over Buick parts counters, but whichever one you opt for, be sure and get the same-model oil pickup assembly.

Ford engines have always been a swap problem because of their front sump, but check out a Bronco oil pan sometime. It will bolt on to your small-block Ford passenger car block (when used with the Bronco pickup), and the sump is further back, usually enough to clear problems in all but the tightest of swaps.

Ready-Made Pan Swaps

In the old days of engine swapping, hot rodders had to fend for themselves when it came to altering a pan so it would fit the new chassis, but we'll get into the how's of this in a moment. If an industrial or marine pan, or an alternate for a given engine, didn't work, then cut, hammer, and weld were the order of the day. Then along came engine swap kits with, at first, just an adapter and a set of mounts to unite the more popular engines with the more popular chassis (as 289 Chevys into Jeeps). But as available kits grew in terms of numbers of builders, as well as increasing engine/chassis combinations, the manufacturers began offering custom pans as part of their kits, if one was needed. Now there are scads of aftermarket pans, designed to be a part of a specific kit but sold separately as well. It just might be that your own needs can be satisfied using a pan from a different swap than yours, but one that will work for you just as well. Before cutting your stock pan, wander by your corner speed emporium. You may just find what you want ready-made.

Pan Modifications

There will be occasions when you can't find what you need in the industrial engine or marine parts books, or at a speed shop and you'll be stuck making a new pan or modifying the old one.

When making a special oil pan, keep in mind that the biggest single problem is going to be the oil pump pickup. In the case of a Ford pan, where the sump is in front and must be reversed to clear the linkage (as with the Thunderbird swap), cutting the pan is only one-tenth of the work. The other 90 percent is getting the pump pickup back to the new sump in workable order.

Consider the pan modification first. An oil pan is made from relatively soft sheetmetal, deeply drawn by the factory press. There is a reinforcement included around the drain plug and around the mating surfaces where it bolts to the engine. However, this reinforcement may not be super-good on some engines. Therefore, no pan work should be attempted without the pan sections actually being bolted to a block to eliminate distortion. Because the pan is of a deep-drawn structure, there are many stresses retained in the metal that will distort badly when the pan is cut apart.

The type of cutting will depend upon the modification. If the lower part of another pan is going to be installed to the stock upper lip, the initial cut may be made with a torch and later trimmed with tin snips (the actual cutting operations can be achieved with the pan removed from the engine). If the pan is to merely have the sump reversed and welded back again, start the cut at a drilled hole and use a metal blade saber saw. This will give an excellent cut that is easy to reweld.

To find the location for the cut, mark a scribe line around the pan circumference at least 2 inches from the bolt lip. This line should be equal all the way around. When the sump is reversed, the bottom part of the sump should then be flat (or as stock), but at the rear of the engine. The cut line may be slightly higher if there are any baffles in the pan that might interfere.

After the pan is cut apart, the bolt lip section must

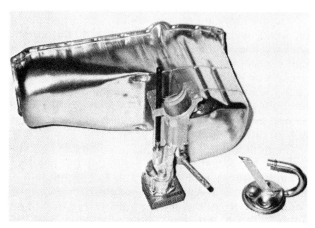

Deeper-than-stock pans require an extension to keep the pickup near the bottom. You can use an extended pickup (right) for street use or a special longer pump (left) for drag racing or heavy-duty usage.

Oiling

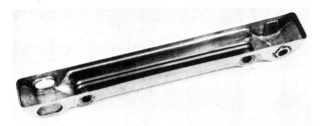

Your stock in-the-radiator trans cooler is nothing more than a tube inside the lower tank, and not good enough to cool your transmission oil in any high-performance application.

be secured to the engine block and the bottom section then tack-welded in place. After the tack welding, remove the pan and use a body hammer/dolly block to align all the edges. If the pan has been tack-welded every inch or so, it can be final-welded off the engine; otherwise final welding should be done on the block. This will reduce further distortion.

A pan is no place to learn how to weld. The bead should be small and of perfect fusion, with no small holes. After the bead has been run (brazing is acceptable), all the slag must be removed with a wire brush and the weld carefully inspected for flaws.

This is a good time to determine if extra baffles are necessary in the pan. Most modern high-performance engines run a windage tray below the crankshaft, which tends to keep the whirling crankshaft from beating the oil to a froth. Some engines, such as the Chrysler 273-340, do not use this tray as it restricts oil drainage back to the oil pump. Before you install such a tray on your engine, check with the speed shop to see if it is acceptable. While the windage tray may not be okay to use in your particular engine, all engines can have extra baffles added to restrict the movement of oil around the pan. On hard acceleration or deceleration, it is possible for oil in shallow sumps to completely surge away from the pump, leaving it high and dry momentarily. This can spell disaster to some engines and should be avoided.

A baffle may be nothing more than a small piece of metal, welded at the front edge of the sump, which will keep the oil from sloshing forward in the pan; it may have a counterpart at the sump rear (especially on center sumps). In the most sophisticated cases, such as the baffles in the racing pans created by Aviaid, Milodon, or other pros, they'll be hinged in one direction so oil can flow *to* the pump but not away from it.

The necessity for a deep sump will be dictated entirely by the swapper. A deep sump is not used so much to get more oil capacity as to get the oil further from the crankshaft. Nevertheless, if an engine is prone to run hot all the time, an extra quart of oil in the pan may prove all that's needed to help the cooling. A deeper sump might be necessary around the oil pump if a special pump is needed, but, as a rule, most engine swaps can generally get along with a stock capacity pan.

Oil Pumps

On the problems of oil pumps, Milodon Engineering is one saving grace. They have come up with a full line of swap items and one of the more exciting designs is a single and double-line pump for Fords. The single-line unit uses a high-capacity line to the rear-mounted truck gears and a secondary line off this bottom plate. Stock Ford engines use the same pump for 289 through 428 engines, but the capacity is not enough to feed the large oil passages in the block. The truck gears used in the special Ford pump are a full ¼ inch longer, which means no rise in pressure but a definite increase in the volume.

The small-block Chrysler engines also get a bigger gear for the pump, since they can use the extra volume. In all cases, oil from the pickup is handled by a special race car hose, which is #12AN (aircraft quality) neoprene with braided steel covering. These hoses are a full ¾ inch inside diameter (which does away with any possible restriction), and are the high-pressure, non-contaminate type used for most hydraulic applications. Milodon carries a complete line of parts to modify stock oil pumps.

If it is impossible to modify the oil pan to eliminate steering linkage interference, it might be wise to modify the steering tie rod(s) to clear the oil pan if the clearance required is minor. If such is the case, the tie rod should be made up of much heavier stock and gusseted at all bends. Of course, if the material is strong enough, no gussets will be needed when used on a light car. Special dropped tie rods are sometimes included in swap kits.

Oil pans can make or break a good swap, so they should be treated as a very special part of the transplant.

Depending on your application and the kind of driving you'll be doing, coolers are available with two, four, or more tubes through the core.

Swap-Ready Pumps

Don't forget the possibility of finding an aftermarket pan from another engine/chassis swap, which might work in your case. If you do find one that'll work, see if that kit also provides a pre-modified oil pump and/or pickup (if required) to match the needs of that pan. While it may seem less expensive to go ahead and modify your own pump and maybe tweak the pickup a little while you're about it, it will undoubtedly be a lot less frustrating, and definitely less time consuming, to go ahead and opt for the professionally-built unit.

Bolt-on Oil Coolers

The majority of letters automotive magazines receive concerning a swap include the question of adequate engine cooling. But the enthusiast hardly ever considers the possibility of controlling engine temperature by cooling the oil. This is the most direct route to temperature control and will ensure a swap life well beyond that without oil cooling.

Here's the way it works. Assume we have an automatic transmission fluid designed to give 100,000 miles of service before a change is required because of oil oxidation. Normal fluid temperature in the transmission will be about 175 degrees F., which seems to be about average for most modern cars. For every 20 degrees increase above this norm, the rate of oxidation will double; and as the oxidation rate doubles, the useful life of the oil is cut in half. Although transmission fluid is used as an example, the same rule applies to engine oil. With this information, the following chart shows how critical transmission oil temperature is:

Oil Temp	Oil Life
175°	100,000 miles
195°	50,000 miles
215°	25,000 miles
235°	12,500 miles
255°	6250 miles
275°	3000 miles
295°	1500 miles
315°	750 miles
335°	325 miles
355°	160 miles
375°	80 miles
395°	40 miles

Temperatures in excess of 300 degrees F. might seem far-fetched to the enthusiast, but consider that merely rocking a car back and forth when it's stuck in mud, sand or snow will cause the transmission fluid to exceed this temperature after a minute or so. If this back-and-forth rocking continues for 15 or 20 minutes, transmission temperatures can exceed 500 degrees. That means the fluid is ruined before the car is freed.

Heat, then, is the big enemy of any engine and automatic transmission. In an engine swap, where an engine-trans combination of a specific size may be mated to a radiator and/or oil cooler of a different size, the control of oil temperature becomes a real

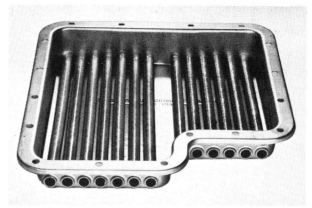

Relatively new to the transmission cooler market is Integrity Koolers of Denver with its trick pans. The Integrity unit has no external lines to run so it's a cinch to install. It holds more fluid than the stock pan, and air going through does the cooling as well as radiator types.

Oil filters can be a problem for a swapper with limited chassis room around the engine. In such cases, a spin-on filter adapter should be used to take advantage of some of the very short filters available.

problem. Most cars are designed to have the engine operate somewhere between 175-190 degrees, which means the oil cooler fitted to the bottom tank of a radiator can never cool the oil below this point. This is no problem so far. But engine temperatures as high as 220 degrees are now considered fairly normal, especially when the engine is under load or in heavy traffic. Most automotive oils start to deteriorate at temperatures above 200 degrees, leading to the formation of gum and varnish. Thus the oil coolers adequate for a small 4-cylinder engine will hardly do the job for a 454-cubic-inch V8 with automatic transmission. Perry's *Chemical Engineers Handbook* points out that the rates of chemical reactions increase rapidly as the temperature rises. Generally, for homogeneous reactions, the rate increases two to three times for an 18 degree rise in temperature. Oil temperature is always measured in degrees Fahrenheit, since all automotive gauges are Fahrenheit.

Oiling

A remote filter adapter is the answer for real problems of clearance around the oil filter. This Chevy rat in a Ford Torino had to use one, and the owner wound up with a cooler location for the filter plus easier and cleaner oil changes.

Now might be the time to define a couple of terms. A homogeneous liquid is made up of various liquids uniformly distributed. A mixture may include suspensions or solids in a finely dispersed state, and the properties of the mixture remain the same regardless of the size of a sample. Oil is a homogeneous mixture. Oil oxidation is the chemical reaction of oxygen and the hydrocarbons and olefins in oils which form new and undesirable compounds. The unwanted agents are varnishes, waxes, acids, and water or hydration compounds, all normally referred to as sludge.

Those who work with oils use a special test to check for acid formation. Without water present in an oil, the acid is less hazardous, but just the slightest trace of water acts as a catalyst and activates a more rapid reaction on the engine and transmission metals and seals, plus the oil itself. It is the acid that forms the gums and varnishes so harmful to the mechanical apparatus of the car.

It is possible for engine oil to be too cold, which is one of the reasons Hayden has a special engine oil cooler thermostat, which keeps engine oil temperature constantly between 180-200 degrees. Unless such a thermostat is used, the oil temperature can fluctuate and be too far on either side of the ideal. Because an engine oil cooler is not factory equipment, most engines operate with an oil temperature between 220-290 degrees, which is getting on the dangerous side of things (remember the chart above). But factory cooling must rely entirely upon the water radiator and normal radiation through the engine block and the oil pan.

Hot rodders and race car builders have worked to control oil temperature through the use of special coolers for years. In some cases, the oil pans have been modified with tubes and fins, or even cast from an aluminum alloy in an effort to reduce engine temperature through swifter heat dissipation. When the oil temperature is lowered, the water temperature also goes down, which is one more reason the engine swapper should automatically consider the installation of such an oil cooler.

But this brings up a paradox with thinwall casting engines. It is generally conceded by engineers that an engine will wear less if the temperature in the cylinder wall metal is high, or above 350 degrees. This, of course, directly contradicts the requirement to keep the oil cool, but it is just one more of the automotive compromises we must live with. It has been found that oil additives will help reduce the problems of upper cylinder lubrication at these high temperatures, but even then little can be done to eliminate the combustion products that actually do the "wearing" of engine parts. This is not the case in the area of a bearing, however, and the temperature must be kept lower. In this case, oil becomes more of a coolant than a lubricant, and it is the reason high-performance engines are set up with increased bearing clearance. The additional clearance allows a greater flow of oil over the bearing surface and cools it.

This control of metal and oil temperature has plagued VW and Porsche engine builders for some time. Because cylinder head temperatures vary widely, any kind of consistent tuning is difficult. Tom Leib of Scat Enterprises found that cylinder head temperatures could be standardized by placing an oil cooler ahead of the engine air fan, thus curing two problems at once. Most oil coolers, whether for engine, transmission, or power steering, are mounted ahead of the radiator to take advantage of the air drawn through by the engine's fan. Because this is not always possible, each situation must dictate cooler location. However, a cooler should never be placed so that it radiates into a stagnant air zone. That is, a cooler tucked away on the fender splash panel away from any kind of ambient air flow will be hard pressed to provide any kind of cooling, and becomes little more than extra capacity with little efficiency.

At the same time, an oil cooler should always be protected from damage by foreign materials. The grille may do this, but if there is any doubt a loose-weave screen may be installed at least 1 inch ahead of the cooler fins, as it will tend to restrict air flow somewhat and will clog with bugs easily. Do not use a tight-weave screen or the type of material sold in service stations as a bug screen. The addition of this small amount of restriction is often all it takes to make a marginal car overheat.

It's an interesting sidelight to the oil cooler installation that oil life seems to be longer. It is, because oil doesn't wear out, as the filter ads read, but is contaminated to death. Metal particles, varnishes, gums, waxes and other contaminants cause a change in oil viscosity and ultimate mechanical part failure. Two decades ago, oil was changed every 1000 miles, but under today's driving conditions, which are much more demanding, the interval has increased up to 4000-6000 miles. Engine design and better oil are to be credited.

It's also interesting to note that not only engine and transmission oil can use a cooler. Most pro road-racing teams use a cooler for the transaxle, too. The Hewland transaxle temperatures were running between 280-320 degrees until oil coolers brought this down to a reasonable 170-180 degrees. This reduced transmission overhaul require-

Ford engines are notorious for poor filter clearance due to stock location at the left front of the motor; so when they are swapped, a remote filter is generally advised.

ments from after each race to after each *tenth* race.

Oil coolers, at least on a mass production basis, have come to the automotive sport through the back door. Until the Hayden Trans-Cooler was introduced in the 1950s for heavy-duty applications, mostly for cars towing trailers, about the only way to get a cooler was to convert some other type of radiator. This made a cooler rather impractical for the average driver and not especially attractive to the engine swapper. Because the Hayden met with such success in recreational vehicle applications, engine swappers started picking up the idea for their cars and practically all race cars now use oil coolers. There is now a long list of cooler manufacturers, including Chrysler Corp. The Chrysler unit came about as a direct consequence of the drag racing and Daytona race car program, but has met with good reception in the recreational vehicle field.

Of all the brands on the market now, most are of the tube and fin design in traditional radiator styling. Some are lengths of finned tubing that can be adapted anywhere, however, and are especially useful when there is very little room for an ordinary radiator. These too are particularly suitable for swaps involving older cars and sports cars, where the grille is usually very close to the radiator. Check with your nearest speed shop.

These companies make a variety of models for different cars, and the swapper is advised to consult the company before selecting a particular cooler. If this is not possible, always try to include a cooler to match the engine and/or transmission.

Don't worry about the chassis, other than problems of mounting and possibly plugging the oil cooler outlets in the stock water radiator. The addresses of all oil cooler manufacturers can be found in monthly automotive magazines and recreational vehicle publications. In addition, local radiator and automatic transmission repair shops often are dealers for these products. Look in your Yellow Pages.

These units are not inexpensive, and the price will range from around $35 to $65. But the value of keeping engine heat under control cannot be explained in terms of cash. Increased oil life, transmission life, and life of engine parts will more than pay for the unit within the first year. The swapper who does not need an oil cooler hasn't completed his swap yet.

As long as you're mounting your filter remotely, why not do your motor a favor and install a dual-filter setup as in this big-block Camaro.

The Exhaust System

Your friendly wrecking yard has exhaust manifolds galore. Boy, does he ever! Careful shopping here might save you the expense of a set of custom headers. Most engines can use any of several different exhaust manifolds in various chassis.

The exhaust system has always been a problem area for the engine swapper, but luckily it's one aspect of a car that can be easily modified. As long as your system has no leaks and isn't too loud, there's no safety problem related to the exhaust system, and the sky's the limit on the shape and dimensions of a custom exhaust system. Basically, there are two routes you can take with the majority of engine swaps. Either you can retain the cast iron exhaust manifold(s) (in stock or modified form), or you'll have to purchase ready-made headers, or even make up your own set. As a rule, whenever the stock manifolds *can* be retained, they should be, assuming that they have a good, free-flowing design. They will be quieter than headers, and certainly a lot less expensive.

There are many swaps, though, where use of the stock manifolds is impossible, and you'll have to resort to a tubing system of some kind. How you build your system will determine the noise level, vibration, and whether you get a performance gain.

Cast Iron Manifold

Sometimes it is necessary to modify the stock cast iron manifolds for steering or crossmember clearance; this can be an extensive modification. If the manifold must be cut and reshaped, the cast iron can be either arc-welded or brazed, the latter being the most common method and quite acceptable. However, unless some kind of high-strength brazing rod is used (such as that from Eutectic) the manifold may break if it is under stress.

If the cast iron exhaust system must be cut and changed, try to keep away from undue exhaust restrictions, especially around the left rear port. This is where the biggest problem crops up, due to steering gear clearance. Rather than reduce the size of the exhaust hole, cut away or flatten the steering mast jacket. Above all, do not inadvertently mask any spark plugs either with the modified exhaust or relocated steering.

Sometimes it is possible to get clearance by swapping manifolds between different year engines. Perhaps the head pipe flange should be further forward, or at a different angle, or the left-side pipe can be put on the right side. Sometimes high-performance cast headers from the factory give better clearance, but this is not generally the case. However, industrial engines usually have a much more compact, but still free-flowing, exhaust system than the same engine in cars. The Olds 425-455 is a prime example of this. The automobile headers are big and bulky, while the industrial engine headers tuck down next to the block and give excellent clearance at the rear.

In the case of the newer Buick V6, there are three different cast iron manifolds available for the right side of the '79 and '80 versions, and one might solve a clearance problem when swapping-in this engine. One of these manifolds is a gargantuan thing designed for use with the factory turbocharger, but because the outlet is in a little different position, and is aimed in a somewhat different direction, it might just solve a problem that the others won't, although you'll have to cap the turbo inlet. In any

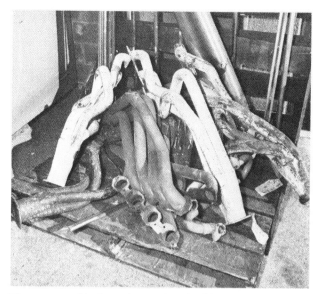

The same yard just may have a bunch of headers they've removed from wrecked cars. Again, careful shopping may turn up a set you can use with just a little revamping to fit your particular application or, with luck, they'll bolt right on.

case, this is just one example of assorted factory manifolds for a given engine.

While on the subject of the Buick V6, keep in mind that the currently-produced engine has been around since its introduction in the '62 model, and while exterior dimensions have remained generally static, minor modifications (especially the substitution of the "even-fire" design to replace the older "odd-fire" in mid-'77, and revised heads introduced for '79) make it essential to know what engine you're dealing with.

If you opt for a wrecking yard engine, get *all* the pieces you can: manifolds, heads, distributor, and so forth. If not, be certain of the year and model so you can order the right parts from the Buick agency. All of this is a digression from the exhaust story, but what we're trying to point out is that there may be a variety of factory exhaust manifolds for your engine.

The only way you'll be able to check what manifold will fit what engine is to make a tour of the wrecking yard. Place the engine in the chassis minus the manifolds, measure the clearances, then start looking. Before going to the trouble of modifying a manifold try to locate a replacement that will work. If the head bolt pattern is the same, this won't be too hard a job.

In the event an older-model exhaust manifold is used on a later engine, it is wise to hog out the manifold ports to fit the newer head ports. If there is not enough material in the manifold to do this gradually, at least make a good taper at the entrance to alleviate some of the restriction.

The headpipes should be the same size as the exhaust manifold, with 2 inches being common on most of the larger engines, and 1½ inches on the smaller-displacement V6's. Stock headpipes can always be modified to fit, and the proper flange to mate against the manifolds is easy to weld on. Although a crossover pipe can be made to fit all swaps, it is advisable to switch to dual pipes.

Exhaust pipes and mufflers from the original vehicle can be retained, unless they happen to be for a substantially smaller engine, such as a 4-cylinder Chevy II or a Falcon 6. In that case, it is better to change to the larger capacity muffler.

Another common mistake in the exhaust system is mounting the pipes and mufflers to the chassis without some kind of rubber insulation. If this isn't done it sounds like the changing of the guard inside the car. As for the selection of a muffler, any of the quiet straight-through designs can be recommended.

As a final word, always work with new material, don't try to use that rusty old exhaust pipe or muffler.

Tubing Headers

Because they add to the car's performance and gas mileage, a good set of tubing headers is recommended for any street machine. The engine swapper, however, has an engine and chassis combination that isn't stock, therefore he can't just pick a header off the shelf at the local speed shop. There are some excellent headers manufactured for certain popular swaps (a list of which is at the end of this chapter), but unless your swap is one of them you must whip up your own, or you don't put the engine in the car.

That would be a shame, since headers are so very simple to make and require nothing more than the basic ability to weld. You don't even have to be an expert welder when you start, but we guarantee you'll be a good welder by the time you finish. Besides, there is a great pleasure in saying: "The headers? Oh, I made them myself."

As mentioned, the only reasons for a set of tubing headers are either for maximum performance or for engine-to-chassis clearance. Either reason is substantial in itself, and may be accompanied by the simple desire to have a "nutty-looking" exhaust system. The latter ego salve is common to older cars that fit more readily into the hot rod category.

From the standpoint of performance, a set of headers will usually increase engine power from 10 to 20 percent, depending upon design. In some

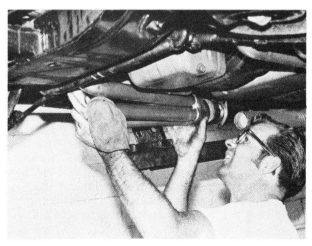

If under-hood space prevents use of stock exhaust manifolds, any good muffler shop can build a set of custom headers in the event a ready-made set isn't offered for your swap.

Exhaust

There's usually some sort of exhaust system clearance problem in any swap, but forethought may provide an easy solution. In this case, the exhaust flange and frame interfered, and the solution was to simply bend the frame flange a little.

cases, the figure will be much greater, as with the 273 and 340-cubic-inch small Chrysler V8. This engine has a very poor stock exhaust system, dictated by the extremely close quarters of MoPar compacts. When specialty headers are created for such a car, they usually sweep upward, by the cylinder heads and out through the fender splash panel. Most manufacturers report a 40 horsepower gain with these headers, and that's power not to be sneezed at.

As noted, commercially available header sets are expensive because they require a great deal of labor to build. But since you have the time to make a swap, you can probably spare another 10 or 12 hours to make a set of headers. The professional can make up a set of headers in much less time, but the amateur can plan on a "long" day getting the job done.

It will cost between $40 and $60 to buy a "do-it-yourself" header set, but this is really the only way to go. Pieces of a kit are available separately—such as header flanges, port stubs, U-bends, and bolts, but it's best to buy the complete kit which is usually cheaper. Companies such as Cyclone, Hooker, Vipar, Douglass and Mercury Tube Ind. have various kits and kit parts available; most speed shops carry their catalogs if the products aren't stocked, or you can write them directly. For others, check auto enthusiast magazine advertising.

With a header flange kit and some pieces of bent tubing, a good set of headers can be spun up by the amateur in a couple of days, assuming he knows how to weld. Even if he can't weld, he can make all the cuts and get the pieces to fit closely, then call on the professional welder to finish the job. Welding header tubing is probably the easiest of welding chores, but the common mistake is to set the torch improperly and throw too much oxygen. This causes a kind of crystallized bead and the system will break later.

Rather than making an exotic set of tuned "banana" headers, the average swap should get no

more than the conventional header, designed to tuck in against the engine. Along these lines, some of the exhaust specialists produce header kits that are already cut and need only be welded. One caution: When the header is finish-welded, it should be bolted securely to the engine or a spare block and allowed to cool in position. Stress concentrations caused by the welding will make the header flange warp otherwise. Furthermore, when a header flange kit is purchased, get the kind where the pipe stubs have already been arc-welded to the flange itself.

Most kits are designed to keep the headers as tightly against the engine as possible so the kits can be used in any situation. This is critical to the engine swapper since the header may need to clear a very narrow frame on an older car, or clear the suspension towers of modern cars. At the same time, there may be a clearance problem around the steering on the left side, and this is where the swap header comes into its own.

Most header kits have an obvious way they can go together, but the swapper may find it necessary to change the steering area slightly. This may mean the extreme rear exhaust port on the left side is too close to the steering shaft. In which case, the tubing for that header may have to be routed down, up, or to the rear for clearance, then it must intersect the main tubing further toward the collector pipe. Often, the rear exhaust port is slightly behind the steering shaft, which means the rear tube must swing to the rear and then outward before coming back to the main tube. If this happens, it may be necessary to cut the flange apart between the rear and middle ports so the header can be slipped over the steering shaft. This is not an uncommon problem.

If the steering shaft or gearbox is extremely close to the rear port, the rear tube may need to be welded into the flange at a very tight angle, then the tube should be reshaped (usually flattened) for extra clearance.

There is not a great deal of clearance necessary at the steering, since the engine torques upward and away from the box or shaft (torques to the right); therefore, creating something in the neigh-

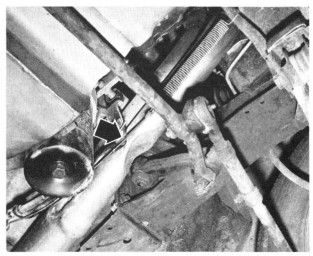

In this case, an apparently easy way out of a clearance dilemma resulted in reduced engine efficiency. The swapper caved in the exhaust pipe, but increased back pressure.

borhood of ⅜-inch clearance is usually enough. About the only chance the header would have of hitting the steering would be if the car's suspension bottoms heavily, allowing the rubber engine mounts to give slightly. This seldom happens.

If there is a problem of clearance between the header and the steering column on an older car, the steering column shaft can be flattened almost ½ inch. Modern cars leave the shaft exposed beyond the firewall, so this will not be the answer with later-model vehicles.

Headers can be fashioned only with the engine installed, as each tube must be built around existing interference. The left-side header will usually be the most difficult to make, so it should be started first. A little bit of extra pipe used here may be taken from the excess material for the right-side header.

A note about working tubing: It's easy to cut exhaust tubing with a hacksaw, but it's easier to trim with tin snips. When trying to mate one piece of tubing to another, always trim each piece until a perfectly flush fit is obtained. Trying to fill large gaps in exhaust tubing is the surest sign of an amateur, and the resulting weld will break in short order. To make a precise trim, hold the pipe pieces together and mark with a pencil the approximate shape necessary. Trim to that shape and test the fit. Any gap more than an ⅛ inch must either be filled with a scrap or the pipe trimmed further. Do not waste tubing since the kit will contain just enough for the job and usually no more.

Once the stubs are trimmed, the major down pipe must be cut and tack-welded in place. This may be the front pipe, or a combination of two pipes leading into one. At any rate, there will be a major pipe involved and it's the reference point for all the others. Bring this pipe in at a smooth flowing curve down from the port, then tuck it in closely to the block and oil pan. There is no relative movement between header and engine, so a minimum ⅛-inch clearance can be squeezed if necessary. Run the down tube to the rear, making necessary swings to clear the steering and starter. Do not weld any of the joints solid, just use a simple tack weld for the moment.

After the major down tube is installed, work around the clearance problem next. If this is the two rear ports, make up both pipes for that section, carefully fitting as you go until the pipes reach

The do-it-yourself project begins by bolting the exhaust flanges to the block, trimming and angling the outlets to aim them out of the way of obstructions, then tack-welding them in place. Remove the flanges for final welding.

either the main down pipe, the collector, or the secondary down pipe (in the case of a split primary system). Keep trimming and tack welding the pieces of pipe together until the entire system is assembled back to where it will connect with the head pipe. This will probably be through a collector tube, which makes up as easily as the smaller connections.

When absolutely certain that everything clears the header (steering, depressed brake and clutch pedals, and emergency brake levers), weld up as many of the joints as are easy to get to. This will make the unit more solid before it's detached from the engine. Remove the assembly and weld up all the remaining joints. If there have been any large cracks filled, expect a considerable stress at that area, which may cause the header to warp. Check the header flange for warpage with a straight-edge. Grind off any little bits of slag that might be on the flange's mating surface and bolt it up to the engine. Run the torch over each pipe to remove any stress that would cause the flange to distort (this will probably be taken out the first time the headers get hot anyway).

When making up the design, try to use as long a piece of pipe for each section as possible to eliminate extra joint welding, which will in turn eliminate some of the time necessary to make the header. A bit of careful planning will disclose what pipe will work where. In the event you come up short for a piece of pipe, the local muffler or parts store will have something you can use. Before header kits were sold, it was common to make your own header flange from a gasket pattern and make up the bends from factory pre-bent exhaust pipe having lots of bends.

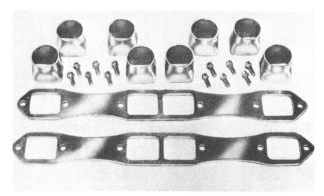

Do-it-yourself header-starter kits are offered through speed shops and come with the flanges, short outlets and small-headed bolts. But you're on your own for the rest of the system.

Exhaust

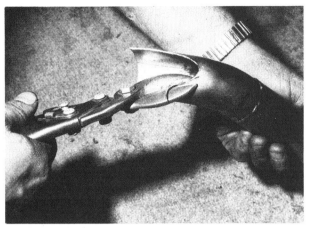

Often it'll take a lot of fit-and-try to snake the header pipes from the exhaust flange outlets around obstructions. Judicious trimming of this pipe with sheetmetal shears will make a smooth flow into the pipe it must join.

Keep in mind that the header must be removable, so don't tuck any pipe over a bolt head, and leave room for a wrench. Chances are you'll be fitting most of the system while lying on your back, so wear a good, heavy coat or coveralls to keep torch slag from burning your hide. Once completed, the custom header will look so much better than the original that you'll want to show off your swap.

Bigger muffler shops have their own hydraulic tube-bending machines. Rather than stock an inventory of hundreds of different tailpipes, they have a simple set of specs for each car's pipe shape and a lot of straight tubing. When they need to make, say, a '76 Chevy Caprice tailpipe, they look up the specs, and in about 5 minutes they can bend up the new pipe to fit exactly. While this has obvious benefits for them, it also has benefits for the engine swapper. Since they can make any bends that they need in just about any common size of exhaust tubing, shops that have such equipment often do custom work as well, and may even specialize in it to capitalize on their machine.

Not only can they fabricate a new system from the headers back to the rear bumper for you, they might also be persuaded to do some or all of the work in making your headers. You could bring them patterns for your various pipes and have them bent. This is definitely a lot easier and faster than having to laboriously cut and weld short lengths of tubing and U-bends to come up with a header to fit your swap.

After the Headers

The exhaust system presents a unique potential for the hot rodder, since it is the one area of the engine where performance can be gained without sacrificing gas mileage or reliability. In fact, an improved exhaust system generally *increases* gas mileage, if all other factors remain equal. A good set of tuned headers can add 40 horsepower when open and as much as 20 horsepower when closed, (with a muffler) with gas mileage increasing several miles per gallon. A pair of glasspack mufflers should be worth about 10 horsepower, depending on how restrictive your stock mufflers were. On many cars, there is perhaps another 40 horsepower to be gained by improving the rest of the exhaust system, the headpipes and tailpipes—at much less expense than a set of headers.

Most tubing headers have a flanged collector bolted to cone-shaped adapters which connect to the pipes leading to your mufflers. Most folks just connect the headers to their stock system in this manner, not realizing that the size of their stock headpipes (the pipes that lead into your mufflers) and tailpipes (the pipes that go from your mufflers to the back of the car) may still be restricting the exhaust gases after they leave the header. While this doesn't affect the engine while running on the dragstrip (since the headers are open then), it does make a difference in street driving, which is what most of us are concerned with anyway.

A case in point: someone we know has a late Chevy station wagon; he took out the stock 400-cubic-inch small block and swapped in a big 454 rat motor. He used headers but connected them to his stock pipes, in which he had already installed four glasspack mufflers, two on each side to keep the noise down. In his search for more power, he later made up a complete new system of straight tubing 2½ inches in diameter, and he used just two mufflers, the big L-88 Chevy ones. Having the larger size tubing and a straight path instead of the many restricting bends of the stock system, and using the large capacity mufflers added up to a whopping 50 horsepower at the rear wheels, measured on a chassis dyno!

Not everyone can expect the same gains, but similar modifications to your own car will definitely make a difference you can feel in the seat of your pants. For engines up to 350 cubic inches, the 2 or 2¼-inch tubing should be adequate; use 2½-inch tubing for the bigger motors. There are a number of stock factory mufflers around with big inlets, out-

If some of your header tubing needs so many angles and bends that you'd spend a week cutting and trimming many short sections, seek out a muffler shop with a tubing bender. They can form a pipe from a single length of tubing in short order.

lets, and cores. Besides the Chevy L-88, there are some biggies from Cadillac, and about the best one available is at your local International-Harvester dealer, of all places. Their muffler (part No. 376607-C1) has a 2½-inch inlet and core and 2¼-inch outlet! One of these on each side of the car is easily quiet enough to be street-legal.

Even if you can't afford a set of tubing headers, you can still modify your exhaust system to get more power and that certain sound you associate with a high-performance machine. Installing some form of nut and bolt device for opening and closing the exhaust will provide you with a street 'n' strip capability, and you can even utilize your exhaust system to give your car a different look, something with a competition flavor.

Still popular on the street are sidepipe conversions to gutsy "off-road" pipes. A number of speed equipment manufacturers offer sidepipe kits on the aftermarket, and you can even make your own or have any muffler shop do the work.

Unlike cast iron exhaust manifolds, tubing headers dissipate heat much easier and faster. Cast iron manifolds tend to retain heat. This means that wiring, fuel lines, and hydraulic brake lines that were adjacent to cast iron manifolds and were in no danger of being affected by heat generated by the exhaust system may now be too close when you install headers. In addition, headers may take up more space than cast iron manifolds and be closer to existing plumbing and wiring. When installing headers, don't just bolt 'em on and let it go at that. Check the proximity of all wiring and plumbing to make sure that it's a safe distance from the headers. You haven't lived until your headers boil your brake fluid. A minimum of 2 inches is recommended to allow for movement of the engine due to torque reaction.

Headers will increase the noise level of operation, and there are two reasons for this: (1) the thinwall tubing used for headers transmits the sounds of exhaust pulses to the engine compartment where they

Just having a set of headers isn't the final answer to a good exhaust system, you need efficient plumbing all the way back. In this case, large-diameter straight pipes lead back to free-flowing turbocharged Corvair mufflers. In fact, these mufflers are so popular, muffler shops still stock them.

are amplified, and (2) your engine will breathe more freely, with less back pressure, and will ask the mufflers to work harder to silence the engine. Keep this in mind when selecting mufflers. They may pass reasonable noise requirements without headers, but when headers are added, they *will* become louder.

In many cases, the addition of a crossover pipe will reduce the noise of your exhaust system. A crossover is added close behind the collectors, connecting the two sides of the system. It will help smooth out the firing pulses and modulate the flow more evenly. If you've got one of the thumper big blocks, like an L-88 or a 440 Magnum, the installation of small factory resonators (in addition to mufflers) will quiet things down quite a bit. The idea is that what small increase in horsepower you'll gain if your system is too loud isn't worth the trouble.

You should either run your tailpipes all the way to the rear bumper or use a pair of sidepipes that are available at local speed shops and muffler outlets. Having the exhaust terminate under the car isn't good practice because of the obvious danger of carbon monoxide fumes. Also, check your state laws about sidepipes because they are illegal in some areas. If this is the case, you can add the sidepipes if you like the appearance, leaving them nonfunctional, but run the real tailpipes out to the rear bumper area.

When installing headers or dual exhausts, allow at least 1 inch of clearance around all pipes to compensate for vibration in the system. Support the pipes with rubber-mounted straps in at least three places per side.

A high-performance exhaust system can do wonders for the way your machine responds. You can help power, gas mileage, and even appearance with the proper selection of components. If you choose wisely and use practical good judgement, the addition of these parts will result in an improvement to your car.

It may look wild and seem to be the only solution to clearance problems, but actually just swapping the right for the left side exhaust manifold on this small-block Ford/Pinto swap would have saved untold amounts of fabricating.

Clutch Linkage

The shifter and clutch linkage are important parts of your swap, since they are actually used by the driver at all times. Making them safe, reliable and comfortable is of paramount importance in any swap.

Making linkages that link can be a gruesome challenge for the inexperienced. When doing a swap, try to duplicate the original conditions as best as possible. Usually, the enthusiast thinks of the shifting equipment as just a wiggle stick hanging off the steering column or jutting from the floorboards. But there's more to it than that. Shifting includes the linkage from the clutch pedal to the throwout arm, and no amount of fancy floor shifters are going to improve gear changing if this initial linkage is poor. So when thinking of manual transmission shifting, the pedal linkage must also be considered. This isn't the case with automatics, where emphasis is on the shifter only.

Experts continue to advise swappers to use the transmission that came with the engine selected, unless a very good adapter is available and the transmission that came with the car is a good one. While using the transmission that matches the engine will ease the engine hookup, it will increase the problem of rear mounts and clutch linkage. This problem will be eased somewhat if the car is post-1955 (just a general year for a guide, not a hard and fast date), after which date the swinging pedal became common.

Trying to hook up the transmission linkage can be a bag of snakes unless the swapper is very aware of the problems of linkage ratio. Swinging pedals usually reach the clutch throwout arm only after transferring operational direction through an idler shaft (called an equalizer bar). This shaft is connected to both the engine/transmission and the car frame via a ball and socket at both ends, and is usually located on the frame immediately ahead of the firewall. As can be expected, the shaft will be different for each and every vehicle made. This is really an advantage for the swapper.

Making it Work

The shaft itself will be available in any number of strange shapes, because the ball on the frame may not necessarily align with the ball on the engine. The swapper can move the ball location, but it is easier to find a shaft that either fits, or comes very close, than to modify the bar. Be advised, however, that ball alignment must be relatively close or the shaft will bind. At the same time, the balls should be horizontal to each other to compensate for the engine torque, which will tend to rock the shaft through a slight arc.

The leverage available between the swinging pedal and the throwout arm will dictate how hard the pedal is to depress. In stock form, the pedal will be relatively easy to push down, and the pressure will seem to "fall through" at some point in pedal travel. If a high-performance clutch assembly is added to the car, pedal pressure will be noticeably higher because the linkage ratios have been figured for the stock pressure plate. If the stock clutch is retained and any one of the pieces of linkage modified, the pedal pressure will also be affected, becoming either heavier or lighter. This is what happens when equalizer bar crossbreeding is attempted.

On the vehicle common to the new transmission, one of the operating arms of the equalizer may be

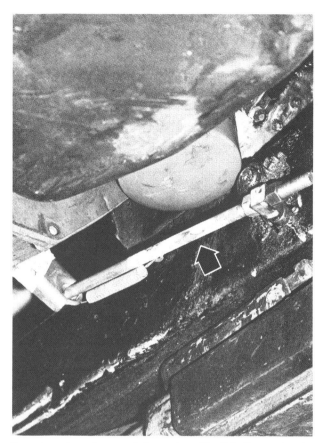

If you have to make up a linkage piece like this throwout rod (arrow), make it twice as heavy as it should be and it'll be just right.

and can easily be adapted to fit. The problem in using a slave cylinder on an engine not designed for one is in getting a direct line between cylinder and throwout arm. It is possible to modify the throwout arm length slightly to get alignment, but this will again have an effect on pedal pressure.

Factory clutch linkages, while usually trouble-free, are a hodgepodge of rods and arms at best, and once you fool with some trying to make your own setup work, you'll appreciate the fact that Detroit has seen the folly of its ways and wised up. In some GM and Ford cars they're now using a clutch *cable* assembly that runs from the clutch pedal arm right to the clutch fork. It's a sheathed cable like the one first used a few years back for throttle linkages, but much stouter. This eliminates the need for the equalizer bar between the engine and frame, and it can be curved and routed just about anywhere you want it to go. If you find one that's too short for your

longer than the other, thus multiplying or subtracting leverage. The vehicle's swinging pedal will remain unchanged (minor linkage changes here usually lead to trouble), so the swapper will want to very nearly duplicate the lever lengths of the new transmission. These lengths will not be available in parts books—only the measuring stick or a duplicate car will give the correct answer.

Try to use stock linkage rods and rod ends as much as possible when using an equalizer shaft, since the pieces have been designed for the high loading involved. Avoid any radical kinks in a rod just for the sake of alignment; instead, it is better to move the shaft lever to align. The levers at the transmission and the inside end of the shaft will most likely be very close, but the lever on the outside will seldom be close to alignment with the pedal. There is no problem in cutting and modifying the levers, if they are rewelded adequately and do not cause interference with the firewall or steering.

Professional swappers tend to use the equalizer rod for linkage rather than the hydraulic slave cylinder, simply because the equalizer is easier to set up in most cases. Chevy equalizers come in a large assortment of sizes, and provide a good place to start looking. This does not rule out the slave cylinder, however.

Slave cylinder kits are available from speed shops to fit several different engines through use of a master mounting bracket that must be drilled to fit. Similar slave units are used on Chevy and Ford trucks,

When you have to install a clutch cross-shaft bracket on the chassis of your vehicle to complete a swap, make it out of heavy plate like this.

Clutch

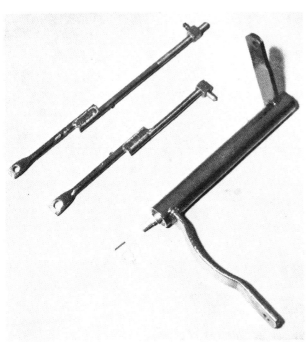

Don't weld up clutch linkage rods like these. Better to make new ones from threaded rod and heavier than these, especially if clutch is a heavy-duty unit.

use, well, that's the way it is. But if it's too *long,* just curl it around to make up for the excess length.

It's quite possible to use a cable assembly together with older clutches and pedal assemblies, but you'll probably have to do a little head-noodling to make the leverage ratio work out. At any rate, it's a logical way to go and should help modern swappers out of their predecessor's dilemma.

Shifter Background

After the clutch linkage has been modified, and works smoothly, then the swapper can give serious thought to the shifting levers. While it may be desirable to maintain a column-mounted shifting arrangement for an automatic transmission, a floorshift is almost always better for the manual transmission.

Back just before WW II, Detroit began placing the shifting linkage on the steering column as a means of gaining true three-passenger front seats. This remote linkage—as it was called—created quite a stir in the hot rod ranks, and since drag racing wasn't known at the time, every rodder wanted to switch to column linkage. This trend started to change in the early 1950s, when drag racing began to show that a column shifter was far inferior to the old floor model. However, the problem of gearboxes prevented the wide popularity of floor shifters. Earlier gearboxes with the lever in the floor were rather weak

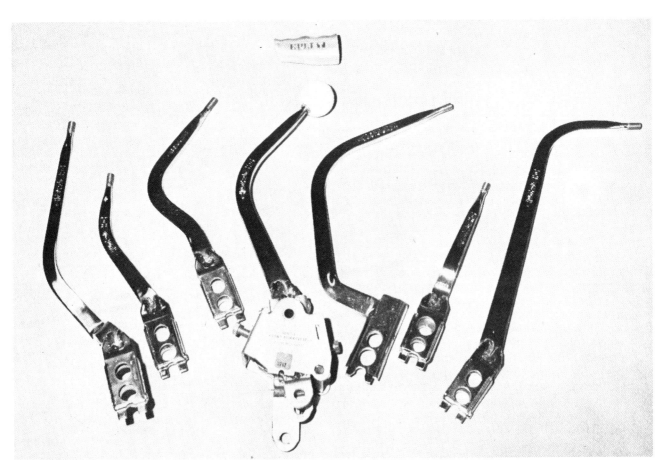

Standard-shift shifters are made in a variety of handle shapes to fit any transmission and body combo. The usual point of interference is where the handle hits the front seat; several handles are available that sweep forward to clear the seat.

In some swaps, you do have to cut a large hole to fit the shifter and transmission in the tunnel, but more work is required to make a new panel to rivet or screw in to cover the hole after installation. Original shifter hole (arrow) in this sports car swap must also be filled in.

and could not take the punishment meted out by the early OHV V8s. There were a few exceptions—namely, the early Cad-LaSalle and Packard transmissions. For a number of years, the only way to get a good floorshift was to have such a gearbox, but as engine performance continued to increase, even those monsters began to heave a sigh of anguish and show signs of giving up.

The first floorshift-for-sideshift box we ever saw was installed on a 1951 Ford, and consisted of the column shift unit cut down to about 6 inches long and mounted on brackets above the floorboard. This home-grown affair was crude, but it did work and it definitely was faster shifting than the column parent. It was not strong, however, and the slightest miscalculation on the driver's part meant a new set of gears.

By the end of the 1950s, it was apparent to almost everyone except Detroit that a floorshift was absolutely essential to drag racing. In 1960 there was a flurry of hot rod-oriented shifters on the market, several of which are still in existence.

Problem Areas

There are several problems involved in designing a good floor shifter, not the least of which is low manufacturing cost. From an engineering standpoint, though, the problem boils down to getting a rather compact shifter located very near the transmission and having the shifter mechanism work flawlessly time after time. This becomes even more of a problem when the unit will be used for drag racing, where the slightest delay in getting from one gear to the other may spell defeat. To this end, there are all kinds of shifters now on the market, all featuring a form of straight-line shifting. That is, unlike the old open-top transmission where the

distance between low and 2nd gears may be 2 feet forward and 1 foot to the right, the modern floor shifter has a very short, positive throw. For the swapper this is a boon, since space is always at a premium.

Most aftermarket shifters will bolt directly to the transmission at the tailshaft mating flange and exit the shifting lever through the floorboards. This means there will be a 4x5-inch hole in the flooring. Some of the Detroit linkage mounts to the flooring and leads to the transmission through a smaller hole. Whichever type the swapper selects will largely be dictated by how much room he has available. In most late-model cars, the transmission hump—or tunnel—is very pronounced and fits around the transmission like a glove. This limits the amount of room inside for a transmission-mounted shifter. When this is the case, the floor-mounted shifter may prove better from an installation standpoint.

As a rule, however, the transmission-mounted shifter is superior. Definitely do plan on spending a few extra dollars to install a quality shifter. There are shifters available for an "almost nothing" price, but they usually perform with satisfaction to match. Get a shifting assembly that will work well time after time, and the best guide here is the drag strip—poor equipment is not going to be used for the ¼-milers. Another good example to follow is Detroit; whatever style they prefer, chances are it will be good for a swap.

When installing a floor shifter, follow the instructions to a tee, and use insulation washers if possible. This will eliminate some unusual "buzzing" from beneath the car, as will a rubber band—cut from an old tire tube—wrapped around the linkage. Like so much about an engine swap, good work here will immediately pay off because it is something the driver can feel.

The Steering System

Small domestic or imported cars with non-power rack-and-pinion steering might make use of the power-assist unit from a Mustang II.
When the engine replacing the 4-cylinder engine on a small car ends up with more engine weight on the front end, power-assist rack-and-pinion is a must. In Ford's unit, steel lines from the pinion part of the box carry fluid to either side of the sealed rack's center, and the fluid pushes the rack left or right in response to signals from the box.

Problems involving a car's steering system often crop up unexpectedly during an engine swap. More often than not, the problem is one of physical clearance between some part of the steering system on the front side of the firewall and some part of the engine. Occasionally, the swapping of a much heavier engine than was originally installed will mean more weight on the front wheels—enough to make steering very difficult. In such a case, serious consideration must be given to substituting a steering system pirated from a heavier car.

Steering Compatibility

If interference is discovered during an engine swap, it's likely to be between the steering box—or the column leading down to it—and a part of the engine block, exhaust manifold, or headpipe. It's evident that something has to be shifted. But many swaps we've seen were complicated unnecessarily by the swapper who shifted the steering gear outboard on the frame—which means cutting and welding, etc.—when simply milling the stock exhaust manifold along the block-mating surface would have accomplished the same thing. It's in cases like these that using forethought is important. Remember the rodder's adage: "There's another way to do it." Some of the reasons for not arbitrarily relocating the steering box, if it can be avoided, will become clear as we get further along.

The steering box is no more than a simple leverage device, with the ratio designed to do a certain job as easily as possible. For this reason, the entire system will be a compatible unit, with length of the pitman arm and steering arms at the spindles an important consideration in the gearbox ratio. The steering wheel diameter is also part of the total and must never be overlooked.

The enthusiast will want to keep steering system components as nearly stock as possible. If this is not possible, a change in one place will mean a similar change elsewhere. For instance, anytime the pitman arm angle or length is changed, a similar change must be made at spindle arm and steering wheel if a particular gear ratio is to be maintained. Such a change will also affect geometry, which must be considered.

Getting Clearance

Alignment of the gearbox is particularly critical. Moving the box just 1 inch to either side or fore or aft will affect the steering, usually allowing the car to turn tighter in one direction, since the gearbox lock will be in the incorrect location relative to pitman arm travel. If the gearbox is moved, then the drag link-tie rod assembly must be equally modified.

Perhaps even more important is the angle of the gearbox and pitman arm to the steering linkage. One common mistake is to raise or lower the existing gearbox to gain clearance. When this is done, relationship of the pitman arm small end to the remaining linkage is changed. The result is misalignment that shows up as hard spots in the steering—caused by binding—and erratic steering.

Installation of different engines in the chassis

sometimes calls for slight gearbox movement to clear exhaust manifolds. It is a mistake to move the box downward a significant distance, more than 1 inch, since the idler arm must then be lowered the same distance. This places the shorter connecting rods from drag link to spindle at the wrong angle, and front-end alignment is almost impossible to attain without changing the spindle arms accordingly. It's better to build a set of tubing headers.

Another example would be any vehicle with side steering, such as the early Fords or a 1939 Chevrolet. If the Chevy gearbox is moved forward or aft, the drag link must be shortened or lengthened a like amount. Otherwise the pitman arm no longer rests at the exact halfway point of travel and turning will be less on one side. If the box is moved up or down, the drag link will no longer be parallel with the springs, which will cause erratic steering upon wheel deflection.

System Geometry

Here's what happens. The connection point of the drag link at both pitman arm and spindle arm must be in a line parallel with the spring or wishbone (in the case of early Fords). This way, when the axle moves up and down, the drag link moves in the same plane. However, if the gearbox is moved, the centerlines of the drag link and spring or wishbone are no longer parallel. When the axle moves up and down, there are diverging arcs between steering linkage and wheels. As these arcs change, the wheels will wander from side to side, and steering will be miserable.

In a typical side steering modification, in which the gearbox might be lowered 1 inch, the solution is to reduce the length of the pitman arm by the same amount. This will effectively reduce the speed of the steering system (lock-to-lock turns of the steering wheel will increase). The spindle steering arm can be shortened or lengthened a similar amount, but this is not a common practice, nor is it recommended.

Connecting the relocated gearbox with the drag link or tie rods is not to be left to poor quality parts. As a rule, tie-rod ends supplied on the original car will do the job for a reasonable period of time. If the vehicle is more than eight or nine years old, or has seen heavy mileage, it is best to replace all steering rod ends. Always purchase the very best. Moog rod ends are excellent. If the engine swap has created a car that is heavier by 200 or 300 pounds, it is wise to make one size increase in rod ends on small cars. For example, on a Chevy II go up one size to regular Chevy, etc. When installing new rod ends, make sure the taper is correct and that the rod end attachment bolt does not pull through the arm too far, thus binding the rod end. Also check that there is no interference between the rod end and the linkage to the steering arm or pitman arm through the full travel.

In some cases where extreme engine/steering clearances are found, it's best to leave the steering box as near its original location as possible—but do away with the stock steering column, and U-joint your way around the difficulty as shown in the accompanying photos.

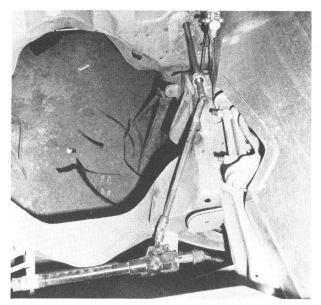

A physically large Chevy rat motor is slated for this Camaro, so steering must be snaked around the sides of the compartment. Industrial aircraft U-joints may be used in such an instance. Here, shaft leads to a Pinto rack-and-pinion unit.

If the newly transplanted engine is much heavier than the one it replaces, a power steering unit will ease the steering chores. On this swap, the power steering cooler is mounted ahead of the box for advantageous air blast.

Steering gear/engine interference may be relatively minor. Small-block Chevy V8 in this '50s-era Chevy pickup needs only a little outboard shifting of steering box, done with shims (arrow). A shift of the box by more than an inch, though, would mean revamping of drag link and tie rods.

The Fuel System

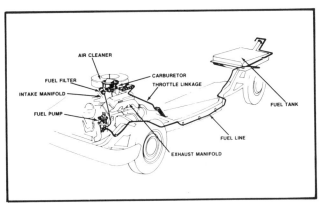

Most American cars incorporate a fuel system that runs something like this. It's best to double-check the components before subjecting them to the fuel requirements of a big engine.

Engine swapping, as the reader may have deduced from browsing this far in the book, involves many areas in addition to the actual replacement of the engine. Some, like beefing up the brakes or driveline to accept greater horsepower and torque, are obvious. But there are other items that should be checked into that the novice swapper may be blind to. Take the fuel system, for example.

If the engine swap is being done with an older car—not necessarily a piece of vintage tin that may have rested unused behind a barn for many years, though the following still applies—it's wise to check out the fuel tank and lines for an accumulation of dirt and debris, possible rust or even water from condensation. It's possible that the older boiler you're ash-canning ran just fine on fuel supplied by the original system. But, fitted out with new-found power, that healthy rig of yours may draw fuel far faster than it did previously; however, a partially blocked pickup tube or line may not supply it quickly enough. The result will be a stumbling engine that gasps when floored, leading to a lot of head-scratching in an effort to solve the problem.

Tank Removal

Most fuel tanks are suspended beneath the rear of the car, just under the trunk floor, by a couple of metal bands bolted to the flooring. If your tank has a drain plug, remove it and let all the old gas run into a container of suitable size. You don't want this stale fuel anyway, and with a weight of about 6.5 pounds per gallon, you'll have problems removing the tank if you're working by yourself.

Next, remove the filler neck if it appears necessary. Most tanks have just the stub of a tube as part of the tank, then a short length of neoprene hose, held with hose clamps, joining the upper metal tube that on many cars is held in some way to the fender or its inner panel. Undo the hose clamps and work the upper section of tube off. Remove the main fuel line fitting, usually at the front of the tank. Loosen the restraining bands; then, if it appears there is still some heft to the tank due to fuel that didn't drain out, slide a floor jack under the car to support the tank while you take out the band's bolts. Now, let the jack down slowly. There are still fuel gauge wires connected to the sending unit on the top side of the tank; watch that these don't stretch and break or pull loose from their terminals. They may not be long enough to let the tank all the way down to the garage floor. Finally, remove the sending unit wires and work the tank out from under the car.

The local radiator shop is equipped to boil your tank out for a nominal fee. They may also be able to pour in slushing compound, swirl it around, then pour out the excess. This will coat the inner surfaces of the tank and make it rust-free. If they don't, slushing compound is available at some speed shops and major brand paint stores. If all else fails, try your local airport. Cleanliness of aircraft fuel tanks is so important that most aircraft overhaul shops stock slushing compound.

It probably won't be necessary to completely re-

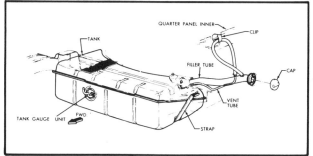

A closer look at the fuel tank itself and arrangement of components as found in most cars. The fuel tank should be removed from an older car during engine swap, for cleaning and inspection of fuel lines, etc.

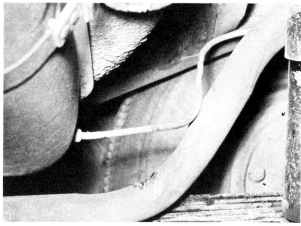

When checking the fuel line, look for such obvious faults as this: line and exhaust pipe interference.

move the fuel line from the car, but inspect it for kinks or areas worn thin by long rubbing. Inspect any lengths of neoprene hose that may be a part of the line. If in doubt about its condition, replace it. If the old line is visually okay, blow through it with compressed air just to be sure.

Fuel Pump

With the tank and line up to snuff, there are still some things regarding the fuel system that bear looking into. You may discover, for example, that some part of the car's frame, front suspension, or other component, interferes with the engine's fuel pump. Often, this has caused swappers to locate the engine to provide access to the pump. This isn't the right way to do it, and it's caused many a firewall to be unnecessarily "massaged" in order to position the engine so the fuel pump can be installed.

If anything prevents you from installing the pump after the engine is permanently bolted in, don't worry. You can go a different route by blocking off the fuel pump opening and adding a remote electric pump. Speed shops will have a block-off plate for most popular engines. If not, one may be easily made and bolted on.

Electric Fuel Pump

Electric pumps come in four types—plunger, diaphragm, bellows, and impeller. They can be mounted anywhere in the line between the gas tank and the carburetor, but their main advantage is eliminated if they are not placed as close to the tank as possible.

The advantage of an electric fuel pump, besides being an alternative to the stock pump, is elimination of vapor lock. With the pump mounted at the tank, the whole fuel line between tank and carburetor is pressurized. With the fuel under pressure, it is extremely difficult for vapor bubbles to form, even if the fuel line gets hot. It's a pretty safe bet that any time a fuel pump is mounted at the tank, vapor lock will be eliminated. Also, it's much cooler back there, so the pump is not likely to become overheated.

The disadvantage of electric pumps is in educating the driver to use them. Electric pumps are ordinarily hooked up to the ignition switch. Any time the switch is on, the pump is maintaining pressure in

Typical tank sending unit. Float rides at fuel level, and through movement of the arm acting on the resistor, "tells" the gas gauge what to indicate. Old floats may have leaked gas inside, so they won't register accurately.

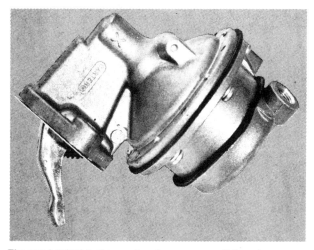

The mechanical fuel pump has become something of an engineering marvel, and seldom causes any problems. But it frequently causes head-scratching in an engine swap since it may interfere with some part of the chassis. The only way out is to eliminate it.

Fuel

But when the stock pump goes, something else has to be substituted to keep the fuel going from tank to carburetion. A remotely-located electric fuel pump is the best solution, ideally mounted as near the tank as is practical.

Here are a pair of electric pumps (to assure adequate line pressure to a fuel-hungry engine) mounted near the fuel tank.

Somewhere in the line between the tank and carburetor, install a fuel filter to trap sediment.

the fuel line. This is fine, until the switch is left on accidentally and the carburetor happens to have a needle valve that leaks a little. In such an unfortunate combination of circumstances, the complete contents of the gas tank will be pumped into the float bowl, filling the engine and overflowing messily onto the ground.

The plunger is without any rings or seal. Fuel constantly leaks between it and the cylinder wall, so that even when the engine is not running, the pump will slowly tick away, maintaining pressure in the line. With age, the pump will operate faster due to wear between piston and cylinder wall.

The strong point of the electric fuel pump, besides its being a dire necessity if you can't use the stock mechanical one, is its reliability. There is no diaphragm to rupture, and the piston and valves can easily be removed in case they get loaded with dirt. A strainer and sediment chamber can be cleaned simply by removing the bottom cap.

No matter what electric fuel pump is selected, it should be mounted as close to the fuel tank as possible so it will push the gasoline rather than pull it. This doesn't rule out a firewall mounting if that is the only alternative, but the closer to the gas tank the better. It should be mounted slightly lower than the tank so gravity will help that tiny amount, and it is imperative to make sure the pump selected is of the correct voltage. Most of the performance pumps are available in 6, 12, or higher voltage, so check what you have.

All the electric pumps include installation instructions, but one instruction bears an underscore—never connect the pump wire to the hot side of the ignition coil; always bring the power lead from the ignition switch. Mount the pump well away from the exhaust pipe and in as cool a place as possible. It should also be protected from flying debris.

When the large engine has stock carburetion, it may be possible to get good results with a single high-performance pump. But make allowances when installing such an electric pump for a later addition of another pump—just in case a larger carb (or carbs) is bolted to the car later.

Here's a special note on imported cars that have a large-displacement American engine added. Most

An auxiliary fuel tank has been installed in trunk compartment. It's actually the tank from an older car. The electric fuel pump is conveniently mounted below it. Arrow indicates leads from sending unit. The float arm inside has been bent to compensate for vertical mounting position of the tank as opposed to the horizontal one.

of these cars have an electric fuel pump as stock equipment, but these pumps are totally inadequate to feed any kind of engine approaching 300 cubic inches. They should be replaced at the time of the swap if any kind of peak performance is expected.

It will be noted that many new cars feature a return line from the stock fuel pump to the gas tank, as a guard against vapor lock and "lingering" pressure. If this feature is desired, it can be attained by installing one of the special inline fuel filters that also has such a return line (when an electric pump system replaces the stock mechanical pump). Always use a large capacity fuel line filter, and check it often to see that it is not clogged and restricting gas flow.

Gas Cap

If your car is fairly old, it will pay to buy a new gas cap. The gasket on the old one may have dried out or a piece may have broken out of it through long usage. While you're at it, consider a locking cap, for with higher and higher gasoline prices, it sure smarts to park your car with a full tank only to return later to find someone has ripped off your supply. Make certain the new cap is compatible with your tank, though. If the tank isn't vented, then the cap must be. Air must enter the tank to replace the fuel as it is used. I once had a service station attendant replace my fuel cap with another that happened to be lying at hand. The tank wasn't vented, and neither was the cap. The result, many miles later, was an engine that went mysteriously dead and—it was found later—a tank that collapsed inward to the extent of a 6-gallon dent.

Sending Unit

Before you replace the tank in the car, check out the sending unit. Even if the fuel gauge on the dashboard works, chances are, on an older car, that the sending unit float isn't working as it should. Older cars used a simple cork attached to a long hinged arm that, as the cork dropped downward with the diminishing fuel in the tank, activated a rheostat that, in turn, caused the gauge needle to move. With the toll of years, the cork may have become less buoyant through the soaking up of gasoline, and hence caused the gauge to register inaccurately. Later cars use a metal float, much like that in a carburetor. Floats, because they're hollow, must necessarily be made of two parts soldered or simply crimped together. It might be that fuel has seeped into the float, causing it to sink, so your gauge always registers empty. In fact, this is often the cause of a malfunctioning gauge, rather than the electrics of the system or the gauge itself. Most dealers, if they don't stock floats alone, will have new or rebuilt sending units. Parts houses may have a universal sending unit that you can use after bending the float arm in accordance with the depth of your tank. Since gauges don't register in gallons, only the variation between empty and full, a universal sending unit will work for you providing that the float arm is long enough to reach the bottom of the tank when it is empty, and the top when full.

If you must rework an existing steel or copper fuel line, or splice in a new length, a single-flaring tool is used to form end flare.

Don't ever use ordinary rubber tubing for a fuel line—e.g. a piece of windshield wiper hose. Use Neoprene or other specially treated tube.

Hardly necessary for street driven cars, aircraft quality—or A/N—fittings, lines are available from surplus outlets if you want that "trick" look under your hood.
The variety of A/N fittings may be staggering, and these are only a fraction of those available. There's bound to be one to fit your application.

Throttle Linkage

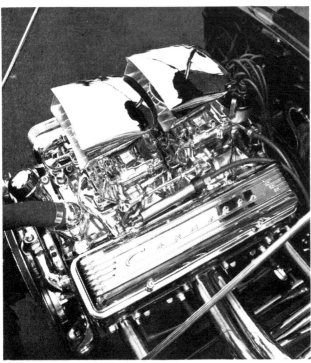

If you can put your dark glasses on amidst the chrome on this street rod engine, you'll see a hydraulic throttle being used. These can be purchased in almost any length and are perfect for problem swaps such as in long vans and motorhomes.

If the throttle system is so simple, how come it causes so many headaches? Everybody who works on cars has some hang-up in some area that they just can't seem to conquer. With us it's wiring and linkages. We long ago gave up trying to subdue those miles of mechanical snakes—but we're still thrashing around in the linkage jungle. Not much headway have we seen in clutch connections, the bane of any engine swapper, but we're beginning to get some smarts with throttle links, mainly because someone in Detroit invented the cable throttle.

Going from the foot to the carburetor lever is such a direct route it seems, but when you live in Podunk the "just right" piece is never available. So you end up making do with whatever you find in the junkyard, and this is where many rodders get into trouble: No two cars have identical throttle assemblies.

Driver comfort dictates in large degree how a foot throttle will be shaped, where it will be located, and how much pressure will be built into the system. All these items are interrelated, and have, in turn, an effect on linkage ratios. Thus, the throttle system for a 1970 Chevrolet will not be the same as that for a 1977 Pontiac. Every time there is a change in carburetion, for instance, there is usually a change in carburetor throttle arm. This will directly affect the ratio of the firewall throttle arm. The carburetor may have different size butterfly valves, which will require a different return spring at the throttle arm; thus, the total pressure required at the pedal will change (lighter or stiffer). The importance of a well-balanced system is seldom appreciated until it isn't there.

Strangely enough, a large percentage of engine-swapped cars have poor throttle systems. One will be so soft that the driver is constantly holding back with his foot, the other so stiff that his foot is always forcing against heavy springs. Another will have linkage that binds, while still another will be so touchy that the slightest foot movement gives great throttle change.

Rod Linkage

Throttle systems come in three basic types: the original rod, the more modern cable, and the hydraulic. All are in use by street rod builders, and all have advantages (and disadvantages). Since form follows function in most aspects of rodding, the type of throttle system selected should be based on what will do the best job; but that is usually the secondary consideration. The main problem is most often one of component supply. Assuming that supply is becoming less of a problem, and assuming that most street rod builders are handy enough with hacksaw and file to cobble up small parts, we're back to choosing the best unit for the job.

The original solid rod linkage is most common to the automobile, although a cable connection was for years included as a control for hand throttle and choke. The great advantage of a rod system is strength—very important with older cars where vibration and the usual poor maintenance was expected. At the same time, the rod system allows for heavier throttle spring return pressures than mod-

The simplest and best throttle linkage for an engine swap is one where you can use stock parts with only slight modifications, such as on this swap where only a simple bend in the rat motor's rod was needed.

ern components. This particular system also had some advantage in simplicity. Considered important with older carburetor designs, it is now obsolete.

A good example of rod simplicity is the Ford Fairlane of recent years. Here, the throttle linkage includes an idler shaft mounted between two brackets, one bracket on the firewall and the other on the engine. The small lever used to connect idler to carburetor rod is spot-welded to the idler shaft at a slight angle, but the entire mechanism is simple and obviously inexpensive to produce. It seems elementary, but unless the linkage is in reasonable alignment, and unless the operating arms are of the correct ratio, the linkage will not work correctly. In essence, this type of linkage (including an idler or bellcrank assembly between foot pedal and carburetor arm) is more prone to give the hot rodder trouble than any other.

Cable Throttle

The cable throttle, introduced several years ago on Detroit stockers because of simplicity and low cost, is by far the most adaptable to most street rods, especially when low assembly spring pressures at the carburetor are involved. The modern cable throttle is much improved over the single wire unit of the past, in that the woven cable of about ⅛-inch diameter moves freely through a loose fitting cover. When first introduced, the new cable units were prone to stick (one of the disadvantages of a cable throttle for years), but working with a synthetic plastic housing the new cables are trouble-free.

Because the cable is essentially a direct route system, most new cars use hanging foot pedals, which is a boon for the hot rodder faced with a pedal mounting problem. However, since the cable is flexible, it is strictly a tension member—it pulls, but does not push. Therefore, the return spring integral with the foot pedal is to return the pedal only (some pedals have no spring). This means that pedal pressure must be at the carburetor or the end of the cable. Rather than rely on the carburetor return spring(s), it is advisable to install one of the accessory springs with a long, soft pull.

Most cars with an automatic transmission will include a separate solid rod linkage system for the

throttle control pressure switch at the gearbox. If this is so, a second spring may be included on the bellcrank or idler arrangement for the transmission control. It is essential to always use the linkage originally produced for the transmission, or at least exactly duplicate the ratios involved!

Keep in mind that a change in carburetion may have an effect upon this automatic control ratio also. To check, measure the length of the carburetor throttle arm (center of throttle valve shaft to center of operating connection point). If the new arm is longer or shorter than normal to the transmission linkage, lengthen or shorten the corresponding arm on the transmission bellcrank. Unless this portion of the system, which is considered a part of the throttle assembly, is correct, throttle manipulation will always seem out of sync with the transmission shifting points.

Hydraulic Throttle

The hydraulic throttle has been known for years, but only during the last decade has it come into widespread use in hot rodding. Because of the complexity of cable and rod linkage routing over a great length—as with buses and boats—the hydraulic unit is preferable. In hot rodding, dragsters began using a hydraulic unit intended for ski boats, because it was much easier to mount than either cable or rod, and it had the advantage of a longer available throw (movement) than was practical with mechanical linkages. Quite expensive at first, these types of fluid couplings are now within reach of the street rodder, although still not as cheap as either cable or rod. In some cases of problem linkages, the hydraulic assembly—including combination foot pedal and master cylinder, high pressure hose, and slave cylinder—is recommended.

As with the cable throttle there should be extra return springs for attendant linkage, as in the case of an automatic transmission; but since the hydraulic

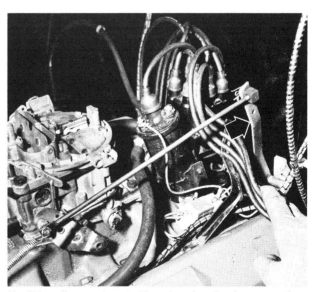

You'll have to experiment with various lengths, leverages to find the most comfortable setup for your car, as each swap is different. You can provide for adjustments by use of threaded rods and extra linkage holes (arrow) for different leverage.

Throttle

In this swap, this Chevy truck had a long throttle arm for the six that was original. This was heated and bent back to line up with the V8 carb. Throttle rod was also bent.

unit is a compression linkage, the foot pedal return spring is effective and the extra carburetor lever spring will pull toward the slave cylinder.

Linkage Mods

Of special interest to street rod builders are modifications to carburetor linkages, and the selection of foot pedals. Since all systems are originally engineered to work together, it's no wonder that the old Ford cross-shaft firewall idler will not fit most modern carburetors; and it is expected that the foot pedal pressure for the 6-cylinder Chevrolet is greater than needed with a late Chevy V8. Further, and of greater importance, is the difference in linkage ratios. The Ford cross-shaft can be narrowed to give a pulling movement (cut shaft between the two mounting cups), but the arm should be lengthened or shortened to approximate what the engine had originally. (Find a chassis and measure to be sure.) Just 1 inch will make a tremendous difference in throttle response.

Modifications may be necessary to all three types of linkage, but are restricted to the carburetor lever and pedal/master cylinder connection with hydraulic, the carburetor lever and foot pedal with the cable, and everything possible with the rod linkage. It is even possible to make the entire linkage assembly from selected pieces. In all cases, however, there are some basic rules of linkage that must not be overlooked.

When modifying linkage, it is imperative that all welded joints be premium. There is not a great deal of strain on the linkage, and brazing is recommended for a better finish. As a rule, it is easier to make one complete unit from two similar links or levers than to actually make something from scratch.

If the carburetor lever must be modified, it should be removed from the carburetor proper if possible. Otherwise, the heat of welding/brazing is likely to cause distortion of the butterfly valve assembly. In some cases, this lever may be cast of quality steel; if so, avoid excess bending (cold). In the event that the lever is a rather complicated mass of bent sheet stock, it might be possible to get the correct alignment and ratio by drilling the connection hole in a different location on the lever.

Many times, the firewall linkage may be bent to give the correct alignment. On practically every car other than Ford, the carburetor is designed for a pulling throttle link, which simplifies the linkage. Yet, it is essential to get the firewall and carburetor levers in line so that the connecting rod ends are not in a bind somewhere during travel. The linkage should work very smoothly at all times, with no rough spots or over-center conditions of any sort.

It is quite easy to build an over-center situation into throttle linkage, especially at full-open position. When working with linkage, remember that the levers are working through specific arcs of travel. Envision two levers in a vertical position: as they both move forward there is immediate response of foot pedal and throttle butterfly; however, as both arms approach horizontal, response becomes spongy. It is then that one or both arms can pass beyond horizontal—and in the case of a full-open throttle, the carburetor is stuck full bore. This is one of the specific safety problems drag race technical inspectors look for, and one of the most common errors in initial street rod linkage.

When trying to establish the correct travel arcs for linkage levers, it is easier to start the travel before vertical and end the travel at about the same number of degrees after vertical. Something starting at around 10 o'clock and ending at two o'clock is the ideal. When an intermediate bellcrank is included in the linkage, it is easy to get an over-center situation in combination if the bellcrank levers are used to modify the ratio (one arm is of different length than the other). Here, neither the foot pedal lever nor the carburetor lever are over-center—but the bellcrank lever is traveling through the last few degrees before it gets to over-center.

Another kind of bind in throttle linkages, almost always due to a modification, is peculiar to rod connections. The rod itself may move so that it's hitting a manifold or head. Although this might seem a slight problem, it is an interference that will cause

In many cases, simple mechanical linkage can be made from a few small rod ends and rods. This Jaguar/302 swap required a Moon bellcrank to change the direction of the original linkage. Note the many adjustment and lever-positioning holes.

the linkage to be tight, as it places extra load on the rod ends. Also check for worn or cocked bushings, particularly at the firewall, and use a good door latch grease to reduce drag. Most firewall linkage does not include a bushing as such, but relies on a short length of tubing to act as both alignment guide and bushing to the lever.

When modifying linkage, include some form of rod end or Teflon bushing for the rod. If a cable throttle is used, the end ball must be free of nicks. Any welding near a Teflon bushing will tend to distort it, so check the hole for roundness.

It's common to change the length of a hanging foot pedal, whether cable or rod linkage is involved. Keep in mind that a longer arm will make the pedal move easier, a shorter arm will make it stiffer. If the arm is made longer, which is the norm, it is often wise to include a footrest alongside the pedal.

On the subject of foot pedal comfort, note that the angle of the foot feed is critical to long distance cruising comfort. The best way to determine the correct angle is to sit in normal driving position and note the angle of the shoe sole when the foot seems comfortable. Usually, the foot will rest easily on the heel, angling slightly to the right at the toe. The foot will also be turned slightly with the outside edge being closer to the firewall.

When cutting the length of rod linkage, it may be easier to install a section of full-thread rod from the local hardware. If you're not handy with a torch, it's easy to modify the rod by cutting and then installing a section of tubing over the cut ends. Drill through tubing and rod and peen over a pin. Another quickie is to use threaded rod and tubing (as found in trophies and desk lamps). If such an adjustable rod is used, include stop nuts at the tubing to avoid change of the rod length due to vibration.

You'll hardly ever find a cable throttle that's the perfect length for your project. It's usually too long. If it's too short, just add a section of rod to the carburetor end. If too long, remove one of the swedged ends from the cable. This is most easily done by cutting the cable at the end, then drilling the remaining pieces of cable from the end. Cut the cable housing to the desired length, reinstall the cable and cut it to the correct length, then swedge the end back in place. A drop of brass will keep it secure. Do not lubricate a cable unit, as the lubricant will attract dirt and eventually cause sticking.

Before you start modification of a cable unit, also check the several different types available and note the various carburetor-end connections. Some use the snap-ball end while others are set with a clevis yoke. They're available from almost any dealer; Ford, MoPar, and GM cars all use the cable type in most applications. Just check out the linkage on a few cars on the dealer's lot and you'll know just what year and model to get. Wrecking yards are also a good source, because you can choose from a wider variety of cars when you shop there. Aftermarket equipment companies should be able to supply any of the pieces you'll need if you decide to build your own linkage rather than go to the cable type. Above all, remember the two most important criteria for building a throttle linkage . . . make it safe, and make it comfortable.

By far one of the easiest ways out for the problem linkage swap is using a late-model cable throttle. Buy a cable at your dealer, make up a bracket, and you can route the new linkage just about anywhere.

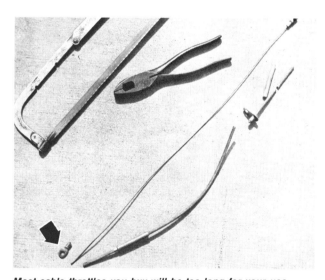
Most cable throttles you buy will be too long for your use. After you cut off the end (arrow), you can shorten the cable, drill out the end fitting and recrimp it on the cable.

Here's a good example of a sturdy, homemade bracket for a cable throttle.

Bellhousing Alignment

A magnetic base is ideal for attaching the dial indicator to the flywheel. This is how the dial indicator must be positioned to check concentric alignment of the rear bellhousing opening with the crankshaft centerline.

Although often overlooked, bellhousing alignment is absolutely crucial to smooth and reliable clutch and transmission operation. What is important is positioning the bellhousing on the back of the engine so that the centerline of the transmission input shaft will *precisely* line up with the centerline of the crankshaft. To compound the problem, the transmission mounting surface (rear of the bellhousing) must be parallel to the clutch engagement surface of the flywheel.

In all too many cases, the bellhousing (scattershield) is merely bolted up, using the factory-installed dowel pins as a guide. But like everything else that is mass-produced, placement of the dowel pins and the positioning of the dowel pin holes in the bellhousing are subject to manufacturing tolerances. Occasionally everything is exactly right or the tolerances cancel each other out, but far more frequently the tolerances "stack up" to produce a totally unacceptable error in alignment.

When the bellhousing is out of alignment, all sorts of problems can occur: pilot bearing failure, transmission bearing failures, clutch chatter, sluggish clutch movement, sloppy shifts, rapid synchronizer wear, or popping out of gear. And of course the first items to be blamed for such malfunctions are the transmission and/or clutch, rather than the assembly procedure.

To check bellhousing alignment properly, a dial indicator with a magnetic base is needed. Using the stock dowel pins, bolt up the bellhousing and tighten securely. The initial check should be the trueness of the flywheel, since all subsequent alignment checks will be measured using the flywheel face. It is essential that the flywheel face be perpendicular to the centerline of the crankshaft if consistently smooth clutch action is to be expected. This can be determined quickly by mounting the dial indicator on the bellhousing. As the crankshaft is slowly rotated, record any variations on the dial indicator, measuring from the bellhousing face to the flywheel (runout of .005 inch is acceptable). If flywheel runout measures more than .005 inch, check the mating faces of the flywheel and crankshaft for burrs or dirt. If this isn't the cause of the problem, the flywheel may be warped and need resurfacing.

Next, affix the dial indicator to the flywheel (the clutch should not be in place during this operation) and attach the indicator so that it contacts the transmission mating surface of the bellhousing about one inch out from the circumference of the rear opening (missing the transmission mounting bolt holes and the clutch pivot ball hole). Slowly rotate the crankshaft by hand and note any variations in the indicator reading to determine if the surface is parallel with the flywheel. The maximum allowable variation between the highest and lowest readings is .005 inch. If the variation is greater, shim stock will have to be placed adjacent to the low point between the bellhousing and the block until variations of .005 inch or less are obtained. Be careful to determine that unacceptable variations are not the result of burrs or paint runs on the mating surfaces or on the surface being followed by the indicator.

Now remount the dial indicator so that it measures the inside diameter of the rear opening in the bellhousing. Again, be sure there is no paint build-up, nicks, or burrs around the edge of the opening. Rotate the crankshaft slowly and check the readings. In this case, the maximum allowable variation is .010 inch, since the actual error is the total variation divided by two, or .005 inch misalignment. If the variation exceeds .010 inch, realignment will be required. Make several revolutions of the crankshaft to verify that the readings repeat.

If the bellhousing must be realigned, there are several approaches which can be used. In either case, the stock dowel pins must be removed from the block and discarded. It is important, however, that care must be used when removing the stock pins to avoid distorting or otherwise damaging the pin hole.

The first method consists of simply loosening the bellhousing bolts to permit moving the bellhousing until dial indicator variation of .010 inch or less is obtained. In some cases, it may be necessary to slightly enlarge the bolt holes in the bellhousing to get sufficient movement. Then tighten the bolts and recheck it to make sure the housing hasn't shifted. With the bolts securely tightened and the housing properly aligned, select a pair of points, roughly 180 degrees apart, where you can drill through the bellhousing flange and into the block mating surface for the installation of new dowel pins. The new pins need not be as large as the stock ones. Something on the order of ¼ inch in diameter is adequate. Most parts departments can supply such dowels. From then on, the bellhousing can be removed and reinstalled in perfect alignment.

The second method utilizes offset dowel pins, which are available from Mr. Gasket/Lakewood. These special pins are offered in three different offsets, .007, .014, and .021-inch, in both ⅝-inch and ½-inch diameters to cover virtually all applications (see chart). Before installing the offset pins, drill and tap a small hole into the side of each dowel pin hole (in the block) so that a small Allen-head set screw can be used to lock the offset pins in the proper orientation after alignment is completed.

When installed, the offset dowel pins can be adjusted with a screwdriver to obtain the proper alignment. In some cases the dowel pins must be polished with a strip of emery cloth to permit them to be rotated in the dowel pin holes with a screwdriver. Adjustment with these offset pins can be tedious and time-consuming, so be patient. After this is completed, tighten all bellhousing bolts and recheck the alignment one more time. If everything is okay, the bellhousing portion of the job is done.

OFFSET DOWEL CHART

Total Indicator Reading	One-Half Total Indicator Reading	Size Dowel To Be Used	Ford & Chrys. Dowel Part Number (½-inch diameter)	All GM Dowel Part Number (⅝-inch diameter)
.012″ to .020″	.006″ to .010″	.007″	15950	15920
.022″ to .034″	.011″ to .017″	.014″	15960	15930
.036″ to .052″	.018″ to .026″	.021″	15970	15940

Use this chart as a guide for selecting the proper Lakewood offset dowel pins to correct your misalignment woes.

Shown is a pair of the offset dowel pins, along with two 10-32 setscrews to lock the dowels in place when the alignment process is completed.

Before the offset dowel pins are installed, a hole must be drilled with a No. 21 drill bit and tapped for 10-32 threads to accept the setscrews.

It may be necessary to dress the dowel pins with emery cloth to permit their rotation after installation in the block.

When bellhousing alignment is complete, tighten the setscrews to secure the dowel pins for future reassembly without the hassles of realignment.

But before we pat ourselves on the backs, there's one more item to be checked: the front bearing retainer on the transmission. It is the outer diameter of this retainer that determines the concentric placement of the transmission on the bellhousing, not the transmission bolts. Therefore, it is important that the bearing retainer be the right one to work with the bellhousing being used. The retainer should be a snug fit into the opening in the bellhousing. If it is not, another retainer of the proper diameter must be found. (Most manufacturers have produced bearing retainers in a number of different diameters.) Another alternative is to use a spacer bushing in the bellhousing opening. Ansen Automotive Engineering (P.O. Box 1426, Gardena, California 90249) can supply several such bushings if you tell them the exact inside and outside diameters required.

A little time and effort spent aligning the bellhousing will save untold hours of future grief and should help you "zero-in" on your performance goals.

Trans Spotter's Guide

One of the basic foundations of hot rodding is parts swapping or, if you will, adapting new/old assemblies to new/old vehicles. Rare is the "rodney" that doesn't boast a different engine, rearend, braking system, wheel/tire combination, or transmission happily taking the place of an OEM part. Rare are the rodders who didn't sweat bullets trying to figure out how these old/new assemblies would fit into their predetermined packages. And rare is the storehouse from which exact weights, dimensions, prices, and availability can be extracted to help them in their quest for practical adaptations. In that we're devoting considerable space to the old torque multipliers, we thought we would take the opportunity to show you what the experts agree is the best way to get your rod (or machine) in gear.

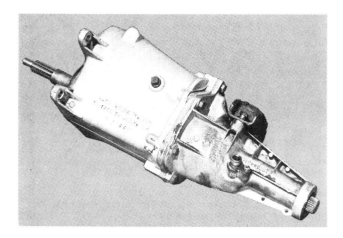

Some Buick extension housings may vary in appearance.

Early models have only these tapped holes.

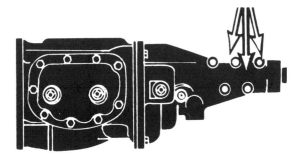

4-SPEED TRANSMISSION
Borg-Warner T-10, 9-bolt curved bottom side cover, aluminum case, and tailshaft housing (early model). Good for light-duty applications. Cast-iron case approx. 10 pounds heavier.
YEARS/MODELS OFFERED
'66-'69 Avanti; '65-'66 Buick Gran Sport, '62-'66 Skylark, '62-'66 Special; '57-'63 Chevy, '57-'63 Corvette, '59-'60 ½-ton truck; '62-'63 F-85 Olds; '60-'64 full-size Pontiac, '62-'64 Gran Prix; '59-'64 Studebaker Hawk, '62-'65 Studebaker Avanti.
CASE LENGTH/WEIGHT/APPROX. COST
21½ inches; 84 pounds; $125

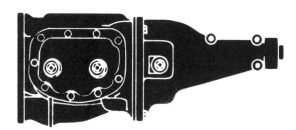

4-SPEED TRANSMISSION
Borg-Warner, 9-bolt curved bottom side cover. Used on light to medium cars.
YEARS/MODELS OFFERED
'65-'69 Mustang, '67-'68 Cougar, '65-'69 Shelby GT 350.
CASE LENGTH/WEIGHT/APPROX. COST
21½ inches; 84½ pounds; $125

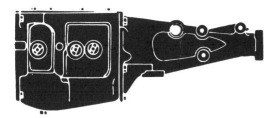

4-SPEED TRANSMISSION
Ford T&C, 10-bolt top cover.
YEARS/MODELS OFFERED
'70 Mustang
CASE LENGTH/WEIGHT/APPROX. COST
24 inches; 96 pounds; $125

4-SPEED TRANSMISSION
New Process, 10-bolt side cover. Used on medium-duty cars.
YEARS/MODELS OFFERED
'66-'67 Dodge Demon and Dart, '70-'73 Demon and Dart, '66-'67 Barracuda, '70-'73 Duster, '66-'68 Valiant, '76-'80 Aspen-Volare.
CASE LENGTH/WEIGHT/APPROX. COST
23½ inches; 116 pounds; $195

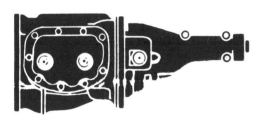

4-SPEED TRANSMISSION
Borg-Warner Super T-10, 9-bolt curved bottom side.
YEARS/MODELS OFFERED
1970. Found only as speed shop item to be used on drag racing or off-road applications on GM products only.
CASE LENGTH/WEIGHT/APPROX. COST
21½ inches; 84 pounds; $425 +

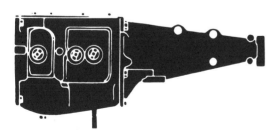

4-SPEED TRANSMISSION
Ford T&C, 10-bolt top cover, used with big block (390, 428, 429-inch) applications.
YEARS/MODELS OFFERED
'66-'73 Fairlane, '66-'73 Torino, '66-'67 Falcon, '67-'69 Mustang, '66-'73 Ranchero, '66-'69 Comet, '66-'69 Cyclone, '67-'69 Cougar, '67-'69 Shelby GT 500.
CASE LENGTH/WEIGHT/APPROX. COST
24 inches; 103 pounds; $195

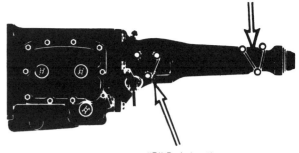

"E" Body location

"B" Body location

4-SPEED TRANSMISSION
New Process, 10-bolt side cover. Used on heavy-duty applications.
YEARS/MODELS OFFERED
'70-'72 Challenger, '70-'72 Barracuda
CASE LENGTH/WEIGHT/APPROX. COST
23½ inches; 116 pounds; $195

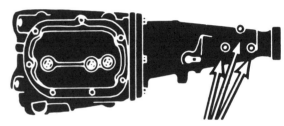

Holes may not be tapped.

4-SPEED TRANSMISSION
Saginaw, 7-bolt side cover.
YEARS/MODELS OFFERED
'66-'67 Buick Gran Sport, '75-'80 Skyhawk, '66-'67 Special; '66-'67 full-size Chevy, '67-'68 and '70-'77 Camaro, '66-'72 and '78-'80 Chevelle, '68-'79 Nova, '78 Corvette, '75-'80 Monza, '66-'72 and '78-'80 El Camino, '78-'80 Monte Carlo; '78-'79 Olds 442 and Cutlass, '75-'80 Starfire, '74-'78 Astre; '76-'80 Sunbird; '67-'68 Firebird, '78-'79 Grand Prix, '78-'79 Le Mans, '71-'77 Ventura II.
CASE LENGTH/WEIGHT/APPROX. COST
21½ inches; 84½ pounds; $125

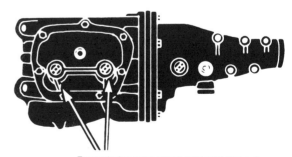

Transmission arms attach with stud and nut.

4-SPEED TRANSMISSION
Muncie, 7-bolt side cover, used from 1955 to 1968.
YEARS/MODELS OFFERED
'65-'68 Buick Gran Sport, '65-'68 Skylark, '65-'68 Special; '63-'68 full-size Chevy, '67-'68 Camaro, '64-'68 Chevelle, '64-'68 Chevy II and Nova, '63-'68 Corvette, '64-'66 Olds F-85, '67-'68 full-size Olds, '64-'66 Olds 442; '67-'68 Pontiac Firebird, '64-'68 GTO, '64-'68 Tempest.
CASE LENGTH/WEIGHT/APPROX. COST
21½ inches; 68 pounds (aluminum case); $175

Trans

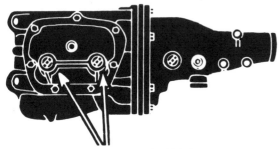

Transmission arms attach with bolt.

4-SPEED TRANSMISSION
Muncie, 7-bolt side cover, 1969 and later.
YEARS/MODELS OFFERED
'69 Camaro, '69-'72 Chevelle, '69-'70 Chevy II and Nova, '69-'74 Corvette, '69-'72 El Camino, '70-'72 Monte Carlo; '70-'72 Olds 442, '70-'72 Cutlass; '69-'72 Pontiac Firebird, '69-'73 GTO, '69-'72 Tempest and Le Mans, '71-'73 Ventura.
CASE LENGTH/WEIGHT/APPROX. COST
21½ inches; 68 pounds (aluminum case); $175

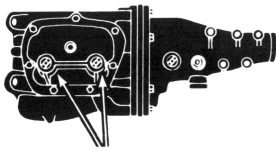

Transmission arms attach with bolt.

4-SPEED TRANSMISSION
Muncie, 7-bolt side cover, 1970, 454 Chevelle.
YEARS/MODELS OFFERED
'70-'74 Camaro, '69-'74 Chevelle, '71-'72 Nova and Chevy II, '69-'74 Corvette, '69-'74 El Camino, '70-'72 Monte Carlo; '70-'74 Pontiac Firebird, '69-'73 GTO, '69-'72 Tempest, '70-'72 442, '70-'72 Cutlass, '69-'72 Tempest and Le Mans, '71-'73 Ventura II.
CASE LENGTH/WEIGHT/APPROX. COST
21½ inches; 72 pounds; $275

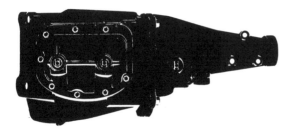

4-SPEED TRANSMISSION
Borg-Warner T-10, (AS-9), 1974 and later, 9-bolt curved bottom side cover.
YEARS/MODELS OFFERED
'74-'80 Camaro, '74-'78 Corvette, '74-'80 Pontiac Firebird.
CASE LENGTH/WEIGHT/APPROX. COST
21½ inches; 72 pounds; $275

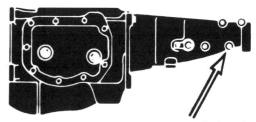

Holes may not be tapped.

3-SPEED TRANSMISSION
Borg-Warner T-16, 9-bolt side cover, first gear synchronized.
YEARS/MODELS OFFERED
'67-'68 Camaro.
CASE LENGTH/WEIGHT/APPROX. COST
21½ inches; 78 pounds; $60

Extension housings may vary in appearance.

3-SPEED TRANSMISSION
Ford, 9-bolt top cover, first gear synchronized.
YEARS/MODELS OFFERED
'63-'69 full-size Ford, '66-'77 Bronco, '63-'71 Fairlane and Torino, '63-'69 Falcon, '63-'71 Ranchero, '63-'79 ½-ton pickup, '69-'79 van, '63-'67 Comet, '63 Meteor, '63-'64 full-size Mercs; '65 full-size Pontiacs.
CASE LENGTH/WEIGHT/APPROX. COST
24 inches; 80 pounds; $60

3-SPEED TRANSMISSION
Ford, 9-bolt top cover, first gear synchronized.
YEARS/MODELS OFFERED
'65-'73 Mustang; '67-'69 Cougar.
CASE LENGTH/WEIGHT/APPROX. COST
24 inches; 80 pounds; $60

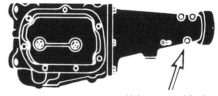

Holes may not be tapped.

3-SPEED TRANSMISSION
Saginaw, 7-bolt side cover, first gear synchronized. Caution; this transmission closely resembles Muncie.
YEARS/MODELS OFFERED
'66-'67 Buick Gran Sport and Special; '66-'70 full-size Chevys, '67-'80 Camaro, '66-'74 Chevelle, '66-'78 Chevy II and Nova, '66-'74 El Camino, '71-'80 Chevy and GMC vans, '73-'75 Vegas, '67-'80 ½-ton pickup, '69-'80 ¾-ton pickup, Blazer and Suburban, '68-'80 GMC ½-ton pickups; '66-'72 Olds F-85, 442 and Cutlass, '73-'76 Omega; '67-'68 Pontiac Firebird, '66-'73 GTO and Tempest, '74 GTO, '74-'78 Ventura.
CASE LENGTH/WEIGHT/APPROX. COST
21¼ inches; 75 pounds; $60

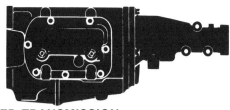

3-SPEED TRANSMISSION
Muncie, 7-bolt side cover, first gear synchronized. Caution: This transmission closely resembles Saginaw.

YEARS/MODELS OFFERED
'68-'72 Chevelle, '69-'80 ½ and ¾-ton pickups, Blazers and Suburbans (2-wheel drive), '68-'77 GMC ½-ton pickup (2-wheel drive), '71-'80 Chevy and GMC vans.

CASE LENGTH/WEIGHT/APPROX. COST
21¼ inches; 95 pounds; $85

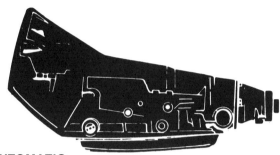

AUTOMATIC
GM Turbo 400, used in heavy-duty applications. (The Turbo 375 is externally identical, used in some GM trucks '65-'80).

YEARS/MODELS OFFERED
'66-'78 GM full-size products except Chevy which began in '67.

CASE LENGTH/WEIGHT/APPROX. COST
28⅝ inches (plus 4 or 9½-inch tailhousing); $225

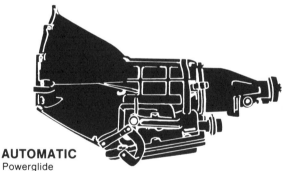

AUTOMATIC
Powerglide

YEARS/MODELS OFFERED
Used by GM '63-'73, primarily Chevys but some other applications as well. (Do not confuse this transmission with the Super Turbine 300).

CASE LENGTH/WEIGHT/APPROX. COST
28⅝ inches; 105 pounds; $50

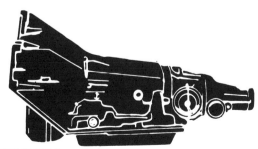

AUTOMATIC
GM Turbo 350, used in light and medium-duty applications.

YEARS/MODELS OFFERED
All '68-'80 GM products.

CASE LENGTH/WEIGHT/APPROX. COST
27⅝ inches (plus 5¾-inch tailhousing); 125 pounds; $125

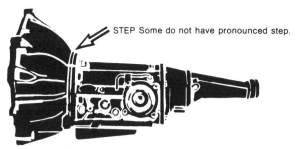

STEP Some do not have pronounced step.

AUTOMATIC
Ford C-4, used in medium and light-duty applications.

YEARS/MODELS OFFERED
All '64-'78 Ford products.

CASE LENGTH/WEIGHT/APPROX. COST
27¾ inches; 109 pounds; $75

AUTOMATIC
Ford C-6, used in medium and heavy-duty applications.

YEARS/MODELS OFFERED
All '66-'78 Ford products.

CASE LENGTH/WEIGHT/APPROX. COST
429 and pickup: 28¾ inches; 351, 427 and 428: 28½ inches; 140 pounds; $100

AUTOMATIC
Torqueflite 727 and 904 (cases will vary between small and big-block applications).

YEARS/MODELS OFFERED
Early version ('62-'64) used flanged output shaft; later version '62-'64 was cable-shift. In '65 applications both button and cable-shifts were offered. The 904 was used '60-'80. These versions used in Dodge, Plymouth and Chrysler with 318, 340, 360, 400 and 440-inch engines.

CASE LENGTH/WEIGHT/APPROX. COST
34½ inches; 138 pounds; $75

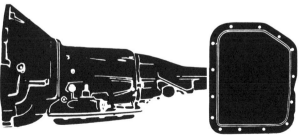

AUTOMATIC
Torqueflite 904 used in light-duty applications. Trans case virtually identical to 727 Torqueflite, but overall dimensions are smaller. Easily differentiated from 727 by differently shaped oil pan.

YEARS/MODELS OFFERED
'70-'76 Dodge and Plymouth equipped with 273 and 318-inch engines.

CASE LENGTH/WEIGHT/APPROX. COST
30½ inches; 105 pounds; $70

4-Speed Trans

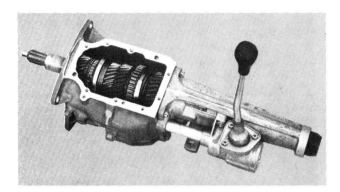

There's been a lot of talk that manual transmissions are on the way out, but don't you believe it! In the hands of a competent driver, the 4 or 5-speed still offers, in most cases, the quickest way down the track. The proof of the pudding is that in the lower classes of drag racing, where sticks and automatics run separately, a given engine combination will have a faster index and/or class record in its stick class than the same motor in the equivalent automatic class. And recent Bracket Nationals have been won by stick-shift cars, proving that, at least in the hands of the right driver, a manual trans *can* be consistent.

Going beyond drag racing, there definitely is no substitute, at this time, for the manual trans in roundy-round competition or road racing, and for good reason. These forms of racing generate tremendous heat buildup that would fry an automatic to a crisp. Even manuals must be specially modified to live under these intense conditions. When you combine this heat with constant up and down-shifting, you have conditions which more closely approximate hard street driving than drag racing, where transmissions need to go "only" from low to high at extreme high rpm in under 13 seconds.

That's why when we decided to explore the best 4-speeds, we went to a man who had learned how to make them live in the harsh, no-compromise world of stock car racing—Gordon Arbitter of Stick Only in Sun Valley, California. What he told us is that in most cases a stout dual-purpose street/strip General Motors Muncie, Chrysler New Process, Ford Toploader or Borg-Warner T-10 could be built relatively economically, using many factory parts. Gordon has also discovered that two very popular 4-speeds can be converted to economical overdrive transmissions, again using factory parts.

Interested? Now that we've got you in our clutches, here's how to get your act in gear. We'll start with the widely used Chrysler A-833 4-speed and Borg-Warner T-10 series. Both have proven to be quite popular with racers, due to the wide selection of gear ratios available. Then we'll cover the General Motors Muncie, Ford Toploader and Doug Nash 5-speed.

Chrysler New Process A-833

Chrysler's A-833 New Process 4-speed has been around in various forms since 1964 and is still in production today. Two different lengths were offered—a short version for compacts and one with a longer tailshaft for intermediates and full-size cars. The 1970-'74 Barracuda/Challenger and 1971-'74 Coronet/Charger/Satellite/Road Runner transmissions have a mounting pad location lower and farther forward than other models. Because of Chrysler's heavy involvement in racing, there have been many heavy-duty pieces available, including a large selection of gear ratios. Currently, an overdrive version is offered as well.

All production cases were cast-iron, except for 1975-'76 Feather Dusters, which had an aluminum case. At one time, a special racing aluminum case was offered under part No. P3690980. Unlike the production aluminum case, it featured steel coun-

tershaft bushings to keep the shaft from pounding a hole in the trans case. This part is no longer available new. However, both long and short aluminum extension housings are still listed under part Nos. P3571016 and P3571028, respectively.

Two different-diameter drive pinions (MoPar's terminology for "input shaft") have been used. The 1966 and later 426 Hemis and 1967 and later 440s used a beefy 1 3/16-inch-diameter shaft with 18-tooth clutch splines. All other motors used a 1-inch drive pinion with 23 splines.

That sounds simple enough, but here things begin to get confusing. There are currently at least seven different drive pinion bearing retainers used to retain two differently sized drive pinion bearings. Neither the drive pinion bearing retainer's base diameter (technically known as the "pilot diameter," since it's this part of the trans that pilots into the bellhousing) nor the size of the bearing itself necessarily correlates to the particular drive pinion being used. There's a lot of uncertainty as to what size retainers and/or bearings were used with a particular combo, although some more common applications are fairly definite: all 1964-'67 transmissions used a small No. 307 bearing, retained by a retainer with a small 4.35-inch-diameter pilot, 1966-'67 Hemis and '67 440s requiring a special retainer no longer stocked; since they used a larger drive pinion, it had a larger-diameter snout.

Starting in 1968, the large No. 308 bearing came into use, and the proliferation of retainers really began. It is generally accepted that most 440s and 426 Hemis used a 4.807-inch-overall-diameter pilot retainer (again with the larger-than-standard snout to provide clearance for the fatter drive pinion) and large No. 308 bearing. The '68-'69 383 continued to use the small No. 307 bearing, but with a special 4.807-inch-overall-diameter pilot retainer. The '70-'71 340s used the small No. 307 bearing with the small-diameter (4.354-inch-pilot) retainer. The '70-'71 383 used the large retainer and large bearing with the standard-diameter snout, as did many '72-'74 regular performance engines. From 1975 to 1980, the overdrive trans used retainers with an extra-large 5.125-inch pilot. Most have used the No. 308 bearing, although some '75s had the No. 307.

Now admittedly all this leaves a lot of loopholes, and there may even be some exceptions to what we've just listed. The best way to find out for sure is to measure your pilot diameter and check what bearing size you have. (Chart C-1) gives the current drive pinion bearing retainer usage (1970-'80). Earlier parts have generally been discontinued, but usually these later parts can be substituted (an exception being the pre-'68 coarse-spline trannys).

Many different gear sets have been used over the years (Chart C-2). High-performance engines with the 1 3/16 coarse-spline drive pinion have mainshaft gears that are bushed internally to prevent seizure on the shaft caused by severe operating conditions. There are also special racing-only slick-shift gear sets (Chart C-3) that have had every other tooth removed from the drive pinion and forward gears, and every other spline removed from the 1-2 and 3-4 synchro sleeves. The synchro ring, struts and synchro springs are discarded entirely. Although these parts are available over the counter,

A-833s with the small retainer pilot bolt pattern (left) cannot be redrilled to that of the larger retainer's (right) because of bolt hole interference. Several manufacturers, such as Lakewood Industries (Division W.R. Grace & Co., 4566 Spring Road, Cleveland, OH 44131), offer a bushing to adapt retainers with small pilots to bellhousings with the larger pilot hole.

CHART C-1

Current Pinion Retainer Usage

Drive Pinion Type	Bearing Size	Retainer Pilot OD	Retainer Part No.
Fine	No. 307	4.354	3410395
		4.807	2892256
		5.125	2960122
	No. 308	4.807	3410247
		5.125	3873596
Coarse		4.807	2801892*
			P3690062**

*Production
**Lubrited for racing

Three of the more common pinion retainers are shown here. From left to right, we have the 4.354-inch pilot OD retainer and small No. 307 bearing (part No. 3410395), 4.807 OD large retainer for fine-spline transmissions (part No. 3410247) and special 4.807 OD large retainer for coarse-spline transmissions (part No. 2801892). The two latter retainers accept the large No. 308 bearing.

4-Speed

CHART C-2

A-833 Gear Ratios

Input Spline	Application	Ratio			
		1st	2nd	3rd	4th
Fine	1970 & earlier (most)	2.66	1.91	1.39	1.00
	'70 Trans Am, '71-'74	2.47	1.77	1.34	1.00
	'65 6 cyl., '74-'75 318	3.09	1.92	1.40	1.00
	'75-'80 overdrive	3.09	1.67	1.00	.73
	1970 & earlier*	2.65	1.93	1.39	1.00
Coarse	'71-'74	2.44	1.77	1.34	1.00
	Race Red Stripe**	2.65	4.64	1.19	1.00

*Also available slick-shifted
**Has been available in the past as a conventional fine input spline gear set and as a conventional coarse input spline gear now available slick-shifted only with the coarse input. Liberty and Nash also offer special racing gear sets in addition to those listed here.

Three different gear designs are offered (left to right): standard, bushed, and bushed with every other tooth removed for the slick-shift race transmission.

CHART C-3

High-Performance Gear Sets

Fine-spline transmissions with the large pilot diameter retainer (4.807-inch) can be converted to the heavy-duty coarse-spline setup by using the following parts, in addition to the correct retainer and bearings designed for coarse-pitch transmissions (see Chart C-1). Of course these gear sets will fit in existing coarse-spline transmissions. For gear ratios, see Chart C-2.

Part	Conventional		Slick-Shift	
	'71-'74	'70 & Earlier		Red Stripe
Drive pinion	3410402	2538196	P2892320	
Cluster gear	3410407	2801109		P3681315*
First gear	2801107		P2892325	
Second gear	3410403	2801105	P2892323	P3681313
Third gear	3410405	2538202	P2892321	P3681311

*Discontinued. Purchase equivalent part from Doug Nash or Liberty Gears.

regular transmissions can be converted with a hand grinder.

Since 1975, overdrive 4-speed (part No. 3878005) has been offered for increased fuel economy. Unlike other Chrysler gear sets that had all coarse gear teeth, both fine and coarse-tooth overdrive gear sets are available. All early production overdrives received coarse gears, but some passenger car owners complained about excessive noise, so Chrysler quickly introduced the finepitch set. However, trucks retain the stronger coarse overdrive gears to this day.

Regular 23-spline input shaft, short-extension housing transmissions can be converted to over-

drive (Chart C-4) by changing the cluster, first gear, second gear, third gear and drive pinion. The output shaft will also have to be changed, since it's smaller in diameter where the overdrive gear fits. (This is also why the long trans can't be converted, as no special long output shaft was ever made.) Since the third-gear position in the overdrive version is actually occupied by the overdriven gear, to retain the normal "H" shift pattern with high (overdrive) gear at the bottom of the right-hand leg of the "H," the front 3-4 shift lever must be inverted downward and the linkage readjusted.

That linkage can be one of two types, for Chrysler changed the shifting mechanism and side cover in 1970, when the new double-lever interlock side cover was introduced on 340 6-barrel AAR 'Cudas and

Two types of synchros have been used. The 1971-'72 synchros (right) are best and can be installed in any of the older transmissions, where they decrease shifting effort while curing clashing problems.

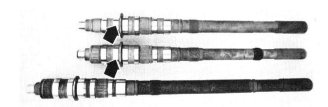

CHART C-4

Overdrive Conversion

Coarse-tooth gears, found in trucks and early '75 production cars, are preferred for strength, fine-spline for noise reduction.

Part	Coarse	Fine
Drive pinion	3743690*	3878647
Cluster gear	3878432	3878651
First gear	(Use existing gear)	3878650
Second gear	3878431	3878649
Third gear (OD)	3878430	3878648
Output shaft	4058228 (26-spline)	
	3878433 (30-spline)**	

*3.09:1 first gear transmissions already use this part.
**Use correct part needed to mate with your driveshaft and U-joints.

A new output shaft (top) is required because of overdrive (third) gear's smaller diameter (arrows). Shaft at bottom is for the long-extension housing trans; since there is no equivalent overdrive shaft, long trannys cannot be converted.

Trans Am Challengers. By 1971, the unit was being installed on all Chrysler 4-speed cars, replacing the older "ball-and-detent" unit in use since 1964. The new unit consists of a cover; two interlock levers; an interlock pin, clip and spring; two gearshift lever assemblies; and two steel forks (1-2 fork, part No. 3410141; 3-4 fork, part No. 3410038). Chrysler recommends using the old-style unit with the Slick Shift transmissions, although the new unit's steel forks can replace the brass ones in the old cover if the necked-down end is cut off.

That about wraps up the MoPar, except for a reminder that if you're converting from an automatic trans to the manual, be sure to verify that your crank is drilled for a pilot bushing; many production automatic cranks weren't. Additional info on Chrysler manual trannys, clutches and shifters can be found in Direct Connection Racing Bulletin No. 7: Chrysler Manual Transmission. It's available for $1, under part No. P4007912, from your Direct Connection Dealer or by writing: Direct Connection, Chrysler Performance Parts, P.O. Box 1718, CIMS 423-13-Q6, Detroit, MI 48288.

Borg-Warner T-10

First introduced in 1957 on the Corvette, the T-10 series has been used in one form or another by all U.S. manufacturers and is still produced today for General Motors cars. It can be distinguished from GM's Muncie by the differing number of bolts used to retain the side cover: T-10s have nine bolts, Muncies only seven. Easy to shift, and with over 20 different gear ratios to choose from, the Borg-Warner 4-speeds have always been great favorites with many racers.

There have been two basic T-10 designs: The fine-spline-geared early T-10 was produced from 1957 to 1965, when it was superseded by the Super T-10, which had coarse-pitch gears. Other than the synchros, there is no interchangeability between what are essentially two different designs.

The original early T-10 was used by all the Big Three manufacturers. GM used the trans from 1957 to 1965, although the Muncie began replacing it in mid-1963. The 1957-'59 General Motors versions used a cast-iron case and aluminum extension housing. Starting in 1960, Corvettes got an aluminum case and extension housing, with passenger cars following suit in 1962-'63. By 1964-'65, those GM divisions still using the T-10 had gone back to the cast-iron main case/aluminum extension. The 1957-'60 GM T-10s had a 16-spline output shaft and a bushed third gear; in '61 and later, third gears were unbushed. Buick Specials and F-85 Olds got

One problem with Second Design Super T-10s is seizure of rear output shaft bushing on yoke. Many racers drill and tap housing for zerk fitting and lube bushing before each run.

CHART T-1

T-10 9310 Gear Set Ratios

Needed for conversion are a main drive gear, first gear, second gear, third gear and cluster gear. For specific gear numbers, see your Borg-Warner dealer or write Automotive Parts Division, Borg-Warner Transportation Equipment, Borg-Warner Corporation, 11045 Gage Ave., Franklin Park, IL 60131.

Version	Variant	Gear Set	1st	2nd	3rd	4th
Early	GM	T-10A	2.54	1.92	1.51	
		T-10E		1.89		
		T-10K	2.20	1.64	1.31	
	Ford	T-10L	2.36	1.76	1.41	
	GM/Ford* GM	T-10M		1.62	1.20	
		T-10N	2.54	1.74	1.30	1.00
Super	First Design	Special close T-10S	2.43	1.61	1.23	
	First and Second Design**	Spl. competition T-10X	2.64			
		Special wide T-10W		1.75	1.33	
	Second Design	Extra-low T-10Y***	2.88			
		Ultra-low T-10U****	3.44	2.28	1.46	

*Specify manufacturer when ordering, as part numbers may differ.

**Available for both first and second designs. Specify which when ordering, as part numbers may differ. 9310 cluster gear not available for Second Design T10-X/W. T10-X/W main drive available in 10-spline only, so Second Design transmissions must change clutch.

***Available as complete assembly AS10-T10Y

****All parts 8620 alloy only, except first and second gears

The 9310 gears have an identifying dimple to distinguish them from regular gears.

4-Speed

Second Design 9310 Gear Set Part Numbers
(Fits GM-pattern bellhousings only)

Gear Set	Main Drive	1st	2nd	3rd	Cluster
T10W	T10W-16D*	T10W-12A	T10S-31B	T10S-11A	T10W-8B**
T10X					T10X-8A**
			T10X-31	T10X-11	
T10Y	T10Y-16A				T10Y-8A
T10U	T10U-16A**		T10S-31B	T10U-11**	T10U-8A**

*10-spline; must change clutch
**This part is 8620 alloy; 9310 not available at this time

a 21-spline output shaft with a companion flange in 1963-'65. Other 1964-'65 GM models changed to a 27-spline output to prevent twisting under high torque loads. Some '62 and later T-10s had 9310 nickel alloy gears for increased strength.

Ford used the early T-10 from 1960 to 1965, although its sister Mercury division didn't start installing the trans until 1962. All Ford's output shafts had 28 splines. The 1960-'62 versions had a 23-spline input shaft, while '63-'65s had a coarse 10-spline input. Two different length inputs were used: The 427s received a special longer 8 15/16 input; all other motors got one 8½ inches long. Ford cases and extension housings were always all cast-iron, except for Shelbys, which were all-aluminum. The Toploader began to replace the T-10 in the big Fords, starting in mid-1964. Like GM, Ford offered some 9310 gears for increased strength.

Chrysler used the early T-10 for only one year: 1963. All cases and extension housings were constructed from cast iron. The input shaft had 23 splines, as did the output, which also had a companion flange.

The Super T-10 was introduced in 1965 with the T-10P, used as original equipment on American Motors products. The '66 Ford Mustangs also used the new design, before it was completely replaced by the Toploader. Some GMC vans got the trans in 1968 only. No matter which manufacturer used the trans, all had cast-iron cases and extension housings. In addition to numerous production ratios, special American Motors, Ford and aftermarket GM versions were offered with competition ratio spreads. Super T-10s can be distinguished from early T-10s by the aforementioned coarse gears, a larger case and increased mainshaft diameter. To accommodate the larger mainshaft, the number of mainshaft pilot roller bearings was upped from 14 to 16 and the inside diameter of the main drive gear was increased to accommodate them. The new mainshaft also used a flange to separate second and third gear, instead of the removable bearing used on early T-10s.

The improved, or "heavy-duty," Super T-10 was phased in during 1972 and can be identified by the thicker thrust flange between second and third gear that requires a new second gear.

Finally, in late 1974, the T-10 assumed its ultimate form, with the introduction of the Second Design Super T-10. The impetus behind the new model was the renewed use by General Motors of the T-10, since the Muncie had been discontinued. Second Design Super T-10s can be distinguished from earlier versions by the following design changes: the input shaft spline count was upped from 10 to 26, a 1-inch-diameter countershaft (⅛-inch thicker than early Super T-10s) is used, first gear is sleeved, the snap ring behind the second gear synchro assembly is removed, and the ¼-inch-thicker mainshaft is retained by 112 needle bearings (all other T-10s used only 80). The new mainshaft has a thick second/third gear thrust flange like the improved (heavy-duty) Super T-10, but with 32 (instead of six) splines for reverse gear (for noise reduction), a splined speedometer gear and 32 (instead of 27) rear output splines. Besides second gear (which interchanges with heavy-duty Super T-10s) and third gear (the same in all Super T-10s), no other Second Design parts interchange directly with earlier versions. In some cases, GM-style main drive gears will interchange, but in that case the clutch must also be changed, in order to work with the different input spline count.

Although individual component parts are offered for early T-10s and Super T-10s, at present only the Second Design Super T-10 is produced as a complete transmission assembly—and only for GM-pattern bellhousings. Aftermarket versions have a nodular-iron case 50 percent stronger than the cast-iron cases previously used, along with an aluminum tailhousing. GM original-equipment models have all-aluminum cases. For racing, always use the cast-iron case if the rules permit, since the aluminum case tends to expand under the high heat conditions encountered; this pulls apart the mainshafts and countershafts, resulting in gear contact on the extreme ends of the gear teeth that can lead to gear failure.

Second Design T-10s are optimized for heavy-duty use, with aftermarket versions featuring a "max-type" main drive gear bearing and different synchros designed for greater durability and easier high-rpm shifting, along with new shift forks that have better alignment and contact with the sleeve for faster shifts. The GM factory models don't have the heavy-duty bearings and synchros, but can be upgraded if desired.

When the Second Design Super T-10 first came out, the gears were cut from 8620 alloy, but now 35-percent-stronger 9310 nickel-alloy gears are offered. If you cannot afford to upgrade the entire trans, Borg-Warner says, "Special consideration should be given to replacement of the main drive gear with the 9310, as it represents the greatest improvement in terms of strength and durability."

Transmission assemblies with 8620 gears, known as AS9s, are followed by a gear-set designator to indicate what ratio is installed in the transmission (example: AS9-T10X for the special competition gear set with 2.64/1.61/1.23/1.00 ratios). Complete assemblies with 9310 gears are called AS10s; at present only the AS10-T10Y is offered complete.

The 9310 gears are available to fit earlier T-10s as well (Chart T-1). In addition, a nodular-iron case is offered for GM-style first design Super T-10s, under part No. T-10W-1A.

General Motors Muncie

GM has produced two 4-speeds: the Saginaw and the Muncie; only the latter is strong enough for serious performance use. Produced from 1963 to 1974, it was used at one time or another by all the corporation's divisions (except Cadillac, naturally!). Muncies make a fine street/strip or roundy-round transmission but aren't as popular in drag racing as some other 4-speeds, due to the limited selection of factory gear ratios. Complete transmissions are no longer available, although they can be built up from component parts.

At first glance, the Muncie may appear to be externally similar to the Saginaw and Borg-Warner T-10, but it's easy to tell them apart, once you know what to look for: Saginaws have cast-iron cases, while Muncies have cases made from aluminum; Borg-Warner T-10s have a nine-bolt side cover, but Muncies use only seven bolts.

Distinguishing the various Muncie subvariants is not nearly so easy. There are three basic versions: a heavy-duty close-ratio, a high-performance close-ratio and a regular (wide-ratio). Over the years, the high-performance close-ratio and regular wide-ratio trannys underwent a three-stage evolutionary process. From 1963 to 1965, these Muncies had a 7/8-inch-diameter countershaft, which rode on 80 needle bearings. Two versions were available: a wide-ratio unit with a 24-tooth main drive gear (input shaft), featuring a 2.52 (first), 1.90 (second), 1.50 (third) and 1.00 (fourth); and a close-ratio, with a 26-tooth main drive gear and ratios of 2.20 (first), 1.64 (second), 1.27 (third) and 1.00 (fourth). No matter which gear set was installed, these early Muncies were all known as the "M20."

Starting in 1966, the countershaft diameter was increased to one inch, retained by 112 needle bearings. The wide-ratio-box gear ratios changed to 2.54 (first), 1.88 (second), 1.46 (third) and 1.00 (fourth), brought about by the new 21-tooth main drive gear. Close-ratio gears and main drive tooth count remained the same.

In 1966 the customer was allowed by Chevy to specify which transmission (close or wide-ratio) he wanted behind his engine, so a new RPO (Regular Production Option) designator was required. "M20" was retained to designate the wide-ratio box only, while the close-ratios were now called the "M21." All this invariably leads to some confusion, so we suggest that when ordering replacement parts, you specify the transmission's year of production, countershaft diameter and first-gear ratio, rather than attempting to identify it by the sometimes misleading factory option number.

In 1971, the number of splines on the main drive gear was upped from 10 to 26, increasing the transmission's ability to handle torque, since there were now over twice as many load-bearing surfaces. A 32-spline output shaft replaced the 27-spline unit previously used, requiring a new extension housing.

There is one more version of the Muncie to discuss: the infamous M22 close-ratio heavy-duty model, also known as the "rockcrusher." It was introduced as an option on the new 396 engine in 1965, and featured stronger gears and a one-inch

Special first-gear sleeve 3978781 (right) has machined striations that prevent gear seizure by increasing oil flow in Muncies with conventional first-gear assemblies.

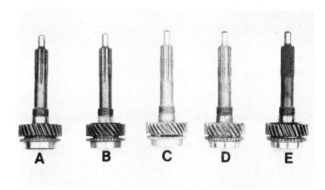

Original factory-installed input shaft had identifying groove on spline end. M22 (A) was grooveless, as were '63-'65 wide-ratio M20s (B). To tell them apart, check gears—the M22s are much more straight-cut. The '66 and later standard Muncies and all M22s also had a 1-inch-diameter countershaft, compared to the early version's 7/8-inch diameter. One groove in input shaft identifies close-ratio standard Muncie (C), two grooves, a '66-'74 wide-ratio M21 (D). In 1971, input shafts were changed from a 10-spline design to 26 splines, with identifying grooves remaining the same. Since (E) is grooveless and has 26 splines, it's an M22, provided it was installed in a production car, since some replacement shafts have no grooves at all!

4-Speed

Parts needed to convert standard Muncie to M22: reverse gear, 3879997; first gear (non-needle bearing), 3924796; second gear, 3879999; third gear, 3880845; cluster gear, 3905466; and either 10-spline main drive, 3925691, or preferred 26-spline version, 3978761. Pre-'66 Muncies with ⅞-inch-diameter countershaft must be bored out to accept 1-inch countershaft (357233).

countershaft from the beginning, with the same ratio spread as the standard close-ratio Muncie. Originally, its input shaft had only 10 splines, like all other Muncies, but during 1970 (one year earlier than the standard versions), it got the new 26-spline input shaft and 32-spline output. Earlier M22s can be upgraded to the more desirable input shaft by using part No. 3978761.

The only sure way to identify an M22 is by the angle of the gear teeth. M22s used a noisy low helix-angle gear set for greater strength; that's why the trans is called the ''rockcrusher.'' By contrast, standard Muncie gear teeth are much more sharply raked. Some claim the M22 can also be identified by the presence of a gear case oil drain plug. This isn't necessarily so, since *all* Muncie replacement cases have drain plugs. Others have tried to distinguish the M22 from regular versions by counting the circumferential grooves on the input shaft, with no grooves indicating an M22. Unfortunately, some replacement input shafts are unmarked, as were all M20s with the wide-ratio gear set. A regular Muncie can be converted to an M22 by changing the mainshaft gears, cluster gear, reverse gear and main drive gear, but it's not cheap, even doing it yourself, the parts will cost around $500. However, by doing your own converting, you'll have a trans that can handle anything you can dish out on the street.

For racing, there are some trick factory parts available for upgrading the Muncie even further. To get from one gear to another, a synchronizer blocker ring slotted for quicker shifting (part No. 344243) can be used. Unlike the stock piece, it features wipers to help get oil out of the grooves between the gears faster. Once in gear, you'll want to stay there, so install a longer high-load 20-pound side detent spring (part No. 3831718) to help prevent hopout from all gears.

Additional hopout protection for first gear can be obtained with the special 344241 synchro assembly, which features a spline lock design. Use a 357239 synchro assembly to help the trans stay in third gear when you let off the throttle. Finally, for an M22 used under ultra-severe racing conditions, there's a special first-gear needle-bearing unit that offers increased durability over the standard M22 first gear.

No matter how many trick parts are used, care should always be taken during assembly. Especially critical on the Muncie is the clearance between the end of the cluster gear and the gear case; Gordie (Arbitter) likes to see .015-.016-inch, achieved by varying the thickness of the thrust washer. Also, be sure not to leave out the input shaft oil slinger, or the trans won't go into high gear as well. It may even help to use one that is .025-inch thicker than stock. For long-distance racing, the '69 and later side cover that uses bolts to retain the shifter arms should be converted back to the earlier arrangement that used studs to retain the arms, since the bolts have a tendency to work themselves out.

Synchronizer blocking ring 344243 (right) has slotted wipers to help get oil out of gears more quickly for faster shifting.

For all-out competition, a special needle-bearing first-gear assembly can be installed in M22s. It consists of a 3965752 first gear, 326578 sleeve, 9433516 needle bearing and 326579 washer.

Ford T and C Toploader

It's not hard to identify the Toploader. Unlike all the other transmissions, the gears load in from the top, rather than the side. The beefy trans began to be phased-in during 1964, to replace Borg-Warner T-10s, and remained in production until 1973. Both close and wide-ratio gear sets were offered (Chart F-1). In 1977, the Toploader was reintroduced as an OD (overdrive) transmission, with 1979 versions going to an aluminum case to save weight. All the OD versions are built by Tremac in Mexico, but other than the overdrive gear set, it's still basically the same trans, and the new gears will practically bolt right in to many old Toploaders (more on that later).

Over the years, many variants have been produced. Three different tailshaft lengths were offered, with varying shifter mounting locations and speedometer cable hookup points. For ground-up race cars, Stick Only (Sun Valley, California) prefers the 14-inch short Mustang tailhousing (C6OZ-7A-039-C, cast D0ZR-7A040-A), due to its ease of installation, relative light weight and two shifter mounting locations.

Most early transmission cases have the five-bolt bellhousing mounting pattern necessary to mate with the Ford bellhousings of that era. Beginning in 1965, when the six-bolt bellhousing mounting pattern was introduced, the trans case was produced with eight mounting bolt holes, so it could be used with either bellhousing.

Toploaders produced from 1964 through mid-1965 have a 1 1/16-inch-diameter 10-spline input shaft and a 25-spline output shaft. In late 1965, the output shaft's strength was upgraded by increasing the number of splines to 28. For performance use, the early shaft (C4DZ-7061-A) should be upgraded to the 28-spline shaft (C5ZZ-7061-C). There was also a close-ratio-only heavy-duty trans used on some high-performance 427/428/429 engines that had a 1⅜-inch-diameter 10-spline input shaft (C4AZ-7017-H), special bearing retainer (C5AZ-7050-K) and 31-spline output shaft (C7OZ-7061-A). Different extension housings were also required. Most of these parts are no longer stocked, but the 1 1/16 input and 28-spline output will handle anything up to 600 horsepower. Any more than that and you'll have to go to Doug Nash Engineering, who offers 1⅜-inch-diameter 9310 alloy input shafts for both close and wide-ratio gear sets. He also has 9310 internal gears for the two stock ratios and his own special 2.98/2.02/1.45/1.00 set.

But even that only partially solves the Ford's biggest problem: the lack of different gear ratios. The trans was strong and durable, but it lacked flexibility. Notice the past tense—for now Tom's Differentials has come out with modular gear sets, featuring splined third and fourth gear positions on the cluster gear and a splined main drive gear. Three different input shafts are currently available, the 1⅜ Ford, 26-spline Chevy and small 1 1/16 Ford. The latter's spline count was raised from 10 to 26 for increased

One problem with the Toploader is gear seizure on mainshaft caused by heat buildup during racing and the very tight .002-inch gear-to-shaft clearance used by factory. To cure the problem, Stick Only bushes the insides of the gears and opens clearance up to .004-inch max (.003-.0035 preferred).

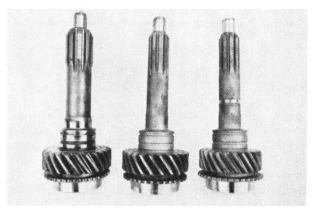

CHART F-1

Factory Toploader Gear Ratios

	1st	2nd	3rd	4th
Wide-ratio	2.78	1.93	1.36	1.00
Close-ratio	2.32	1.69	1.29	1.00
Overdrive, except				
'79 302 V8	3.29	1.84	1.00	.81
Overdrive, '79 302 V8	3.07	1.72	1.00	.70

Ford input shafts, left to right: 1⅜-inch-diameter big-block high-performance (available in close-ratio only), 1 1/16-inch-diameter standard close-ratio and 1 1/16-inch-diameter wide-ratio (note identifying groove). Internal gears on both standard and high-performance close-ratio trans were the same.

Want to use the tough Ford behind your Chevy? Get a standard 1 1/16 input shaft. Use either a cast-iron retainer (part No. C5AR-7050-J, cast C5AR-7050-B or C6AR-7050-F) or new aluminum retainer (D9DZ-7050-A). Turn retainer in lathe and remove .055-inch from its overall diameter, then shorten the snout by .60-inch. A special pilot bushing is also required: Either bore out an early Chevy '57-'61 Turboglide bushing or use a McLeod 8618 bushing. You might also consider their 8610 scattershield that's drilled for both Chevy and Ford trans mounting patterns.

4-Speed

Thanks to Tom's Differentials' modular gear sets, a variety of gear ratio spreads are now available.

strength, so it requires a late Chevy clutch disc and throwout bearing. Both conventionally synchronized gears and special slider gear sets for drag racing are available. The slider gears completely eliminate the production synchros, instead replacing them with 12 engagement teeth, thereby creating a "semi-clutchless" transmission. Right now, over 48 different gear ratio combinations are offered, but soon there could be, in Tom's words, "potentially an infinite amount" available, including several overdrive sets.

In the meantime, Stick Only has discovered that you can put the new stock Ford overdrive gears into the earlier direct-drive transmissions with only minimal mods required, provided you have a Falcon, Fairlane or Mustang with the short extension housing and 23 11/32-inch-long mainshaft. So far, they have used the gears from '77-'78 cast-iron OD Granadas only (Chart F-2), and haven't verified whether or not the newer '79 aluminum-case gear sets will fit, although a cursory inspection seems to indicate compatibility. If they do fit, you'll have a choice of two different overdrive gear sets, since '79 302 Mustangs/Capris had a different ratio set than the other overdrive boxes. To make the conversion, you must change the cluster, main shaft gears, input shaft (main drive gear) and output shaft (mainshaft). Similar to the Chrysler OD conversion covered last month, the 3-4 shift rail must be reversed to preserve the correct "H" shifter pattern.

By now you're probably wondering if you can go the other way and put the direct-drive gears into the aluminum case which would sure save some weight. The answer is "maybe," as the completely internal shift linkage does present some problems. While Stick Only feels that the internal linkage can be desirable, since it shifts "like butter" and is less susceptible to damage than normal external shift linkage, considerable modification is required to mate the arms and detents to the early gears. Currently, an aluminum box is being run experimentally on an IMSA Monza road racer; if, and when, it becomes a "standard" Stick Only production item, we'll let you know.

At any rate, it now appears that modern technology and the reintroduction of the Toploader as an overdrive box have combined to give new life to a very sound design that had apparently suffered a premature demise in 1973.

CHART F-2

Overdrive Conversion

Pieces are from '77-'78 Granada transmission with 3.29:1 first gear. Aluminum trans gear fit has not been verified.

Cluster	**D7DZ-7113-A**
1st gear	**D7DZ-7A029-A**
2nd gear	**D7DZ-7102-A**
3rd gear (OD)	**D7DZ-78340-A**
Main drive gear	**D7DZ-7017-A**
Mainshaft	**D7DZ-7061-A**

New mainshaft (right) is needed because it has a relocated second-gear snap ring (A) and indentation (B) to eliminate third-gear seizure problems.

To fit OD gears in old case, the reverse idler boss must be ground for clearance and .150 inch must be taken off the reverse idler tip.

Doug Nash Engineering 4+1 Quik Change

No guide to the best 4-speeds would be complete without mentioning the Nash 5-speed, which is becoming the dominant transmission wherever it's allowed to compete. A "streetified" version is also offered and is gaining in popularity.

Officially called the DNE₂ 4 + 1 Quick Change, the racing version features a magnesium case and tailhousing, and can be used as a 4-speed in those classes where rules prohibit the additional gear. In the 5-speed mode, the extemely low first gear ratios used allow the car to launch harder, due to increased torque multiplication. The additional gear also allows the engine to remain within its peak horsepower band longer, with less rpm drop between shifts. Designed from the ground up as a virtually bulletproof slider-style transmission with 9310 straight-cut spur gears, the Nash race 5-speed features a splined cluster shaft to allow maximum gear interchangeability, making possible an almost unlimited number of gear ratio combinations. Stock synchros are eliminated, and are replaced with 12-lug rings suitable for high-rpm crashbox-style shifting.

The street version uses an aluminum case to prevent corrosion, but is only 10 pounds heavier than its racing forebear. Variable extension housing and input shaft designs are offered to allow bolt-in Ford, MoPar or GM replacement. Readily available Borg-Warner Super T-10 synchro components are used to facilitate replacement, while the helical-cut gears are machined from 4617 steel alloy, selected for its superior wear properties compared to the more shock-resistant 9310 alloy used in the race box. A redesigned case allows the shifter to be tucked in close for maximum tunnel clearance, with the shifter mounting pads coinciding with the factory 4-speed mounting location as much as possible. Provisions are included for hooking up the speedometer.

Both street and racing versions utilize the same bearings and SAE 8620 shaft material, although the street shafts are slightly redesigned to accommodate the helical gears' increased thrust loads. The street version also uses a splined cluster to broaden the choice of gear ratios.

Currently, there are no overdrive ratios offered for the street 5-speed, because Doug Nash believes they are unnecessary, due to the greater torque multiplication allowed by an additional gear and the fact that the added gear permits lower intermediate gears to be run. For example, an economy rear axle ratio like 3.08:1 run in conjunction with the Nash 5-speed, gives the same overall torque multiplication in first gear as a 4.56:1 rearend, yet still permits great fuel economy with the direct-drive fifth gear. And there's no strain on the transmission caused by using an indirect high gear, as is the case with overdrive transmissions.

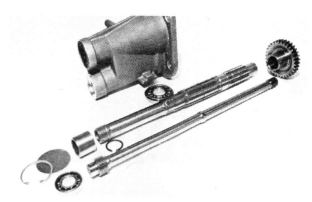

In addition to its splined countershaft gears, what really makes the Quik Change a quick change is the case design. Instead of the usual rather small access cover, the whole case splits in half for access to the internal components. RTV sealant is used in place of gaskets.

An optional torsion bar cluster shaft is available to reduce driveline shock, minimizing parts breakage in drag racing and smoothing entry into corners when downshifting for road racers. Street version (bottom) can be distinguished from racing version by helical-cut gears and conventional synchros. On both versions, a center main bearing is used on cluster shaft to prevent vibration.

Aftermarket Manual Transmission Specialists

Trans End
P.O. Box 5018
Clinton, NJ 08809
(201) 236-6901

Doug Nash Equipment & Engineering
111 Century Court
Franklin, TN 37064
(615) 790-2900

Tom's Differentials
15551 Paramount Blvd.
Paramount, CA 90723
(213) 634-8431

Stick Only
9900 Glenoaks Blvd.
Sun Valley, CA 91352
(213) 768-4747

The Ultimate T-10
11640 Ilex St. N.W.
Coon Rapids, MN 55433
(612) 757-5210

Liberty Gears
6390 Pelham
Taylor, MI 48180
(313) 278-4040

Brake Plumbing

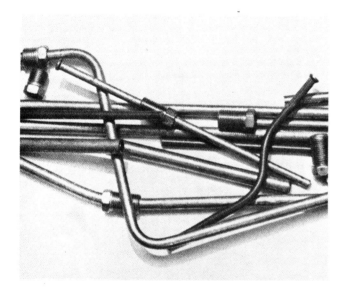

Brake line plumbing seems to be one of those foreboding parts of a vehicle that most rodders don't want to touch. Perhaps it's because brake lines must be carefully cut and bent to specific lengths and shapes, and they must be double-flared and equipped with the right fittings to produce a reliable, durable and leak-free system—a system upon which their very lives could depend. But although brake line plumbing is critical, it is still well within the realm of backyard maintenance that can be successfully tackled by the average enthusiast. All that's needed are a few special tools, care, and patience.

But let's start with a few basics. Since the brake system operates on a principle of hydraulics, which states that fluids aren't compressible, the brake lines must be capable of handling pressures in excess of 1000 psi from the master cylinder to the wheel cylinders without leaks or the likelihood of failure due to cracks or bursting. Consequently, the brake line material must be adequate to meet these demands which is why copper or aluminum tubing is strictly forbidden for use as brake lines. Instead, the lines must be steel or specially constructed high-pressure hoses. Additionally, the system must be free of any air bubbles (which are compressible) to function properly.

But there's more to the basics of brake line plumbing than just material strength. The lines must also be of adequate size to provide an unrestricted flow of brake fluid to the wheel cylinders to assure smooth and even brake application and release. For most passenger cars, this means that the minimum size for a line feeding any one wheel cylinder would be ⅛ inch inside diameter. A line feeding two or more wheel cylinders should have a minimum inside diameter of 3/16 inch. And of course the lines must be free of kinks or other restrictions that might impede their flow potential.

All of that sounds simple enough, and it is. To build or replace a system conforming to these basics, only two common tools are required in most instances: a set of fitting wrenches and a tubing bender. Of course this is presuming you use prefabricated brake lines with double-flared ends. Such lines are available in a wide variety of lengths from most auto parts stores. Assuming you can bend these lines to conform to your specific length requirements, we recommend this approach to avoid the necessity of cutting and double-flaring the tubing ends. Double-flaring isn't particularly difficult, but it does require more expensive tools and some practice.

Unlike conventional open-end wrenches that grip the nut on only two sides, fitting wrenches resemble a box-end wrench with a small opening to allow them to be slipped over the tubing and onto the tubing nut, gripping five sides of the nut to prevent slipping, distortion or rounding of the edges. Such wrenches aren't particularly expensive, and they're available at most tool supply stores or department stores, such as Sears.

Tubing benders are usually available at these same tool outlets. There are quite a variety of benders, ranging from simple spring-type benders (which unfortunately can't be used with prefabricat-

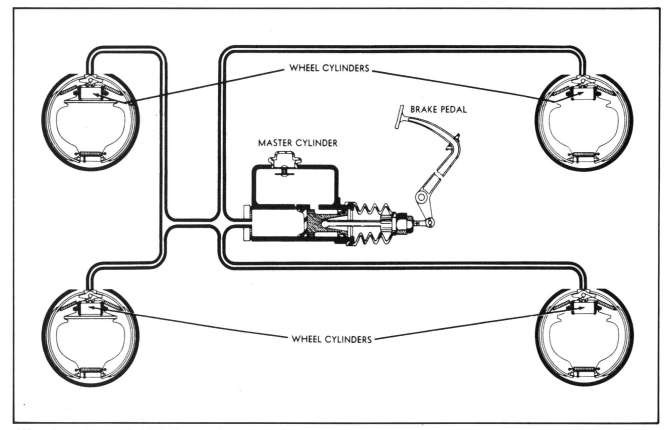

Although greatly simplified, this diagram shows the brake plumbing to be a closed system which must be totally leak-free.

ed lines) to lever-type benders in varying degrees of complexity and price. Such benders are necessary to make smooth, tight radius bends without kinking or collapsing the tubing.

If, for some particular reason, you decide to fabricate your lines to arrive at specific lengths, you will need two additional tools: a tubing cutter and a double-flaring tool. As with the previous tools, the tubing cutter is relatively inexpensive and readily available. The double-flaring tool is a different story. Many tool supply stores handle flaring tools, but in most cases these tools are only capable of producing a single flare. A double flare is required for brake lines because it offers increased strength and resistance to cracking or fatigue where the metal is stretched to form the flare, thus greatly reducing the likelihood of a brake system leak and subsequent failure. There are several different versions of double-flaring tools, again ranging in price, but the more expensive tools generally provide more consistently acceptable results.

One of the most common reasons for replacing a brake line is that it has been crushed or damaged while work was being done on the vehicle. This is especially true of the front brake line feeding the right front wheel, which is frequently damaged during engine installation or removal on many cars. Another need for working with the brake lines is that all the drag racing associations require any brake lines in the flywheel area of the car to be rerouted to the outside of the frame or encased by heavy protective steel shields.

So to provide a guide to both of these projects,

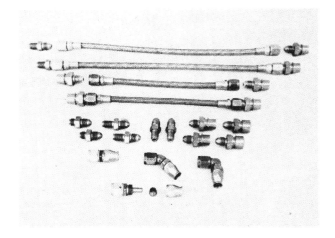

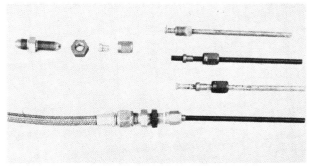

Shown here is an assortment of prefabricated braided line brake hoses and numerous hose ends and fittings available from Earl's Supply. Earl's also has special bulkhead fittings and adapters for attaching braided line directly to steel tubing brake lines.

Brake

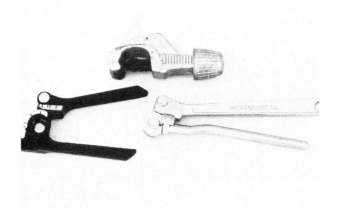

To cut and bend your own steel brake lines, a tubing cutter and benders, such as these, are required to do a neat, professional-looking job.

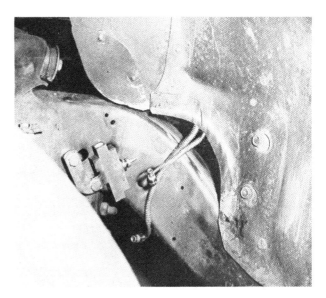

the accompanying photo sequence illustrates the relocation of the brake lines and distribution block on a late-model Chevrolet to the outside of the frame and replacement of the right front wheel line with a new line rerouted inside the front crossmember.

PLUMBER'S HELPER

Much of the hassle of cutting, bending, and flaring brake lines has been eliminated by something relatively new to performance automobiles: braided stainless steel, flexible Teflon brake line hoses. These hoses, although quite expensive, add a custom touch to any specialty vehicle while simultaneously providing excellent abrasion resistance and eliminating line failures caused by metal fatigue and vibration. At the present time, these lines have yet to be approved by the Department of Transportation, so their use is restricted to off-road vehicles, such as race cars and dune buggies.

The lines shown here are available from Earl's Supply Company (Lawndale, California), along with a very complete line of their reusable hose ends and adapter fittings in both SAE and metric sizes. They even have fittings to permit the connection of the braided lines to rigid steel lines.

The braided stainless lines are offered in both -3 and -4 hose sizes with associated A/N hose ends. In most cases, the -4 line is suggested, since the required hose ends and adapter fittings are much less expensive than the smaller -3 ends and adapters. However, if it can be afforded, the -3 line expands less under pressure for a firmer pedal feel and quicker pressure release. This can be important on automatic transmission-equipped drag cars, such as econorails.

Earl's is currently offering complete conversion kits for some of the more popular cars, and of course they'll make up lines to the customer's exact needs. We used one of their -3 lines to reroute a brake line inside the front crossmember of a car in the accompanying story, a task that would have been impossible with rigid tubing. If you have the need, this kind of brake line plumbing offers a nice alternative.

Shown here is the relocation of brake lines to the outside of the frame on a late-model Chevelle, as required by drag racing sanctioning body safety rules. The distribution and warning light switch block was relocated to the outside of the frame and the brake lines rerouted accordingly. A new line was fabricated to supply the left front wheel, and a -3 Teflon-lined braided stainless steel line was routed inside the front crossmember to feed the right front wheel and simultaneously protect the brake line from accidental damage during engine installation and removal.

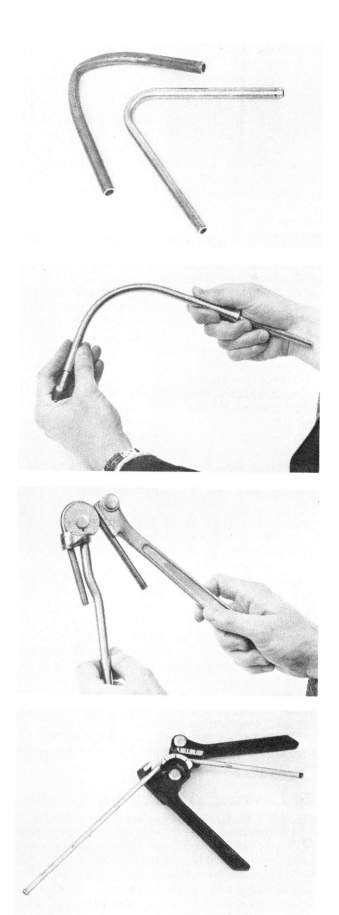

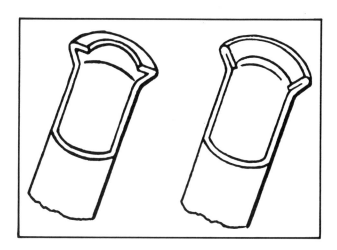

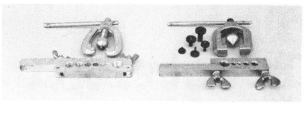

A

B

C

To prevent kinked or collapsed lines, such as shown here, a tubing bender is essential. Spring-type benders are inexpensive, but they can't be slipped over tubes that are already equipped with fittings. Lever-type benders can produce a very tight radius and smooth bends.

Brake line fittings are designed to work with flared tubing ends. For extra strength and to prevent cracking, such flares must be double thick, as shown. At the upper right (A) is a comparison of a standard flaring tool and one with inserts to make double flares. At the lower left (B) is another double-flaring tool. When using a double-flaring tool, the insert is used to gauge how much the tube should protrude from the clamp.(C) The insert then gives the tube end the correct initial shape. The insert is then removed and the taper completes the flare.

The Electrical System

If you like working on or modifying cars, sooner or later you'll be confronted with the necessity of understanding a vehicle's electrical system in order to troubleshoot a problem, rewire a circuit, or modify an existing circuit. If you're like most enthusiasts, you probably don't know very much about electricity and you fear that if you start to reroute wires, splice into existing wires, or whatever, you'll get it wrong and ruin something. Your fears aren't totally groundless, because if you don't have a basic understanding of what you're doing, then you're simply gambling that you'll get it right the first time. And like most gambling, if you don't know the game, the chances of becoming a loser are far greater than hitting the jackpot. The circuits of an automobile aren't really very complicated if they are broken down into individual systems, which is what we'll do here. In this way, you will be able to clearly visualize how each circuit works, and thereby greatly improve your odds of doing the job correctly on the very first try.

There are really only four basic electrical systems in an automobile: the ignition and starting system, the charging system, the lighting system, and the gauge and accessory system. All four of these systems have one common denominator: the battery. And this leads us to the one basic fundamental which you must keep in mind at all times when dealing with automotive electrical systems: Current must always make a complete loop from the positive post of the battery back to the negative post before anything connected in between can work. In virtually all cases, this means that a wire has to run from a source connected to the positive battery post to the light, accessory, coil, starter motor, or whatever, and then another wire must run back from that item to the negative battery post.

However, to save the trouble and expense of having to run two wires from the battery to each electrical item, the entire chassis of the car is simply connected to the negative post, which, in turn, makes the entire chassis of the car the negative battery post. This is called grounding the chassis. Then only the positive wire has to be routed from the battery to each individual electrical item, and the return wire of the circuit merely has to be connected to the closest grounded chassis component, such as the frame or sheetmetal. In direct current systems, which is what we are dealing with on automobiles, there are no exceptions to this complete circuit, or loop rule.

Ignition and Starting System

We'll start with the ignition and starting system, since it is probably the most complicated, and because the other systems won't do you much good unless the car starts and runs. As you can see on the accompanying schematic, a heavy positive wire runs directly from the battery to the starter solenoid or relay. This solenoid or relay is really nothing more than a heavy-duty switch. Such a device is used because of the large amount of current the starter motor uses. Without a solenoid, a heavy battery cable would have to be run all the way up to the dash, through a heavy-duty igni-

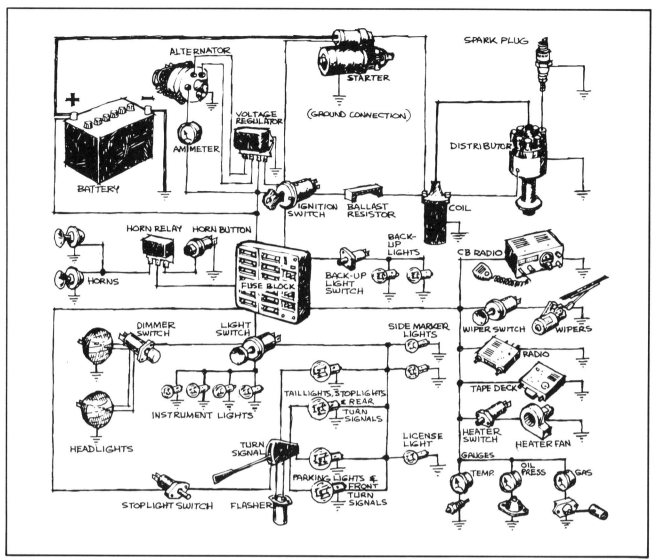

This is a simplified schematic of the basic electrical systems of an automobile. Many cars have additional special circuits not shown here.

tion switch and then back down to the starter motor. The solenoid or relay is controlled by a small positive lead from the battery to the ignition switch and then back down to the solenoid. When the ignition switch is turned to the "start" position, current flows through the small wire to the solenoid, which then closes, sending full battery current into the starter motor. And because the starter motor is bolted and grounded directly to the engine block, the circuit is completed and the starter motor runs.

The solenoid is also fitted with an additional terminal, from which a small wire runs to the positive side of the ignition coil. If you study the schematic, you will see that the ignition switch supplies current to the coil via a ballast resistor. This resistor reduces the normal battery voltage of 12 volts to between 6 and 8 volts. This lower voltage is adequate to run the ignition system during normal driving, and because of its lower voltage, there is less arcing in the ignition points (we'll get to those in a minute). However, during the time when the ignition switch is turned to the "start" position, the extra lead from the solenoid to the coil bypasses the bal-

last resistor to supply a full 12 volts to the ignition system for the hottest possible spark to assist in starting the engine. When the ignition switch is released from the "start" position to the normal "on" position, current no longer flows to either the starter motor or to the positive side of the coil through the solenoid terminals.

Now, back to the ignition system. We've already discussed the flow of current from the ignition switch through the ballast resistor to the coil. At the coil, the current is fed through windings inside the coil and then out of the coil from the negative coil terminal and into the distributor. Inside the distributor, this wire from the coil is connected to the breaker points.

The breaker points are nothing more than a switch that allows the coil current to go to ground when the points are closed, thus completing the circuit. The rotation of a cam within the distributor opens and closes the points at precise intervals timed to movement of the valves and pistons within the engine. Up to this point, everything we have talked about in the ignition system is referred to as

Electrical

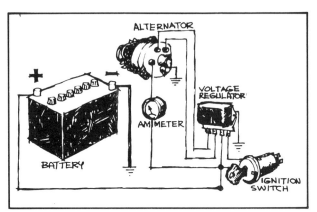

The charging system is composed of the battery, ignition switch, voltage regulator, and alternator (or generator). The wiring between the voltage regulator and alternator may vary with different makes, so check the specific wiring diagram for the car under consideration. If an ammeter is used, it goes between the alternator battery terminal and the battery positive post.

the primary side of the ignition circuit.

As current starts and stops its flow through the primary circuit, as controlled by the breaker points, the current flowing through the windings in the ignition coil generate a magnetic field. Each time the current stops flowing, that magnetic field in the coil collapses, which in turn, induces a very high-voltage current in the secondary windings of the coil. One end of these secondary windings is grounded and the other end is connected to the center tower of the coil. The high-voltage current induced by the collapsing magnetic field then flows from the center coil tower through a short length of spark plug-type wire to the center of the distributor cap.

Inside the distributor, the rotor, which is nothing more than a rotary switch, directs the high-voltage current to the correct tower on the perimeter of the distributor cap. From there the high voltage flows through the selected spark plug wire to the spark plug. At the plug, the high voltage jumps the gap at the end of the spark plug in the combustion chamber, where it goes to ground, returning to the coil. All of the high-voltage part of the ignition system is called the secondary side.

The only difference between the conventional ignition system we have just covered and late-model high-energy systems with breakerless distributors is that instead of breaker points, either magnetic or photocell devices are used to trigger sophisticated electronics packages that start and stop the flow of current to the primary windings of the coil. Most such units also increase the *amount* of current supplied to the primary windings so that an even stronger spark results in the secondary circuit.

The Charging System

This system too is fairly complicated, but not so much as the ignition and starting system. Simply stated, the charging system merely uses power produced by the running engine to generate electricity to replace that power in the battery that is being used by the other three systems on the automobile. The only thing that makes this simple process complicated is the voltage regulator, through which the generator (or alternator) current passes before going to the battery.

As its name implies, the voltage regulator controls the amount of current supplied to the battery, based on the state of charge of the battery. If the battery is fully charged, the voltage regulator supplies a minimal current flow to maintain that full charge. But if the battery is partially run down, the voltage regulator will supply full current from the charging system to replenish the battery as quickly as possible. We won't go into the actual internal workings of an alternator or generator here, because that really isn't relevant to our discussion. Instead, we'll just say that if you have a problem with the charging system, and after you've verified that all of the wires are properly connected as shown in the schematic, then you can be reasonably sure that the problem is in the generator, alternator or regulator, and you should consult a qualified repairman.

The Lighting System

In the two previously discussed systems, almost all the wiring, with the exception of the ignition switch, was in the engine compartment. But both the lighting system and the accessory system have wiring that runs throughout the vehicle. Consequently there is usually a connecting or junction block mounted on the firewall where the wires pass into and out of the passenger compartment.

On most vehicles, the passenger compartment side of this connecting block is also a fuse block, since light and accessory circuits are fused or equipped with circuit breakers (a resettable type of overload protection device). Outside of tracing individual wires through the fuse and connecting block on wiring schematics, these systems are fairly straightforward, with easy-to-follow positive-to-ground paths.

Actually the lighting system is composed of a number of subsystems: the headlight system, the turn signal system and the instrument panel system. Dome lights, courtesy lights, trunk lights, and under-hood lights, along with the cigarette lighter, could also be considered a subsystem of the lighting system, since as with the headlight subsystem, these circuits, although fused, are supplied with

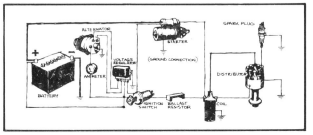

The ignition and starting systems are composed of the battery, starter motor and solenoid, the ignition switch, ballast resistor, coil, distributor, and spark plugs. Notice that the case of the coil is grounded. This is important to the operation of the secondary side of the ignition system (see text).

battery power even when the ignition switch is off.

The turn signal subsystem is the most complicated, since it is interconnected with the stoplight circuit and a flasher unit to provide the blinking of the turn signals when turned on. However, if you study the accompanying schematic, you'll see that the turn signal switch merely makes a complete circuit to either the right or left-hand indicators, interrupting the stoplights if they're on too.

One point that might be confusing is that two positive wires run into the taillight and front parking light housings on most vehicles. This is because the bulbs used in those lights, as well as the sealed-beam headlights, have two separate filaments. One filament is for the tail and parking lights, while the second filament, which is a brighter one, is used for the turn signals or stop lights. Both filaments in each bulb have a common ground. In the headlights, the two filaments provide a high and low beam. And in case you didn't notice it before now, most of the low-beam or outer headlights on quad-headlight cars also have two filaments in them and actually switch from one filament to the other, along with the illumination of the other two when the high beams are turned on.

The Accessory System

This is the simplest of all the electrical systems on a car. In almost all cases they consist of no more than a fused positive lead, routed through a switch, to the accessory, which is in turn grounded. Gauges are also part of the accessory system. Gauges do not usually have switches to turn them on or off, as they are controlled by power from the accessory side of the fuse block, which is on only when the ignition switch is turned on or in the "accessory" position. However, most gauges are fitted with senders. In almost all cases, the sender does nothing more than vary the amount of grounding the instrument gets, thereby changing its reading. Consequently, if the wire from a gauge to a sender unit ever shorts out, it will simply make a 100-percent ground and the gauge will show a full-scale reading.

Taken one at a time, a vehicle's electrical system isn't hard to understand. You may have second thoughts about that statement the first time you slide under the dash and find a bundle of 20 or 30 different, colored wires running up to the instrument cluster, but don't be put off. Grab the correct wiring diagram for the vehicle and patiently trace the circuit that you're concerned with until you know exactly where it goes. You'll find it's not too difficult, and the rewards are bound to be in your favor, since now you've got this game wired!

SCHEMATIC CODES

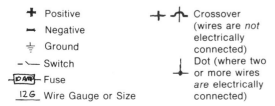

+ Positive
- Negative
Ground
Switch
Fuse
12 G Wire Gauge or Size

Crossover (wires are *not* electrically connected)
Dot (where two or more wires *are* electrically connected)

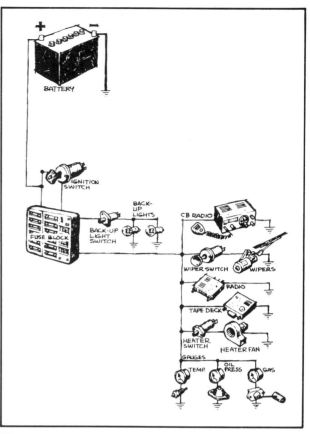

The accessory system consists of virtually all systems that will work when the key is turned to the accessory position, such as the wipers, radio, back-up lights, heater fan, and, of course, the gauges. These are all simple "loop" circuits. (The turn signal system, which doesn't work unless the key is on, was included with the lighting system since it works with the taillights and parking lights.)

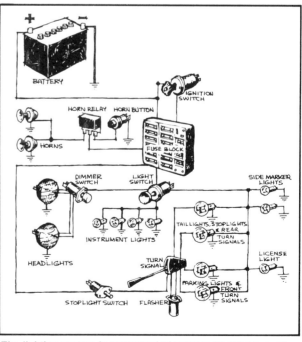

The lighting system is composed of many subsystems, such as the headlight system, the turn signal system, and the instrument light system. Other subsystems that work even when the key is off can also be included, such as the horns, stoplights, courtesy and dome lights, and even the cigarette lighter, although not all of these have been shown here.

MoPar Swapping Guide

The Road Runner and other B-body cars can live up to their image with hemi power—if you're lucky enough to find one of those rare engines.

As early as 1962, Chrysler Corp. was heavily involved in high-performance automobiles. Since that time, they have offered many interesting engine/chassis combinations aimed at the high-performance market. In fact, they once went so far as to build complete, race-ready vehicles, available at the dealer level on a special-order basis and void of any warranty. Cars such as the '65 Hemi Belvederes/Coronets and the '68 Hemi Barracudas/Darts made such an impact on the industry that many of these types of swaps have been duplicated in backyard fashion. For example, 440 Darts and Dusters were commonplace as were 440 engine replacements in the earlier Plymouth and Dodge sedans. Federal emissions laws also have had an effect on guys purchasing older cars and transforming them into modern day super cars.

General Information

The single most important item you need to obtain before attempting any engine swap is a service manual for the car being used. The time saved and the elimination of problems before they arise will more than offset the expenditure.

Now, before getting into specific MoPar engine swaps, let's go over the basic "muscle car era" Chrysler body and engine identification list. This will simplify later explanations and identify the particular combinations. Chrysler car bodies were divided into three groups: A-body ('64-'73 Valiant, '64-'69 Barracuda, '64-'73 Dart, Duster, Demon and Sport), B-body (Coronet, Satellite, Road Runner, R/T, GTX, Belvedere, Charger and Super Bee) and E-body ('70-'73 Barracuda and Challenger). The engines were also divided into separate groups: A-engine (273, '67 and later 318, 340 and 360), B-engine (361, 383 and 400), RB-engine—meaning "raised block" (413, 426 wedge and 440), Hemi (426) and 6-cylinder (170, 198 and 225). From here, when we refer to engine/chassis combinations, we will identify them as A-bodies, B-bodies, A-engines, B-engines, etc.

Engine Swapping Basics

Ideally, all of Chrysler's '62 and newer engine installations are mounted at three points, two engine block side mounts (one on each side) and a transmission mount (attached to a crossmember). All side mounts are made up of brackets (except '73 A and B-bodies, which use a one-piece bracket and insulator) which bolt to the block, and rubber insulators which attach to a front crossmember (known as a K-member). The rear transmission mount consists of a rubber insulator, which bolts to the crossmember; the crossmember bolts to the transmission tailhousing. As an aid to obtaining the correct mounts, insulators and K-member, check the accompanying charts for the specific part number for your application.

Also included is a transmission crossmember and mount usage chart, which shows the correct part numbers for each model year. Because Chrysler retained a very basic crossmember and transmission mount design, special mounts for custom installations can be easily fabricated. The big change in the

The 1974 Chrysler A-body cars (here in a two-door Plymouth) will swallow any MoPar engine, and this one's running a massaged 383 (to 400 inches) B-motor by a simple swap of K-member, two motor mounts, and a handful of nuts and bolts.

trans crossmember and mount area occurred from '65 to '66, when the shape of the mount and its position were changed. Transmission usage within Chrysler's line of bodies was pretty much straightforward. The A-body 4-speed cars used the short tailhousing, the B and E-bodies the long tailshaft housing. However, it is possible to use the long housings in an A-body chassis. The automatic transmission tailshaft extensions were the same for all bodies.

A-body Conversions

Let's begin with the A-body engine swaps. The A-body engine compartment was widened in 1967, which made the '67-'73 A-bodies more desirable for big-block engine swaps. The 273 was introduced into the A-body in '64; therefore, any '64-'66 A-body can be mated to a 273 or 318 by using the '64-'66 A-body 273 engine brackets, insulators and K-member. This type of 273 or 318 swap is a bolt-in. The 340 or 360 engine also will fit quite easily by using the same 273 mounts; however, the left side engine bracket requires modification (see illustration). Due to shock tower and steering positioning, a B-block engine swap is not recommended for the '64-'66 A-body.

Luckily, the '67-'73 A-body had a variety of production engines available, including the 383 ('67-'68-'69) and the 440 ('69). Therefore, these models make logical choices for B-block engine swaps. If the car originally was a 6-cylinder, a new K-member, two brackets and two insulators are all that is required to install virtually any engine. All A-engines used the same basic K-member; however, the part number may differ from year to year due to sway bar clearance. If at all possible, the best plan is to use the K-member made for the specific year car you are using. Any A-engine, A-body swap is a bolt-in operation. Basically, this means that a 318 can replace a 273, and the 360 can be bolted easily in place by using the 340 pieces. The brackets in either case are determined by the engine being used.

The B-engine can be swapped into the A-body by changing the K-member, brackets and insulators. These parts were the same for all three years ('67-'69) they were in production. Although some sway bar problems may be encountered, the '68-'69 K-member 2883999 should be used in the '70-'73 A-bodies. The raised-block engine can be swapped

into the A-body by using the same conversion pieces as the B-engine; however, exhaust manifold clearances get very close with the 440 installation.

The 383 or 440 engine can be installed in any '67-'72 A-body by using the 383 pieces, but if the 383 or 440 is installed in a standard A-body, the heavy-duty torsion bars (2535894-5) are required to compensate for the additional weight of the B-block engine. Another item not to be overlooked is brakes. You can install the Rally package disc brakes, or at least make sure the original units are in good working order and adjusted properly.

As a note of interest, the '73 mounts (bracket and insulator) are a one-piece design. This change requires that the '73 mounts be used with a '73 K-member and the '72 and earlier mounts be used with the '72 and earlier K-members. However, the '72 and earlier K-members will bolt onto the '73 A-bodies, which means you can install any B-engine into the '73 A-body chassis by using the '67-'69 383 K-member.

B-body Conversions

The B-body chassis line can be divided by model year into three groups—'62-'65, '66-'70 and '71-'73 and, because all the various engines have been available in the B-body, engine swapping is quite simple, if the correct parts are used to install the engine.

The '62-'65 B-body has three K-members designed for ease of engine installation: one for the 6-cylinder, one for the A-engine and B-engine families, and the third for the Hemi. In essence, this means you can select any engine you wish; and, by referring to the charts, you can order the correct K-member, brackets, and insulators and have yourself a bolt-in engine swap. It's that simple.

The 318 engine used in the '62-'65 models was the old design, which is not only heavier but larger than the later 318. The original 318 engine can easily be replaced, as the newer 318 bolts directly to the old 318 insulators, brackets and K-member. The 340 and 360 engines are also bolt-in installations;

The 400-inch wedge looks like it was a factory fit in the Plymouth, but uses lightweight (but adequate) 6-cylinder radiator. Battery, heater component, and wiper motor stay in their original locations.

MoPar

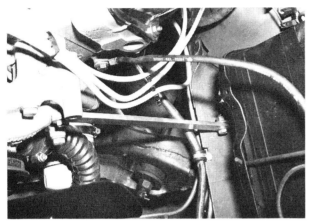

A properly designed torque strap keeps rubber production mounts from severe loads under hard acceleration, and keeps drivetrain components in proper relationship.

however, the left engine brackets must be reworked as shown in the illustration. The B and RB engines will fit these cars by using the same K-member and insulators as the A-engine, but new brackets are required (2268216 and 2268220). The 426 Hemi can also be fitted by using K-member 2460975, brackets 2468150-1, and insulators 2468184 and 2532708. Although the 440 was not used in the '62-'65 cars, it will bolt in using the 383 engine mounts. The same 383 pieces are used to install the new 400 cubic-inch smog motor.

Installing a V8 in a 6-cylinder '66-'70 B-body also requires a new K-member, brackets, and insulators. The B and RB engines can be installed in place of an A-engine by simply changing the brackets (see chart). The Hemi, however, requires a new K-member, brackets, and insulators. The insulators needed are from the '64 Hemi and the brackets are 2780672-3. The 340 was an available B-body option in 1970; however, the 340 and the 360 can be installed in the '66-'69 B-bodies by using the 318 K-member, insulators, and brackets 2536125 and 3418400.

As mentioned in the A-body text, the '73 B-body K-members are completely different than the '72 and earlier units due to the isolated front subframe on the '73 B-body. Because of this, the '72 and earlier K-members do not fit the '73 chassis. The new '71-'73 B-body cars follow a similar pattern to the earlier B-bodies, in that there are three K-members: one for the 6-cylinder, one for the A-engine, and one for the B-series engines. The 360 can be installed in the '71-'73 B-body by using the 340 brackets, insulators, and K-member, and the 426 Hemi can be installed into the '72 B-body by using 3583076 K-member, brackets 3418305 and 2951601, and insulators 2951599 and 2532708.

E-body Conversions

The E-body Barracudas and Challengers were introduced in 1970, and at one time or another the 225, 318, 340, 383, 440 and 426 Hemi engines were available options. Because of this, stock production parts are available to install any MoPar engine into the E-body. For example, in a V8-equipped E-body, the 318, 340, 360, 383, 400 and 440 engines can be installed by merely selecting the correct engine brackets and insulators (refer to charts). You may have noticed that the 360 and 400-cubic-inch engines are not listed on the charts; that's because the 360 utilizes 340 mounting pieces, and the 400 uses 383 parts. As shown on the charts, the Hemi requires a special K-member 3583076, brackets 3418305 and 2951601, and insulators 2951599 and 2532708 for installation into the '72-'73 E-body. The 383, 400 and 440 can be installed in the '72-'73 E-body by using the '71 engine mount brackets and insulators from a 383 or 440 installation.

Hemi A-body Conversions

The Hemi A-bodies were originally built in 1968, and both the Barracudas and Darts used the same conversion pieces. The key item in building a Hemi A-body is the K-member. A special K-member (2836891) was used for the original cars, but it is no longer available. However, a 273 A-body K-member (2883980) can be made to fit by cutting off the 273 engine mount support brackets and welding on the engine mount support brackets from a '66-'70 Street Hemi K-member. The insulators (2468184, 2532708) and engine brackets (2780672-3) to be used are from a '66-'69 Street Hemi. The left motor mount bracket requires the insulator locating hole to be redrilled 1 inch to the rear, and the K-member should be spaced ½ inch away from the longitudinals (by using 2x2x½-inch spacers) for adequate carburetor-to-hood clearance. The spacers are not necessary if an aftermarket hood scoop is used. On the original cars, the right shock tower was reworked to gain valve cover clearance, and for the same reason the master cylinder was offset using a 1-inch thick aluminum plate (2836931). Flexible master cylinder hoses also were used so the cylinder could be removed to adjust valves without disconnecting the brake lines. Tubing headers are necessary for this swap, as there are no production castings available.

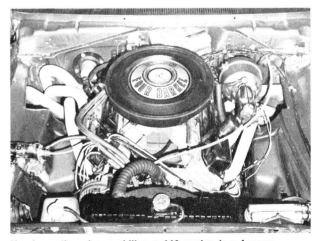

Here's another sleeper/killer; a 440 wedge in a former 340-powered Duster. Air cleaner from a 340 really fools the troops.

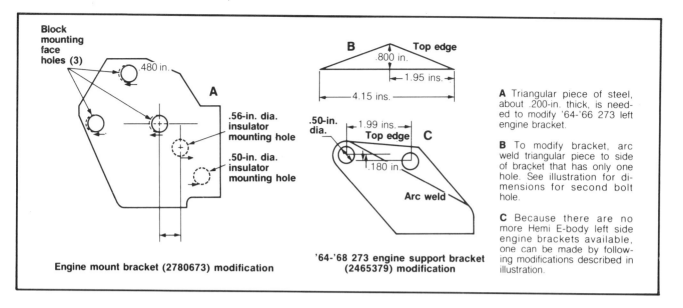

Block mounting face holes (3)
.480 in.

A

.56-in. dia. insulator mounting hole

.50-in. dia. insulator mounting hole

Engine mount bracket (2780673) modification

B — Top edge
.800 in.
1.95 ins.
4.15 ins.

.50-in. dia.
1.99 ins.
Top edge — C
.180 in.
Arc weld

'64-'68 273 engine support bracket (2465379) modification

A Triangular piece of steel, about .200-in. thick, is needed to modify '64-'66 273 left engine bracket.

B To modify bracket, arc weld triangular piece to side of bracket that has only one hole. See illustration for dimensions for second bolt hole.

C Because there are no more Hemi E-body left side engine brackets available, one can be made by following modifications described in illustration.

Automatic Transmission

MoPar engines had three basic transmission/bellhousing mounting bolt patterns. There is one for all 6-cylinder engines, one for all A-engines and a common pattern for all B, RB and 426 Hemi engines. For example, the 340 automatic transmission or bellhousing will bolt to any A-engine, and the Hemi automatic transmission or bellhousing will bolt to any B or RB engine.

Automatic transmission selection for an engine swap is pretty straightforward. Assuming that you choose a 1962 or later aluminum case Torqueflite, all that's necessary is to make sure the trans has adequate capacity for the engine to be used, and that the bolt pattern matches the block. When selecting the trans, choose it for the type of shifting mechanism used and the type of output shaft. The '62-'64 transmissions had a flanged output shaft, while the '65-'73 units have a slip-spline output shaft. The '62-'64 transmissions used a pushbutton-cable shifting mechanism, and the '66-'73 units use a mechanical linkage type shifter. However, both types of shifting mechanisms were used in '65.

Care must be exercised when selecting a torque converter. Of primary concern is the 360 engine, which uses a specially balanced converter. This unit (3515844) must be used with the 360, or extreme vibration will result. The area of concern when selecting a converter is that the input shaft of the transmission must match with the neck of the converter. The A-904 (small automatic) has a smaller input shaft than the A-727 (large automatic) trans. There also have been two different input shafts used in the A-727. The earlier '62-'66 models used a smaller input shaft than the '67-'73 units. However, a conversion kit is available from Chrysler High Performance Parts (P3412071) to convert the small input shaft to the larger one.

The engine-to-torque-converter mating is simple, if the flex plate that came with the torque converter is used. The only exception to this is if you use a Hemi converter with an A or B-engine. In this case you will need an adapter type flex plate (P2466326). This flex plate is required because the Hemi crank flange has 8 bolt holes, while the A and B flanges use a 6-bolt pattern.

Clutch and Bellhousings

Selecting the proper bellhousing for an engine swap is more involved than the automatic transmission selection. In addition to matching the block bolt pattern, you must match the transmission bolt pattern, match the starter and flywheel, and match the clutch linkage to the bellhousing.

There are actually two different pressure plate bolt patterns which we will discuss here; the third was a 9½-inch clutch for the old 273 engine, which isn't of sufficient capacity to be considered. The two remaining patterns are 10½ and 11 inches. The 10½-inch flywheel bolt pattern was used for all 340's, '70-'71 383's, '72-'73 400's, '70-'73 440's, '70-'71 Hemis and '67 and earlier 383's. The 11-inch clutches were used with '66-'69 Hemis, '67-'69 440's and '68-'69 383's. All '70-'73 383, 440 and Hemi clutches are known as 11-inch scalloped pressure plates, but they have a 10½-inch flywheel bolt pattern. To use an 11-inch scalloped clutch pressure plate in a regular 10½-inch clutch installation (such as a '68 340), clearance must be filed on the starter pilot boss on the inside of the bellhousing to provide the needed clutch-to-housing clearance.

The '70-'73 V8 engines use the same ring gear and geared starter. All V8's in '70 through '73 with the standard 10½-inch flywheel have a 10-tooth geared starter and a 130-tooth ring gear. In '69, all 11-inch clutches except the Hemi used the 11-inch flywheel with a 10-tooth geared starter and a 143-tooth ring gear. The '66-'69 11-inch flywheel for the Street Hemi used a 12-tooth straight-through starter and 172-tooth ring gear. An important point to remember when dealing with clutches is that all related components should be considered a complete assembly. Components from one assembly, such as the 10½-inch, should not be exchanged with those of another assembly, such as the 11-inch or 9½-inch, unless all parts of the assembly are changed. Remember, the bellhousing must bolt to the block,

MoPar

In this swap of a 440 in a 1970 Duster, stock 440 engine mounts were used, but the left mount requires a piece of ¼-inch steel to be welded on to move the mount on the engine just enough to mate with the K-member.

driveshaft assembly kit (P3690590), which contains all the necessary parts to fabricate a custom driveshaft; however, this kit is designed to mate the A-833 (4-speed) or A-727 Torqueflite to the 9¾-inch Dana axle. If this doesn't fit your combination, you can modify one of the production driveshafts to fit.

A-BODY K-MEMBERS

Year	6-Cyl.	273-318-340	383	383 w/power steering
'64-66	2260609	2260609		
'67	2768375	2768548	2881925	
'68	2883982	2883980	2883984	2883999
'69	2883982	2883980	2883999	
'70	2962082	2925976		
'71-72	3583062	3583064		
'73	3466466	3466468		

B-BODY K-MEMBERS

Year	6-Cyl.	V-8	440	426 Hemi
'64-65	2204199	2401057		2460975
'66	2467991	2467990		2467993
'67	2768542	2768537	2768537	2768540
'68	2883992	2883990	2883990	2883994
'69	2925932	2925930	2925930	2925934
'70	2962092	2962090	3466479	2962094
'71	3583070	3583100	3583100	3583076
'72	3583070	3583052	3583052	
'73	3642746	(318-340) 3642744	(400-440) 3642748	

E-BODY K-MEMBERS

Year	6-Cyl.	318-340-383-440	340 6-Pack T/A	Hemi
'70	2962010	3466477	3583052	3583076
'71	3583070	3583074		3583076
'72	3583070	3583052		
'73		3583074		

accept the clutch, accept the transmission and hold the starter in correct relationship to the flywheel.

Exhaust System

Exhaust systems sometimes can be a little tricky. It all depends on the intended use of the car and what its expected performance level should be. For example, in many cases it will be far easier to use production cast iron manifolds, headpipes, mufflers and tailpipes rather than to fabricate headers, head pipes and crossover tube, and install large-capacity mufflers and 2½-inch tailpipes. It all depends on what you're looking for from a performance standpoint. If cast iron exhaust manifolds are to be used, a system can usually be found that will bolt on to your swap. The 383-440 engine installation in an A-body requires special exhaust manifolds, which were used with that package (2863897, 2946728). If the ultimate street exhaust system is to be designed for your car, it's suggested you use an adequate four-tube header with a crossover tube (running between collectors); 2½-inch head pipe tubing; Imperial, Street Hemi, turbocharged Corvair or low-restriction aftermarket mufflers; and 2½-inch pipes running back to the rear axle.

Driveshaft

With the engine and transmission installed in the car, the remaining critical item is the driveshaft. With a production engine/body combination, the production driveshaft will work fine. Simply order the matching unit for your combination. If you have a non-standard combination, then a special driveshaft will have to be fabricated. Chrysler High Performance Parts offers a special

TRANSMISSION CROSSMEMBERS & TRANS MOUNTS

Year	TRANSMISSION CROSSMEMBERS Standard Manual & Automatic	4-speed	TRANSMISSION MOUNTS Automatic	Manual	Hemi
1964					
A-Body	2260287	2260287	2265836	2265836	
B-Body	2265423	2208740	2265826	2405872	2401653
1965					
A-Body	2260287	2260287	2265836	2265836	
B-Body	2265423	2208740	2265826	2401653	2401653
1966					
A-Body	2530642	2530642	2533145	2533145	
B-Body	2530692	2530668	2533145	2533145	2660673
'67-69					
A-Body	2768475	2768475	2533145	2533145	
B-Body	2881938	2530668	2533145	2533145	2660673
'70-71					
A-Body	2925943	2925943	2533145	2533145	
E-Body	2962074	2962074	2892471	2892471	3410310
B-Body	2962074	2962074	2533145	2533145	2660673
A & B-Body (June '71)	3583188	3583188	2892471	2892471	3410310
1972					
A-Body	2925943	2925943	2533145	25331·45	
B & E-Body	3583188	3583188	2892471	2892471	
1973					
A-Body	3466462	3466462	3642831	3642831	
B & E-Body	3642794	3642794	3642831	3642831	

B-BODY ENGINE MOUNT BRACKETS

Year	6-Cyl.	273-318	340	361-383-426W-440	426 Hemi
'64-'65	2264679	2402185 (2)		2268216	2468150
	2264678			2268220	2468151
'66	2532277	2806025		2806167	2780673
	2532278	2536125		2536132	2780672
'67-'69	2532277	2806025		2863751	2780673
	2806479	2536125		2536132	2780672
'70	2532277	2806025	3418400	2863751	2780673
	2806479	3418394	3418394	2536132	2780672
'71	2532277	2806025	3418400	2863751	3418305
	2806479	3418394	3418394	2536132	2951601
'72	2532277	2806025	3418400	2863751	
	2806479	3418394	3418394	2536132	
'73	'73 B-body uses a 1-piece bracket and insulator (see B-body insulator listing)				

BELLHOUSINGS

6-CYLINDER / A-ENGINE

Year	6-CYLINDER 3-speed	4-speed	11-in. clutch`	Year	A-ENGINE A-Body 3-speed	4-speed	B-Body 3-speed	4-speed
'64	2402690	2463025	2463565	'64	2463411	2465524	2402696	
'65-'66	2468479	2468431		'65	2463411	2465524	2468482	2465524
'67-'72	2658955		2536918	'66	2463411	2465524	2536941	Use '65
'73	2658955			'67-'68	2780900	2806083	2536941	Use '69
				'69-'71	2892480	2892480	2892480	2892480
				'72-'73	3515732	3515732	3515732	3515732

B-ENGINE

Year	383 A-Body 4-speed	361-383 B-Body 3-speed	4-speed	413-426 B-Body 3-speed	4-speed	440 B-Body 4-speed	Hemi B-Body 4-speed
'64		2402681	Use '65	2406043	2463235		2463235
'65		2468448	2468370		2463235		2463235
'66		2536943	2536945	2536943	2536945		2780510
'67	2536945	2536943	2536945	2536943	2536945	2843235	2780510
'68	2536945	2843925	2892260			2892260	2892257
'69	2536945	2892624	2892624			2892624	2892257
'70-'73		2892511	2892511			2892511	2892511

A-BODY ENGINE MOUNT INSULATORS

Year	6-Cyl.	273-318	340	383
'64-'66	2264140 2265018	2465508 (2)		
'67	2806844 2806842	2806779 (2)		2536121 2465861
'68-'72	2806844 2806842	2806779 (2)	2806779 (2)	2536121 2465861
'73	3642820 3642821	3642810 3642811	3642810 3642813	

A-BODY ENGINE MOUNT BRACKETS

Year	6-Cyl.	273-318	340	383
'64-'66	264668 2265023	2465378 2465379		
'67	2532278 2806841	2843223 2843224		2465862 2536132
'68-'69	2532278 2806841	2843223 2843224	2863443 2863445	2465862 2536132
'70-'72	2532278 2806841	2863443 2b4322	2863443 2863445	
'73	A-body uses a 1-piece bracket and insulator (see A-body insulator listing)			

B-BODY ENGINE MOUNT INSULATORS

Year	6-Cyl.	273-318	340	361-383-426W-440	426 Hemi
'64-'65	2264675 2264674	2402183 2402182		2402183 2402182	2468184 2532708
'66	2658283 2658784	2536121 (2)		2536121 (2)	2468184 2532708
'67-'70	2658283 2806476	2536121 (2)		2536121 (2)	2468184 2532708
'71	2658283 2806476	2536121 (2)	2536121 (2)	2536121 (2)	2468184 2951599
'72	2658283 2806476	2863735 (2)	2536121 (2)	2863735 (2)	
'73	3642826 3642827	3642810-1 3642818-9 (wagons)	3642810 3642813	3642814 3642815	

E-BODY ENGINE MOUNT BRACKETS

Year	6-Cyl.	318	340	383-440	Hemi
'70	2532277 2806479	2806025 2536125	3418400 3418394	2863751 2536132	3418305☆ 2951601
'71	2532277 2806479	2806025 3418394	3418400 3418394	2863751 2536132	3418305☆ 2951601
'72	2532277 2806479	2806025 3418394	3418400 3418394		
'73		3642842 3642843	3642842 3642843		

☆ Superseded by 2780673

E-BODY ENGINE MOUNT INSULATORS

Engine	'70-'72	'73
6-Cyl.	2658283-2806476	
318-340	2536121 (2)	3642850 (2)
383-440	2863735 (2)	
426 Hemi	2951599-2532708	

NOTE: The '70-'71 Hemi E-Body left side engine mount bracket (3418305) has been discontinued. It has been superseded by bracket 2780673, however, the replacement unit is not a bolt-in Hemi E-Body bracket until minor modifications have been performed. The mods include elongating the three holes on the block mounting face (the flat portion which bolts to engine block). These three holes should be moved a full ⅛-in. in the direction shown (see diagram). The next step is to elongate the insulator mounting holes. These two holes must be moved in the opposite direction from the block mounting holes (refer to arrows on diagram). These holes also should be moved ⅛-in.

Theory and Practice

Contemporary engine swaps no longer emphasize the traditional high power-to-weight aims of an engine exchange. The brute acceleration requirements of yesteryear's swapping rodders have given way to the more practical parameters of our times—namely, economy, handling, and everyday utility. There's a whole new generation of enthusiasts out there who are going to have to approach the subject of swapping with plenty of fresh perspectives and not a whole lot in the way of hands-on experience. Hopefully, this review will shed some guiding lights.

Basically, engine swaps can be divided into three categories: common (V8s into Pintos, Vegas, and the like), oddball (super-duty Pontiac power in a Porsche), and strictly OE (original equipment). It wouldn't really be practical to look into all of the permutations and combinations that fall under any of these headings, but there is some common ground to cover. As unlikely as it may seem, all the above groups have their roots in OE—and that's the area most often ignored. In view of the veritable volumes of published swapping material, OE has always drawn the short end of the stick. We're going to do our best to remedy that right now.

Engine Identification

Locating suitable swapping material has always been a somewhat confusing proposition for engine exchange enthusiasts, mostly because there's so much to choose from. Even when a potential powerplant has been found, the problem of determining exactly what lies under its valve covers still remains.

The key to this guide is knowing the car the prospective motor came from. Most of our clues are based on having a complete vehicle to inspect rather than just the engine itself. But as you'll see, there are instances where information applies to separated assemblies as well. In some isolated cases, the same ID code may appear on different engines from one manufacturer. The same may apply to a particular engine used in different model year applications by the same auto maker.

Availability and desirability are the main requirements for our listings, so certain combinations considered rare and hard to find have been passed over. If any doubt remains as to an engine's ID after its manufacturer's codes are deciphered, check out other reference sources. Repair manuals (like *Motor's* or *Chilton's*) or even the original factory service texts can contain the confirming clue as to a powerplant's true identity. The key codes to most popular swap material are listed as follows:

BUICK

Choice Buick powerplants can be identified by a two-letter code stamped into one of two locations. All 400, 430, and 455-cubic-inch engines are marked on the left side of the cylinder block below the two rear spark plugs. The smaller 350-cube engines are also stamped on the left side of their block, but the code can be found below the front plugs.

Year	Engine	Code
1967	400/400	RR
1968	350/280	RP
	430/360	RD
1970	350/285	SB
	350/315	SP
	455/350	SR (Special)
	455/360	SS (Special)
	455/370	SF, SR
1971	455/315	TR
	455/330	TA, TR (Special)
	455/345	TS
1972	455/260	WA
	455/270	WS

CHEVROLET

All Chevy V8s can be identified by a two or three-letter code which can be found following the engine's serial number stamped into the front right-hand side of the block below the cylinder head.

CAMARO

1967	327/275	MK, ML, MM, MN
	350/295	MS,MT,MU,MV
	396/325	MY,MZ
	396/350	EI,EQ,EY
	396/375	MQ,MR
1968	302/290	MO
	327/275	EA,EE
	350/295	MS,MU
	396/325	MW,MY
	396/350	MR,MX
	396/375	MQ,MT
1969	302/290	DZ
	350/295	HQ,HR,HS
	350/300	HA,HE,HB,HP
	396/325*	JB,JG,JU,CJG,CJK,CJU
	396/350*	JF,JI,KA,CJF,CJI
	396/375*	JH,JL,KC,CJH,CJL JJ**,JM**,KE**
1970	350/300	CNJ,CNK,CRE
	350/360	CTB,CTC
	396/350*	CTW,CTX
	396/375*	CKD,CTY
1971	350/270	CGK,CGL,CJG,CJD
	350/330	CGP,CGR
	396/300*	CLC,CLD
1972	350/200	CDG,CKD,CKK
	350/255	CKS,CKT
	396/240*	CLA,CLB,CTA,CTB
1973	350/175	CKB,CKU
	350/245	CLJ,CLK,CLL,CLM

*Early 1969 big-blocks are indicated by a two-digit code and displace 396 cubic inches. Late 1969 and later big-blocks are indicated by a three-digit code and displace 402 cubic inches.
**Aluminum cylinder heads

CORVETTE

1967	327/300	HE,HO,HH,HR
	327/350	HP,HT,HD,KH
	427/390	IL,IQ,IM,IR
	427/400***	JC,JD,JF,JG
	427/435***	IU,IT,JE,JA,JH
1968	327/300	HE,HO
	327/350	HP,HT
	427/390	IL,IQ
	427/400***	IM,IO
	427/435***	IR,IT,IU
1969	350/300	HY,HZ
	350/350	HW,HX
	427/390	LL,LM
	427/400***	LN,LQ
	427/430	LO**,LV**
	427/435***	LR,LT,LX,LP** LU**,LW**
1970	350/300	CTL,CTM
	350/350	CTN,CTO,CTP,CTQ
	350/370(LT-1)	CTR,CTU,CTV
	454/390	CGW,CRI,CZU
	454/465	CZL**,CZN**
1971	350/270	CGT,CJL
	350/330(LT-1)	CGY,CGZ,CJK
	454/365	CPH,CPJ
	454/425	CPW**,CPX**
1972	350/200	CDH,CDJ,CKW,CKX
	350/255(LT-1)	CKY,CKZ,CRS,CRT
	454/270	CPH,CPJ,CSR,CSS
1973	350/190	CLA,CLB,CLC
	350/250	CLD,CLH,CLR,CLS
	454/275	CWM,CWR,CWS, CWT
1974	350/250	CLD,CLR
	454/270	CWM,CWR,CWS

***Three 2-barrel carburetors
**Aluminum cylinder heads

CHEVELLE

1967	327/275	EA,EB,EC,EQ,EE
	327/325	EP,ER,ES,ET
	396/325	ED,EK,EM
	396/350	EF,EJ,EL,EN,EU,EV,EW
	396/375	EG,EX
1968	327/275	EA,EE
	327/325	EP,ES,ET
	396/325	ED,EH,EK
	396/350	EF,EL,EU
	396/375	EG
1969	350/300	HB,HE,HP
	396/325*	JA,JK,JV,CJA,CJB,CJV
	396/350*	JC,JE,KB,CJE
	396/375*	CJD,CJF,JD,KD,KF, KG**,KI**,KL**,KH**
1970	350/300	CNJ,CNK,CRE
	350/360	CRT
	396/330*	CKR,CKS
	396/350*	CTW,CTX,CTZ
	396/375*	CKO,CKQ,CKT,CKU, CTY,CKP**
	454/360	CRN,CRQ
	454/450	CRR,CRV,CRS**
1971	350/270	CGK,CGL
	396/300*	CLB,CLL,CLP,CLR,CLS
	454/365	CPA,CPD,CPG
	454/425	CPP**,CPR**
1972	396/240*	CLA,CLB,CLS,CTA, CTB,CTH,CTJ
	454/270	CPD,CRW,CRX,CPA
1973	454/245	CWA,CWB,CWC,CWD

*Early 1969 big-blocks are indicated by a two-digit code and displace 396 cubic inches. Late 1969 and later big-blocks are indicated by a three-digit code and displace 402 cubic inches.
**Aluminum cylinder heads

NOVA

1968	350/295	MN,MS,MV
	396/350	MR,MX
	396/375	MQ
1969	350/300	HA,HB,HE
	396/350	JF,JI,KA
	396/375	JH,JL,KC
1970	350/300	CNJ,CNK,CRE
	350/360	CTB,CTC
	396/350*	CTW,CTZ
	396/375*	CKQ,CKT,CKU,CKW, CKP**
1971	350/270	CJD,CJG
1972	350/200	CKD,CRL,CDG

*Early 1969 big-blocks are indicated by a two-digit code and displace 396 cubic inches. Late 1969 and later big-blocks are indicated by a three-digit code and displace 402 cubic inches.
**Aluminum cylinder heads

OLDSMOBILE

The popular Olds Eights listed on our ID charts can be identified by a two-letter code located on a tape attached to the front of the oil filler tube.

1968	350/390	TN
	455/365	UN, UD
	455/375	UN, UT
	455/400*	UV, UW
1969	350/310	QN, QP, QV, QX
	400/325	QR, QS (W-30)
(W-30)	400/360	QT, QU
	455/365	UL
	455/375*	US, UT
	455/390	UN, UO
	455/400*	UV, UW
1970	350/310	QN, QP
(W-31)	350/325	QX
	455/365	TP, TQ, TU, TV, TW, UL
(W-30)	455/370	TS, TT
	455/375*	US, UT
	455/390	UN, UO
	455/400*	UV, UW
1971	455/320	UN, UO
	455/340	TA, TN, TP, TQ, TV, TW
(W-30)	455/350	TL, TS, TT, US*, UT*

*Toronado

CHRYSLER

Chrysler Corporation's mix-and-match possibilities are literally endless. There's so much in the way of parts and information covering MoPar interchangeability that a book could easily be written on the subject. In fact, one already has. And rather than getting even further bogged down in particulars and part numbers, we're referring you straight to the source. Send one dollar to Chrysler Performance Parts, P.O. Box 857, Detroit, MI 48288, and ask for bulletin No. 28 on engine conversions. It's by far the most complete reference outlet for interchange facts that we've ever come across.

Deciphering Chrysler Corporation's powerplant ID plan is considerably simpler than most other car makers' markings because each MoPar engine is stamped with both year and size codes. The first thing to determine is where each one of almost a dozen different motors are marked. Code locations can be found as follows:

ENGINE SIZE	CODE LOCATION
273-318-340-360	Right front of block below the cylinder head
361 & 383 (1960-67)	On machined pad on right side below distributor
383 (1968-71)	Left rear of block near the oil pan flange
400 (1972)	Left rear of block near the oil pan flange
400 (1973-77)	On machined pad on right side below distributor
426 (1964-67) & 440 (1966-67)	On machined pad at top left of block above the water pump
426 (1968-71) & 440 (1968-72)	Left rear of block near the oil pan flange
440 (1973-77)	Left front of block near the tappet rail

CODE BREAKDOWN
1965-'67

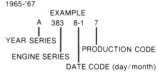

YEAR CODES

A	1965
B	1966
C	1967

CODE BREAKDOWN
1968-'73

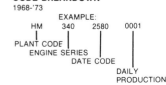

DATE CODE

2164 thru 2529 1968 (D)
2530 thru 2894 1969 (E)
2895 thru 3259 1970 (F)
3260 thru 3624 1971 (G)
3625 thru 3990 1972 (H)
3991 thru 4255 1973 (J)

ADDITIONAL CODE MARKINGS

E Cast crankshaft
H Standard 4-bbl
HP High performance
S Special engine

Additional ID information: Chrysler's A-engine series of small-block engines (273-318-340-360) all have rear-mounted distributors, while all other V8 MoPars have front-mounted distributors.

PONTIAC

The late-model Pontiac V8s that we're concerned with can be identified by a two-letter code stamped into a machined pad located beneath the engine production number on the front of the block below the right-side cylinder head.

1967	400/325	WI, WZ, XN, XW, XX, YF, YT
	400/333	WD, WY, XT
	400/335	WT, WWW, YS
	400/350	XJ, XZ
	400/360	WS, WV, XS, YE, YR, YZ
	428/360	WG, XP, YH, YY, Y2
	428/376	WJ, XK, YK, Y3
1968	400/330	YT
	400/335	WI, WQ, WZ, XN
	400/340	YE
	400/350	XZ, YZ
	400/360	WS, WT, XP, XS
	428/375	WG, YH
	428/390	WJ, WL, YK
1969	400/325	WQ
	400/330	WZ, YT, YW
	400/335	WQ, YW
	400/340	XZ
	400/345	WH, XN
	400/370*	WX, XH
	428/370	WW, XP
	428/375	XJ, XK, YH
	428/370	WF, XF
	428/390	WJ, XG, YK
1970	400/330	XV, XZ
	400/350	WT, WX, XH, YS
	400/366	WS, YZ
	400/370	WH, WW, XN, XP
	455/360	YH
	455/370	WA, XF, YA
1971	400/300	WK, WT, YS
	455/325	WJ, WL, YA, YC
	455/335	WC, YE, WL (Firebird)
1972	400/200	WK, WS
	455/300	WD, WM, YB, YE
1973	400/230	Early—WP, WS, YT, YY, Y3, ZS
		Late—XK, XN, XX, YG, Y6
	455/215	Early—YA
		Late—XJ, XY
	455/250	Early—WT, WW, YA, YD, YK, ZC
		Late—XA, XE, XL, XM, XN, X7, XE, XY (LeMans)
	455/310	Early—W8, Y8
		Late—XD, ZJ
1974	455/290	W8, Y8

*Ram Air IV

Theory

AMC

It's unfortunate that more enthusiasts don't get involved in AMC cars because we've come to learn that they're one of the most practical groups to deal with in terms of powertrain interchangeability. Nearly everything required to blend a Nash body with any one of the half-dozen popular AM Eights can come straight from the parts books. Mechanically, each engine is identical externally, and interchangeability of internals is almost as straightforward. Considering the raw materials and the wealth of information available, we wouldn't be surprised if fast Nashes become the rage of the Eighties.

American Motors' V8s can be identified externally in two ways. The entire series of blocks that we're discussing—290, 304, 343, 360, 390, and 401—have their displacement indicated on a tag attached to the front of the right side valve cover. If time has taken its toll on the inscription, some 1969 and later V8s have their cubic inches displayed as cast-in numbers on both sides of the block between the first and second core hole plugs. If possible, always double-check your findings, because all these engines have interchangeable valve covers.

If an engine is still in its original car body, the seventh digit of the Vehicle Identification Number (VIN) can be used to identify its displacement. The VIN can be found on the left front door panel or in the upper left-hand corner of the instrument panel. The following chart keys AMC vehicles to their original engines:

290 2-bbl.	H
290 4-bbl.	N
304 2-bbl.	H
343 2-bbl.	S
343 4-bbl.	Z
360 2-bbl.	N
360 4-bbl.	P
390 4-bbl.	W (1968-'69)
390 4-bbl.	X (1970)
390 4-bbl.	Y (SS/AMX & Machine)
401 4-bbl.	Z

FORD

High-performance FoMoCo-built automobiles that have their original engines still in place can be identified through their warranty and VIN plates. The two primary tags to look for will provide both year and engine codes as follows:

1967-'78 WARRANTY TAG

EXAMPLE:

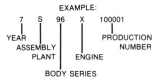

```
7    S    96    X    100001
|    |    |     |    |
YEAR |    |     |    PRODUCTION
 ASSEMBLY |    |    NUMBER
  PLANT |   ENGINE
      BODY SERIES
```

1967	A	289 4-bbl/225-hp
	K	289 4-bbl/271-hp
	P	428 4-bbl/360-hp
	Q	428 4-bbl/345-hp
	R	427 (2) 4-bbl/425-hp
	S	390 4-bbl/336-hp
	W	427 4-bbl/410-hp
1968	A	289 4-bbl/225-hp
	J	302 4-bbl/235-hp
	K	289 4-bbl/271-hp
	N	429 4-bbl/360-hp
	P	428 4-bbl/360-hp
	Q	428 4-bbl/345-hp
	R	427 (2) 4-bbl/425-hp
	S	390 4-bbl/335-hp (GT)
	W	427 4-bbl/390-hp
1969	G	302 4-bbl/290-hp (Boss)
	J	428 4-bbl/Cobra Jet
	M	351 4-bbl/290-hp
	N	429 4-bbl/360-hp
	P	428 4-bbl/360-hp
	Q	428 4-bbl/335-hp (CJ)
	R	428 4-bbl/335-hp (CJ w/Ram Air)
1970	C	429 4-bbl/350-hp (Cobra Jet)
	G	302 4-bbl/290-hp (Boss)
	J	429 4-bbl/370-hp (Cobra Jet)
	M	351 4-bbl/290-hp
	N	429 4-bbl/360-hp
	P	428 4-bbl/360-hp (Police)
	Q	428 4-bbl/335-hp (Cobra Jet)
	R	428 4-bbl/335-hp (CJ w/Ram Air)
	Z	429 4-bbl/375-hp (Boss)
1971	C	429 4-bbl/370-hp (Cobra Jet)
	G	302 4-bbl (Boss)
	J	429 4-bbl/370-hp (Cobra Jet)
	M	351 4-bbl/285-hp
	N	429 4-bbl/360-hp
	P	429 4-bbl (Police)
	Q	351 4-bbl (GT)
	R	351 4-bbl/330-hp (Boss)
1972	F	302
	P	429 (Police)
	Q	351 4-bbl
	R	351 4-bbl (Boss)
1973	F	302
	Q	351 4-bbl
	R	351 4-bbl (High Output)

Motor Plates

In the early days of roll-your-own hot rodding, the catchall, but comic, phrase, "use an adapter," was the reply most often offered to virtually any engine swap question. The advice itself was practical, but due to the lack of hands-on hardware, it was most often proposed in jest.

But leave it to the racers to come up with the answers, even when there are no questions. In this case, a question was asked, and it was the $64 one at that; it was the rodder's perennial "How?" And this time, a common competition car construction practice—the use of flat, transverse mounting tabs or a single mounting plate to mate an engine with a chassis—provided the anxiously awaited answer.

Due to the nature of their forward-facing water pump and timing gear housings, most modern V8 motors have potential mounting points built into nearly all the right places. Motor plates, as they've come to be called, are usually attached to the front of the block (at the gear or pump housings or to other existing bosses or pads), and as long as there is a pair of structurally sound points to attach the plates' outboard ends, the plan becomes infinitely practical for any number of mix-and-match street or strip experiments.

We followed along as Blaine Anderson of Anaheim, California, scratch-built a pair of plates to mate his big-block MoPar wedge motor with an A-body Chrysler car—one of the few muscle machine combinations never offered as an assembly-line option. (We should point out that for this particular application, Direct Connection offers a special front K-frame for a big motor/little car fitting. But although it makes for a very neat, OE-style installation, the motor plate method is cheaper, easier to execute, and it leaves a lot more under-hood room for the exhaust system). After watching Blaine make all the attachments to his own iron, the system appears to be as close to the mythical universal adapter as anything will ever come.

Before diving in under-hood, establish the outer limits of all existing hardware. One point where potential component interference exists is at the K-frame in the area of the oil pan's sump. Here the critical dimension between the oil pan rail (at the very bottom of the block) and the sump is determined.

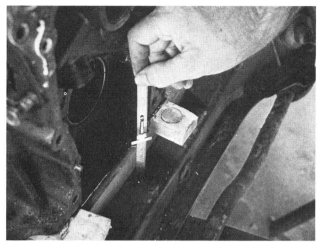

With the block located in the engine bay piloting on its rear (transmission) crossmember and mount, sections of wood are used to position it in relation to the frame. This is where those premeasured clearance numbers come in handy. Since powerplants are usually factory-offset to allow for left-side steering gear clearance, remember to consider this when making mounting maneuvers.

Once the engine is positioned at the proper height and angle, a measurement is taken across the front face of the block to determine the width of the frame stubs at that point. This distance figure is then used to fabricate a dummy plate from common hardboard material. The stuff is stiff, easy to work with, and inexpensive, and it's sturdy enough not to flex in use and upset critical calculations.

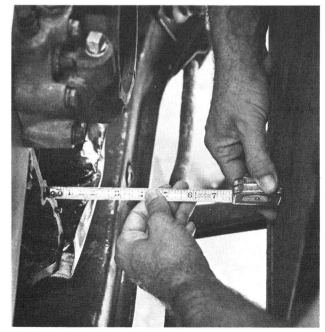

The engine should be referenced to as many fixed structures or components as possible. Here an inclinometer determines the block's lateral attitude in relation to the radiator and its surrounding supports. A simple ruler or tape measure will confirm what your eyeballs can't.

Since the bolts that attach the motor plate to the engine carry all the supporting load, close relationships between these components are critical. Elongating existing bolt holes will weaken the entire system, so try to work to close tolerances. Here a pair of standard water pump-to-block gaskets are temporarily positioned by the housing's hold-down bolts, while silicone sealer applied to the block face is allowed to set up.

Theory

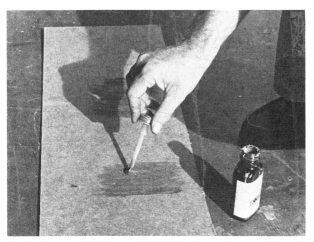

Contact cement is then applied to the face of the gaskets and to the backside of the hardboard template, where it comes in contact with these areas of the block.

With the template positioned under-hood and pressed firmly against the sticky gaskets, a putty knife is used to separate the gaskets from the block so that they stick to the template in their proper positions.

Using the gaskets' outer edges as guidelines on their inboard sides, and then using the points of contact with the frame rails as references for their outboard sides, the shape of the mounting tabs or plates is sketched directly onto the templates.

Although almost any type of handsaw can cut the template patterns to shape, the actual tabs are made from ⅜-inch-thick T6 aluminum stock, and that stuff is slightly harder to work with. A power tool assist will come in real handy right about here, but if it comes right down to the bare backyard basics, a sharp handsaw will work, too.

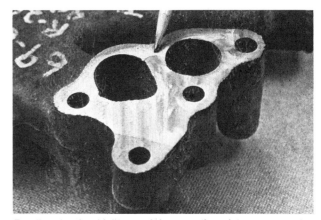

To allow for the thickness of the mounting plate, an amount equal to the aluminum's thickness plus the combined thickness of the two compressed pump-to-block gaskets must be milled off the mounting face of the water pump housing.

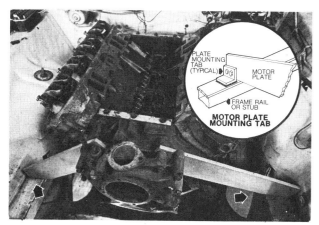

With holes drilled at all appropriate pump housing openings and mounting points, the tabs can then be used to support the block in position. Short lengths of angle iron are then used to attach the plates to the frame at the points indicated (arrows), but we'd suggest avoiding welding the brackets in place until all other related components (like the headers, steering gear, and clutch linkage) are lined up in their proper positions.

The transverse plate mounts to the frame in much the same simple manner as the home-brewed arrangement reviewed earlier in this chapter. (Two pieces of angle iron will handle the job exceptionally well.) One minor drawback of this design is the lack of room for a mechanical fuel pump. The way we see it, however, considering this system's slew of other advantages, it will be of little consequence to anyone except the most finicky OE purist. But then again, someone like that wouldn't be using a motor plate, would he?

Easy On

This hardware from Hooker Headers makes a V8 Vega swap a true bolt-in affair. The yoke-type front plate allows the use of OE exhaust manifolds. Trans crossmember and all attaching parts are included in the kit. Headers are also available from Hooker for this popular swap.

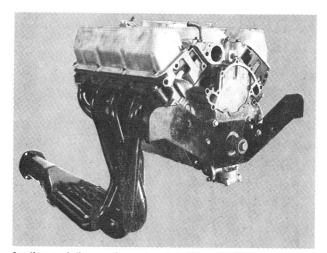

Another variation on the motor plate theme is this arrangement for Ford V8s from Total Performance in Mt. Clemens, Michigan. Proprietor and former FoMoCo Muscle Parts man John Vermeersch has designed this single-plate system to attach any Ford small-block to virtually any FoMoCo frame. As seen here, fitted with "low-profile" JR headers (notice how the tubes are stacked flat for floorboard and ground clearance), the Total setup makes a Boss-motored Pinto a veritable bolt-in.

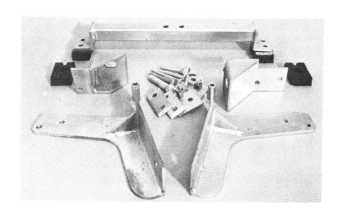

Chevrolet OE Alternate Parts	Engine Tabs		Mounts		Bellhousing Mounts		Bell-housing	Clutch Fork	Oil Pan	Oil Pump Pickup
	left	right	left	right	left	right				
SMALL-BLOCK										
Manual Trans	3836325	3836326	3768180	3768180	3728507	3728508	3755343	3737454	3735640	3754942
Cast-iron Powerglide	3836325	3836326	3768180	3768180	3728507	3728508	—	—	3735640	3754942
Aluminum Powerglide & all THM	Use sidemount kit		3990916	3990916	**	**	—	—	3735640	3754942
BIG-BLOCK ***										
Manual Trans	*	*	3768180	3768180	**	**	3755343	3737454	3902371	3860366
All THM	*	*	3990916	3990916	**	**	—	—	3902371	3860366

* Use aftermarket tabs (Hurst, Cylone, Trans-Dapt) in 6-cylinder frame holes.
** Rear crossmember installation required. Use mount number 3870182 for PG and THM 350 and number 3872248 for THM 400.
*** Tube headers required.
NOTE: All part numbers listed are Chevrolet's, but compatible components are also available from aftermarket sources.

Theory

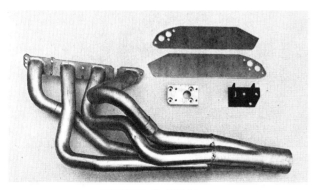

NHOA Kits

These parts and pieces from the National Hemi Owners Association make it possible for a late-model 426 street hemi to be fitted to virtually any Chrysler car. The elephant ears, or Mickey Mouse mounts, as the NHOA refers to them, support the motor behind the water pump housing; and they'll work in more than just MoPars. The shiny metal block shown here is used to relocate the master cylinder if it interferes with the wide engine's left-side valve cover. The darker bracket is used to attach a hemi block to a B-engine K-frame, using the original motor mount bosses on the passenger's side of the block. The headers shown here are designed to mate a hemi with any of the Corporation's A-body (Duster, Demon, Dart Sport) cars. If the NHOA doesn't have the hardware for your particular street hemi swap, chances are they can either locate the parts for you or, at the very least, provide details on the installation.

Buy the Books

Quite possibly, the ultimate source for original equipment interchange information is the *Hollander* manual. It's referred to in the trade as "The Bible," and for many a good reason. Cross-referenced listings identify components and systems, as well as the cars they came in and the other models they'll fit. It takes a bit of practice to become proficient in its use, but like any other source of specifics, it's well worth the effort to learn. Boneyards nationwide depend on *Hollander* for what-fits-what guidelines, and the serious swapper can reap many benefits. Editions are available covering current and past production vehicles and foreign cars as well. Further information can be obtained directly from Hollander Publishing, 12320 Wayzata Blvd., Minnetonka, MN 55343, (612) 544-4111.

Further references to most of the powertrains reviewed here can also be found in another book, *Petersen's Big Book of Auto Repair*. This hefty volume calls the shots for both the beginning and the experienced do-it-yourselfer, with literally loads of step-by-step how-to's. Every approach to an engine swap should start with an open book rather than an opened hood.

Room to Lube

With under-hood space around most V8s usually at a premium, swappers are always looking for ways to cut corners. No actual cutting is required here, of course, but this tip will turn some cramped corners into very usable work room. Both Ford and Chrysler small-blocks can be fitted with a right-angle oil filter adapter designed to tuck the filter canister closer to the block. Both setups provide more space around the exhaust system, and as you can see, the Ford mounting also unshrouds the critical area around the motor mount boss (arrow). The idea is far more practical and much less expensive than a remote system, and each adapter is available right in the neighborhood from the appropriate dealership under the part numbers shown.

CHRYSLER
P3690886—Complete kit
FORD*
C5AZ-6840-A—Gasket, adapter to block
EAA-6749-A—Gasket, head of hollow bolt to block
C5TZ-6881-A—Adapter
EAA-6890-A—Insert, adapter to block
C5AZ-6894-A—Bolt, hollow, adapter to block

*In view of the relatively extensive Ford parts list, and considering that the minimum quantity for all gaskets ordered is 10, we suggest contacting a specialty swap shop.

We should also mention that Ford's adapter will work on all their V8s except the FE's.

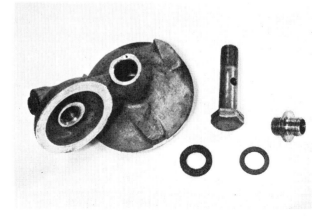

Classic Combinations

Although 1955-'57 Chevrolets don't exactly fall within our late-model musclecar parameters, their mass popularity as swapping material at least merits a mention. Essentially, all three variations on what was basically the same body/chassis platform are easily adaptable to both OE-style small-block power as well as to later-model rat power. The process of mating either motor with an early car has actually been refined to the point where certain combinations make for a better fit than the factory original.

As can be expected, both pure-stock, assembly-line power teams—a small-block backed by either a manual trans or the Powerglide automatic—require the simplest arrangements. With the standard-shift OE bellhousing bolted to the back of a mouse motor, virtually any 3 or 4-speed Saginaw, Muncie, or Borg-Warner GM gearbox will fit. Early cast-iron Powerglide installations are equally easy because the original V8 cars were attached to their 'Glides by a pair of bellhousing mounting ears. Later-model automatic-backed powertrains must be "side-mounted" with an aftermarket kit attached at the side rather than at the front of the engine block, and a late-model rear crossmember must be custom-mounted to match. Big-blocks will fit in under-hood, too, but valve-cover-to-firewall interference problems may require some sheetmetal tweaking. Kits containing all the necessary hardware for any of these combinations are available from a number of the swap shops listed here.

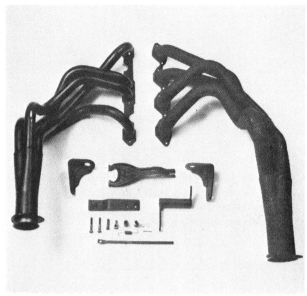

Cyclone Automotive produces quality headers for both big and small-block early car installations. Clutch linkage conversion pieces are also available from the same source.

Popular Swaps

A Plymouth Duster of '70 vintage is one swapper's idea of a street terror—after he went the 440 V8 route and opened it up to 446 inches. Trick wheels and outgoing hood scoop give away what would otherwise be a street sleeper.

If you've read the first chapter of this book, then you already know why we feel engine swapping is on the rise again. Hot rodders will always resort to building something at home if it isn't available over-the-counter, and, unfortunately, high-performance cars are in that category. Yet not all engine swapping being done today is strictly for "street racer" type performance. While the majority of engine swaps are done with the vision of new-found under-hood powers uppermost in the mind of the swapper, there are also swaps done for economic reasons. Dropping a late-model motor into an older car not only results in a vehicle that has more power, but often one which puts out less of the ugly pollutants clouding our skies. In addition, that new motor may also put a few more miserly miles underneath the tires for the same amount of overpriced gasoline. Engine swaps that have paid for themselves are not as rare as they might seem at first.

"Classic" Swaps

By classic, we don't mean that these are the finest examples of the swapper's art, just that these swaps involve older vehicles whose body styles have come in for more than their share of popularity. Resurrecting an older "special interest" vehicle isn't easy when you're stuck trying to find parts for it and you have to rebuild an obsolete engine that's had the life driven out of it.

An engine swap can be the perfect answer if you're not restoring the car to original condition for shows or the like. The best example of such a classic engine swap is the '55-'57 Chevrolet. Ever since these cars appeared in showrooms 20 years ago, hot rodders have been in love with them. They represent a clean-styling oasis in a period when gaudiness was the rule; they're easy to work on, and are fast becoming collector's items. Their easy adaptability to later powerplants and drivetrains has made them naturals for swaps, and it would be safe to say that at least 50 percent of these cars currently on the road are modified in one way or another.

Among the other classics ripe for a weekend affair with a rented chain-hoist would be the mid-sized cars of the '60s: Fords, Plymouths, Chevys, you name it. The desirable elements are the relatively light overall vehicle weight, and oodles of under-hood room, to say nothing of the "sleeper" appeal when one of these oldsters is all dolled up in the engine department but with a stock (but clean) exterior with perhaps a set of trick wheels the only giveaway.

As evidenced by the rapid growth of street rodding, almost any make and body style of vehicle built before 1949 is not only ripe for an engine and driveline swap, but such new/old hybrids are already on the streets in vast numbers, and rarely are two exactly alike. There are few limits to your creativity with these older cars.

Lest we hurt the feelings of some enthusiasts, we might add that '49-'57 Fords and Mercurys are equally suited for fresh motors and make fine street machines; and the '49-'54 Chevrolets are almost as popular with Stovebolt fans as their newer brethren, though they require more work.

The sports car set would do well to look to domestic horsepower to replace what is commonly a sewing machine-4; this '66 MGB is urged by an aluminum '62 Buick V8 and has 30,000 troublefree miles on its clock.

Compact Swaps

The classic swaps are fine for those guys who don't mind dealing with an older vehicle and the restoration hassles it can bring, but there are even more vehicles of recent vintage that lend themselves to the swapper's torch/touch. The popular swaps today can be divided into several categories, the first and perhaps largest of which is the compact-car contingent. Taking an engine out of a full or medium-size car and dropping, or shoehorning, it into a small car is the basic concept behind engine swapping in general, so the little cars we've seen so much of in the past few years make up a good percentage of the swap subjects today. Most popular of all of these would be the Pinto and Vega, both of which can be made into street terrors with a small-block V8 up front. The Pinto swap with a 302 is not as practical or popular as the Vega with a V8. There must be several thousand V8 Vegas running around right now, and the fact that five companies make complete swap kits for this combination tells you something.

Getting a little larger in vehicle size while remaining compact, there are a great many swap possibilities. In the Chevy line there are the Corvair and Chevy II waiting for 283-350 power; Ford lovers can find the 289-351 a good home in an early Falcon or Maverick, and the MoPar camp can fit their high-block 440 into a number of small cars like the Duster, Dart, Demon and Valiant.

Truck and RV Swaps

While most engine swapping can be considered "recreational" when it's done by an enthusiast who loves working on cars, some swaps are more recreational than others. Currently very popular is the trend toward putting big, late-model engines into older pickups for a variety of weekend and vacation duties from hauling car trailers, to boat trailers, to house trailers, to campers.

Unless you've got something like a nitrous oxide injector on your engine, there just isn't much you can do with a stock pickup engine when you're towing a camper, a dune buggy and four kids on vacation and you have to negotiate a steep grade. The answer in some cases is to modify the truck's original engine with headers, an intake system and dif-

ferent gears; but, often, more brute torque can be gained by simply swapping in a later, large-displacement engine which will probably also give you better fuel economy and dependability in the bargain. The mini-trucks like the Datsun, Toyota, Courier, and LUV have also proven fertile ground for swaps, and even a few expensive motor homes have felt the hook of a chain-hoist in quest of more hill-climbing power.

Import Car Swaps

There are some excellent vehicles built outside the U.S. borders; unfortunately, the handful that would meet American hot rodders' standards of performance cost 10 to 20 grand! The answer for the enthusiast who would like to have a "sexy European" body, but something under the bonnet a little more powerful and dependable than the normal sewing-machine-4, has got to be an engine swap. Of course, there'll be raised eyebrows at the thought of such a thing, but judging by the mail we receive, there are thousands of foreign car owners out there willing to brave the criticism.

Many sports cars and compact imports are well suited to small-block American V8 power. They already have the looks, handling and comfort most drivers are looking for, all they need is the torque to "keep up with the traffic."

The following selections of all four kinds of currently popular engine swaps—the classic, truck and RV, compact, and import car types—should be

Mercury Capris, not known for muscle in factory trim, can swallow any reasonable V8—but with shoehorning. But this car is a good example of the types of cars that are receiving a V6 injection, now that these "sawed off" V8s are becoming more common in wrecking yards.

Dropping a large-displacement, late-model motor into an early truck has become very common in the last few years. Such a combination can be practical and economical to run as well as having the power to handle your recreational needs—at a quarter the price of a new truck today.

Swaps

No one knows how many sports cars like this Datsun 240Z are running around with American V8 power, but it's certain that import cars are one of the hottest areas of engine swapping activity today, from mini-trucks to sedans and sports cars.

SWAP SHOPS
The following are some of the more popular sources of supply for engine swapping parts and information.

Motorhome Service
15027 Keswick St.
Van Nuys, CA 91405
(213) 997-1242
(Engine swapping Izusa diesels into RVs, trucks, autos)

Mundorf Conversions
2020 Lomita Blvd.
Lomita, CA 90717
(213) 530-8480
(Jaguar conversions, installing Chevy V8s. Kits available)

KEP Kennedy Engineered Prod.
10202 Glenoaks Blvd.
Pacoima, CA 91331
(213) 899-2612
(Engine adapter plates for various VW engine swaps)

Interjag XJLimited
7622 Talbert Ave.
Huntington Beach, CA 92648
(714) 842-2929
(Chevy V8 into Jag kits, also GM diesels into Jags)

Power Brake Service
13150 Arctic Circle
Santa Fe Springs, CA 90670
(213) 802-1683
(Specializing in power brake conversions for engine swaps, or any brake problems)

Tom Berry
760 Newton Way
Costa Mesa, CA 92627
(714) 646-9703
(Chevy V8s into Mercedes. Kits available)

Rod Simpson Hybrids
P.O. Box 25779
Los Angeles, CA 90025
(213) 826-3304
(Porsche & Datsun specialists, Chevy V8s into 911 & 914 Porsches)

Nobu's Auto Lab Inc.
6366 DeLongpre Ave.
Hollywood, CA 90028
(213) 462-2018
(Specializing in Dyno tune-ups, engine swaps, Chevy V8 into Datsun Z's)

Wenco Industries
7749 Densmore Ave.
Van Nuys, CA 91406
(213) 785-0643
(Specializing in custom driveshafts for 4WD and engine swaps)

Low Mfg. & Dist. Co.
245 W. Foothill Blvd.
P.O. Box 856
Monrovia, CA 91016
(213) 357-4767
(Specializing in 4WD conversions & engine swaps for mini-trucks)

Wilcap Co.
2930 Sepulveda Blvd.
Torrance, CA 90510
(213) 326-9200
(Engine adapters, specializing in custom diesel engine installations)

Advanced Four Wheel Drive Center
2345 E. Huntington Dr.
Duarte, CA 91010
(213) 358-3157
(Conversion parts & kits for Bronco, Scout, Toyota, & Jeeps; also OD kits)

Downey Off Road Mfg.
10023 South Pioneer Blvd.
Santa Fe Springs, CA 90670
(213) 949-9494
(Chevy into Toyota Land Cruiser engine swapping parts and kits)

Advance Adapters
P.O. Box 1923
Paso Robles, CA 94446
(805) 238-7000
(Transfer case adapters, engine adapters, motor mounts, part-time drive conversions, headers)

Con-Fer
300 N. Victory Blvd.
Burbank, CA 91502
(Adapters for GM engines into Toyota four-wheel drives)

Hurst Performance Prod.
50 W. Street Rd.
Warminster, PA 18974
(Motor mounts, transmission mounts, floor shifts)

Andy Herbert Automotive & Marine
8792 Fruitridge Rd.
Sacramento, CA 95826
(916) 381-0677
(Engine swapping a specialty, kits available)

Pete Malone
2612 W. 234th St.
Torrance, CA 90505
(Chevy into Jaguar)

enough to stimulate you into action on your own project. Surely one of the swaps we've covered could find a home in your driveway; the pride and satisfaction in knowing your vehicle didn't come off an assembly line is worth the work every time.

ENGINE MEASUREMENTS

One of the more positive deciding factors in shoehorning an engine into your car is that engine's physical bulk or size. There's an old swapping adage that "anything will fit in anything," but that's predicated on the fact you're willing to cut out the inner fender panels and substitute new ones hand-formed from sheetmetal; move the radiator ahead so far that you'll have to eliminate your grille; revamp the firewall to have most of the engine back under the cowl; or leave the hood off or add a blister that you'll have to crane your neck to see around. These are all possible, but none are acceptable.

If you've fallen heir to a healthy, big V8 engine and are shopping for a car to put it in, or you feel your present car's powerplant isn't up to modern-day standards, then it's time to dig up a ruler. Measure the width of the engine compartment (assuming the engine is already out); measure the distance from the firewall to the radiator, and determine the height from where the bottom of the pan will go to the underside of the hood.

Armed with the above figures, check out the accompanying chart with its physical measurements of most popular engines. Forewarned is forearmed, and the few minutes this procedure takes will be worth it.

Any year Vega of any body style makes a good home for a V8, and there are probably several thousand of them running around.

ENGINE SPECIFICATIONS CHART

Engine	cu. ins.	A	B	C	D	E	F	G	Oil Sump	Starter
American Motors 6	232/258	30	35	24	24	25	26	29	Rear	Left
American Motors V8	304/360/401	28¾	29¼	21½	25½	21¼	28	29½	Rear	Right
Buick V8	350	29	30½	23	28½	21½	25½	28½	Rear	Right
Buick V8	430/455	29	30	23	28	22	27	30	Center	Left
Chevy/Pontiac/ Olds/Buick 6	250	30½	32½	16	23½	24	25½	28	Rear	Right
Chevy V8	265/283 327/350	26½	27	19½	26	20½	25	27	Rear	Left
Chevy V8	396/427/454	30½	30½	22	27	23½	29½	33	Rear	Left
Ford OHV 6 (small)	144/250	29	31	17	17	24	26	28	Front	Right
Ford OHV 6 (large)	240/300	30	32	13	13	24	26	28	Front	Right
Ford V8	260/351	27	29	20	22	22	25	27	Front	Right
Ford V8	232/312	26	29	23	28	25	27	29	Front	Right
Ford V8	332/428	30	32	23	27	28	30	32	Front	Right
Ford V8	Hemi	32	34	32	32	30	32	34	Front	Right
Ford Flathead	221/255	30	30	26	26	22	26	x	Rear	Right
MoPar 6	170/198/225	30	31½	24	30	29½	22	26	Front	Left
MoPar V8	273/318 340/360	29½	29½	20½	25	23½	28	31	Front	Left
MoPar V8	383/400 440	29	30	23½	29½	24	28	30½	Front	Left
Olds V8	350	28¼	28¼	21½	26	20¼	25	27½	Rear	Right
Olds V8	455	29	31	22¼	26½	24	27	31	Rear	Left
Pontiac V8	350/400	28¼	29	22	27	20	26	31	Rear	Left
Pontiac V8	455	29½	32	23	27	27	28½	33	Rear	Right
Chrysler Hemi	426	32	31	28½	29	24	28	31	Center	Left
Chevy 4	153	22½	23½	16	23½	24	25½	28	Front	Right
Cadillac V8 (except Eldorado)	472	30	30½	23½	28	28½	29	32	None	Right

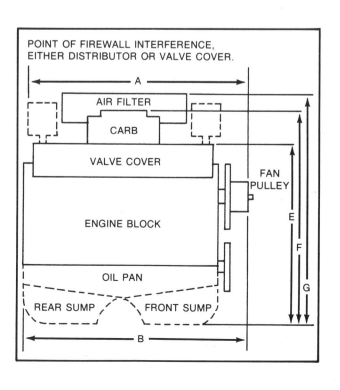

POINT OF FIREWALL INTERFERENCE, EITHER DISTRIBUTOR OR VALVE COVER.

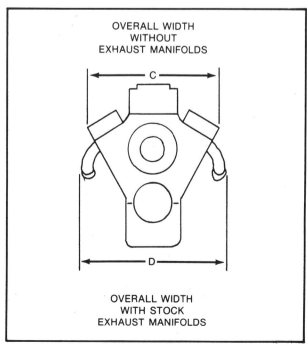

OVERALL WIDTH WITHOUT EXHAUST MANIFOLDS

OVERALL WIDTH WITH STOCK EXHAUST MANIFOLDS

Swaps
302 Chevy V8 in Mercury Capri

Young Californians, mostly male, almost exclusively car fanatics, are into several different automotive "scenes." There is the well-known Van Nuys cruising set, as well as several similar groups in other suburbs like Whittier and Santa Ana. Within this cruising scene there are different factions: vanners, racers, low riders, and mini-pickup guys. Some of these groups engage in competitive events, but for the most part their deportment is low-keyed.

Smaller groups of young Californians are more actively involved in the competitive derivations of cruising. Rather than talk about the merits of one's automobile, they test the mettle of their machinery. Groups involved in this scene include street racers, cafe racers, and the Mulholland group. Brian Mitsuhashi and his ground-hugging Capri are a part of the night-time Laguna Seca crowd. The hills of Los Angeles are laced by moderately traveled roads with endless curves, particularly a wondrous, winding road known as Mulholland Drive, that bring out the best in a good-handling car. In the heart of darkness, some unreal machinery comes out to challenge the clock and the curves.

Brian originally went the suspension route on his '74 V6 Capri, installing a complete Interpart Mulholland suspension package. The new springs lowered the car several inches and the heavy-duty shocks and sway bars gave it control. The Capri was very agile, but not as quick as Brian wanted. The solution, he felt, was more inches in the form of a V8. Since the Vettes and Trans Am-type Camaros were some of the stiffest competition on the "course," Brian decided to beat them at their own game by putting a Chevy small-block in his Capri.

To handle the swap, Brian called on master swapper Son Oliver at Son's Auto Center (17316 Crenshaw Blvd, Torrance, CA). Son is a perfectionist. He specializes in swaps that work so well they look like they were factory installed. Son likes to use as many factory parts as he can to make future repairs and maintenance as simple as possible. The small-block Chevy fits easily into the V6 engine bay. The firewall was untouched, and there is even room for a shroud around the fan. Only the back corner of the left valve cover had to be dimpled to clear the power brake booster.

Son always strives to mount his engines as solidly as possible. For this reason he mounted the front motor mounts to the top of the suspension rather than to the sheetmetal to prevent flexing and fatigue. Son made his own bracket which supports stock Camaro motor mounts. The rear motor mount was made out of a 3-inch-wide piece of 5/16-inch flat plate. The bar has a 1-inch drop in the center to accommodate the Turbo 350 transmission. The rear mount bolts to the stock Capri mounting holes, and uses stock Chevy transmission mounts. The transmission tunnel had to be enlarged to clear the governor housing, the dipstick tube, and the rear section of the transmission oil pan. The transmission is a fully manual unit modified by Son and equipped with a B&M Super Hole Shot converter. The shifter is a B&M cable shifter which aids clearance problems.

To gain room in the engine compartment, the air conditioning was discarded and the battery was moved to the trunk. The radiator is a modified Vega Desert Cooler unit, which combines with a Vega shroud and an aluminum flex fan for ample cooling.

The 302-inch Chevy fits easily into the Capri. The swap was easier than putting the same motor in a Vega. The battery is trunk-mounted for more room.

The swap allows the use of a radiator fan shroud for better cooling. The radiator is a modified Vega unit with a Camaro front brace panel.

The radiator hold-down panel is from a Camaro, with handmade mounting brackets riveted to the front cross brace. The fan is an aluminum flex fan. The oil pan is a Chevy replacement item from a '68-or-later Nova. This universal replacement pan clears the rack and pinion steering because the sump is all the way in the back of the pan; it also has more taper than other Chevy oil pans, permitting the engine to be mounted at the original crankshaft centerline. The driveshaft is a one-piece Chevy unit with a Capri rear flange to accommodate the stock Capri rearend. Brian plans to change over to a 9-inch Ford rearend with narrowed axles to gain strength, easier gear ratio changes, and the ability to run wide tires within the stock wheel openings.

The 302-inch Z28 engine ran 10.30s in its previous home, a '38 Chevy coupe. It has been completely blueprinted with an Isky roller cam, TRW pistons, a Tarantula manifold with an 850 Holley, a Rotofaze ignition, and Overseer headers. The headers are custom-built and use 1⅝-inch tubes. When the motor was first installed, '76 Monza exhaust manifolds were used, but the headers were added for more power.

The healthy-sounding exhaust is the only clue to the Capri's performance potential. The body and interior are completely stock. The car sports a fresh coat of black paint and all the trim has been painted black. The wheels were sprayed gold and the front bumper was removed for a cleaner look. The black sunscreen was made by Brian out of Contact paper. The car looks low, but it actually rose an inch after the swap and the removal of the air conditioning. Right now, the small 185 HR-13 Pirelli radials are the limiting factor of the car's performance. Brian can blaze the tires without even trying, but as soon as the new rearend and wide tires are installed, he'll be able to get all the new-found power to the ground.

The miniature Z28 is Brian's everyday transportation, but what he likes best is to let the car unwind on some deserted mountain road. Brian definitely believes performance cars are made to be driven hard. If you don't believe him, just ask him to show you his yearly $3000 insurance premium.

The motor-mounts are from a Camaro bolted to brackets made by Son's Automotive and fastened to the Capri's front end, not the body.

A sleeper at rest, the Capri appears docile enough and even its nose-down stance and styled wheels don't really give its handling/power potential away.

Swaps
252 Buick V6 in Buick Skylark

We really did it this time! We came up with an engine swap that most people can't believe, in a car that still more people wouldn't even consider; and the result is one of the nicest running engine swaps anybody around here can remember. The car in question is a 1980 Buick Skylark, one of GM's X-bodied, downsized economy/luxury cars that shares the same basic chassis and drivetrain as Chevrolet's Citation, the Pontiac Phoenix and the Olds Omega.

What makes this car unique in terms of engine swaps is that the engine is transverse-mounted, feeding into a transaxle to front-wheel drive. Two "corporate" engines are offered in these cars, the 151-cubic-inch in-line 4-cylinder manufactured by Pontiac and the 173-cubic-inch 60-degree V6 manufactured by Chevrolet.

What we had in mind was installing a 252-cubic-inch 90-degree Buick V6, suitably warmed over with a simple five-step program developed by Smokey Yunick to effectively double the horsepower output of any stock Buick V6 without losing smooth street driveability. In other words, we were looking at plunking 230 + lively horsepower where 115 hp had been quietly sleeping. Since we would be working with a Buick engine, the Skylark Sport Coupe was selected to avoid any crossbreeding conflicts with the factory.

In its stock form, the Skylark Sport Coupe is a very pleasant, though not too exciting, car. The ride is smooth and the handling is fair. It's roomy, quiet and economical, but loaded with every option, our "heavy" Skylark cried out for more power and better handling. Of course, we never could leave a good thing alone, usually resorting to the seldom-achieved premise that we're going to make it bet-ter—only this time we did.

The accompanying photos and captions outline our efforts, although we did run into a few problems during the swap at the Doug Roe Engineering facili-ty, 4025 E. Winslow, Phoenix, AZ 85040. Smokey's five-step plan called for adding a specialty manifold, carburetor, headers and a streetable hydraulic per-formance camshaft, as well as performing a quickie cylinder head porting job. Smokey's own dyno tests record what happens when these mods are done to the 4.1-liter V6, which, incidentally, is factory-equipped with an aluminum intake manifold and a Quadrajet 4-barrel carb. Two-barrel-equipped 3.8-liter V6s achieve an even more significant power gain from these mods.

Unfortunately, we were unable to complete the manifold and carb swap by press time, since hood clearance problems meant hood modification, so our test engine hasn't reached full potential yet.

Since we've removed all the nameplates and low-ered the car, it's become a real attention getter, but it's the unexpected performance and handling that really open the eyes of other drivers. We often get hailed down at a traffic light nowadays, and the question is always the same, "Hey, buddy, what is that thing and what's it got in it?" A simple reply says it all: "It's just a Buick!"

The stock engine in our Skylark was the optional 2.8-liter 60-degree V6, manufactured by Chevrolet Division. This engine exhibited stumbling and stalling when cold, but subsequent carb adjustments cured those problems. In everyday city traffic, this setup delivered a consistent 23 mpg, even with the air conditioning on.

The interior on the Sport Coupe has a definite performance theme with an all black dash and black and white full instrumentation. Red accent striping sets off the dash and console, which houses the cable-actuated shifter for the 4-speed manual transaxle. Completing the interior are bucket seats upholstered in a black and white hound's-tooth fabric with matching door accent panels.

Since Buick does not offer a tachometer in their instrument package, we added a Stewart-Warner Model 997-B Stage 3 tach. The 7000-rpm tach in the Model 289-A housing almost precisely matches the stock instrumentation.

Dragstrip performance of our Skylark was less than spectacular. On the first outing, a best of 17.91 seconds at 75.56 mph was achieved. A second test after some carb and timing adjustments had been made netted a slightly faster 17.48/76.84. A lighter Skylark without so many accessories, such as air conditioning, power windows, etc., would undoubtedly have gone even quicker.

The X-13 GT wheels are shod with BFGoodrich P235/50R13 Radial T/A tires inflated at 32 psi on the front and 28 psi rear. These tires have a full 7½-inch tread width, yet they're 2 inches shorter than the stock P205/70R13 tires that come on the Sport Coupe, thus lowering the car 1 inch overall.

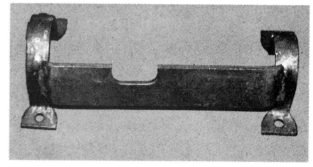

To provide more precise steering control, a revised steering box bracket was installed to reduce firewall flexing. This is a service part available from any GM dealer for X-bodied cars built prior to July, 1980. X-bodies built after that date have a reinforced firewall that eliminates the problem.

To significantly reduce flexing, or compliance in the engine cradle mounts for vastly improved handling, we replaced all four of the upper cradle mounts (left) with front upper mounts (part No. 14002107) surrounded with three GM shim washers (part No. 1366624) to virtually make the upper mounts solid. The lower mounts (bottom) (part No. 14002108) are from the '81 X-11 Citation. This modification helped a lot, but still more can be done (see text).

Swaps

To further improve looks and handling, Jim Welch at Vanowen Brake & Wheel in North Hollywood, California, lowered the front of our Skylark an additional 1½ inches by cutting the coil springs surrounding the MacPherson strut front suspension. He then realigned the front end for ½-degree of positive camber and 3/32-inch toe-out to correct torque steer.

The rear of the car was lowered 1 inch by cutting one coil from each of the rear springs. This made the smaller diameter 50-series tires look right in the wheelwell openings and helped handling. A second benefit is that the rear axle is no longer so noticeable from the rear of the car as it is on most X-bodies.

To stiffen the rear axle for better handling, the axle housing was boxed by stitch-welding a .090-inch steel plate the full length of the assembly. This job was done for us by Brogie Race Cars in Anaheim, California.

The final handling mod was relocating the upper track bar mount for the rear axle to make the track bar parallel to the axle assembly. This was done by bolting two steel plates to the existing bracket after trimming the rolled sheetmetal edge away. After lowering the car, we had to lower our track bar mount 1¾ inches to make it right.

The engine swap at Doug Roe Engineering in Phoenix, Arizona, began by pulling the stock 2.8-liter (173-cubic-inch) Chevrolet 60-degree V6. Although the shop manual calls for engine removal from underneath the car by lowering the engine cradle assembly, it can also be easily done by unbolting the engine from the transaxle, laying the air-conditioning compressor atop the battery (it is not even necessary to depressurize the A/C) and lifting it out the top in the conventional manner. The radiator doesn't even have to come out.

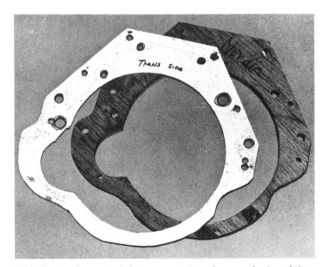

With the engine out of the car, a pattern for an adapter plate was made using the transaxle bellhousing flange and the rear of the Buick 90-degree V6 block as templates. A ¾-inch adapter plate was then fashioned. By the time you read this, a ½-inch aluminum adapter may be available from an aftermarket source, such as Mid-Engineering, P.O. Box 286, Mason, MI 48854.

The adapter plate was then fitted to the transaxle, along with a '62-'68 vintage MoPar-geared starter, such as used on most of their 6-cylinder models with a 122-tooth ring gear. Also shown in this photo is a special McLeod aluminum flywheel, which has been slipped into place to check clearance (some grinding may be required). The Chrysler starter had to be used with this setup, since its gear-drive offset provides the necessary block clearance. The stock throwout bearing is retained, and since the clutch is self-adjusting in the X-bodies, you just bolt it in and forget it.

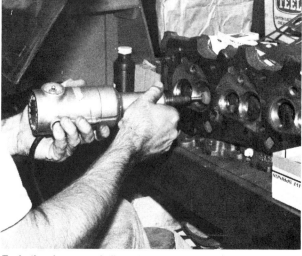

To further improve air flow, the stock heads were given a "dollar port job," which means that sharp edges immediately beneath the valve seats were blended in, and the remainder of the port polished with hard rolls. This only takes a few minutes, but it's worth a bunch of performance.

Before installation, our '80 4.1-liter (252-cubic-inch) Buick V6 was treated to a few modifications for power and durability (see text). The first step was to replace the stock rod bolts with Buick's heavy-duty rod bolts (part No. 25506513), torqued to 40 ft.-lbs. The correct procedure for this is to remove, replace and retorque one bolt at a time to retain connecting rod cap alignment.

Here's where we got a little help from our friends at Buick. The stock V6 front cover (left) has a fairly long water pump and the oil filter is canted forward. The prototype cover (right) keeps everything closer to the block for increased clearance. Look for the new cover to be included in Buick's heavy-duty service parts list in the near future to help hot rodders with this swap.

Next, a Crane H-214/2867-12 hydraulic cam was installed to improve breathing. C.J. dialed in the cam "on time" using the new cam lobe checking fixture from Mills Specialty Products. New Crane lifters were also installed along with the cam.

The last preswap step after bolting on the heads and intake manifold was the installation of the McLeod aluminum flywheel, clutch and pressure plate, which features a heavier-than-stock diaphragm spring. Since Buick V6s are externally balanced, the new flywheel must be balanced to equal the stock flywheel prior to installation.

Swaps

With brackets fabricated to properly locate and align the power steering pump, alternator, and air-conditioning compressor, Murray Turner and C.J. Baker swung the 4.1 into the Skylark. Some wiggling and jiggling was necessary to get the transaxle to properly engage the clutch, but it wasn't too bad.

The standard X-body-type mounts were used in conjunction with a homemade front bracket on the engine. The front mount (engine), upper torque strut and rear transaxle mount that we used were prototype pieces from Buick that featured harder rubber compounds than stock to help control the torque of the 4.1 engine. Again, these mounts may find their way into the heavy-duty parts list soon.

This is the water pump pulley clearance achieved when both top and bottom ⅜-inch spacers are used on the front mount.

To gain a little extra water pump pulley clearance and starter motor clearance, a ⅜-inch aluminum plate was placed atop the front (engine) mount. Another ⅜-inch spacer under the mount would help too, but carburetor-to-hood clearance then becomes a problem. If the hood is to be fitted with a hood scoop, use the second spacer.

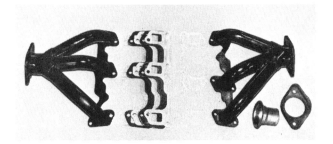

To go along with our ported heads and bigger cam, headers were a must. Happily, the 3-into-1 headers manufactured by Weiand for conventional V6 placement in Regal and Century models fit perfectly. We reversed the headers so that the outlet is inclined slightly toward the passenger side; and two extra header flanges were obtained from Kenne-Bell Enterprises (212 San Lorenzo, Pomona, CA 91766) and used as spacers for the front headers to provide starter clearance. K-B also has the header gaskets required between the flange plates.

Smokey's 5-Step Dyno Test

Stock 4.1-liter Buick V6 .... 152 hp

Weiand manifold & Holley 600-cfm carb added .... 170 hp

Weiand headers added .... 175 hp

Crane H-214/2867-12 cam added .... 202 hp

Cylinder heads given minor cleanup .... 230 hp

The larger size of the 4.1-liter engine precluded the use of the stock, thermostatically controlled electric fan. To solve this problem, we used two Flex-A-Lite (5915 Lake Grove Ave., Tacoma, WA 98499) electric fans mounted in front of the radiator. Shown here is their Model 10 unit with adjustable thermostatic controls and a Model 20 auxiliary fan. We discarded the controls and installed both fans as if they were Model 20s, connecting them to the Skylark's existing thermostatic controls. Either way, these fans really do a job; and we've never seen water temperature climb over 190 degrees, even while stuck in traffic on a 100-degree day with the air conditioning on.

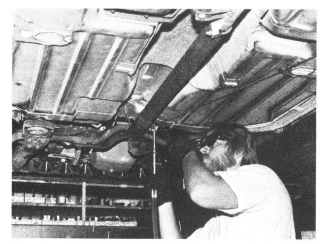

Doug Roe fabricated an exhaust pipe to connect the headers to the exhaust system. The car was later taken to a muffler shop where the remainder of the stock 2-inch exhaust system was replaced with a custom 2¼-inch-diameter system and a turbo-type muffler. However, since the '81 Citation X-11 has a 2¼-inch system, those stock parts could be used equally well.

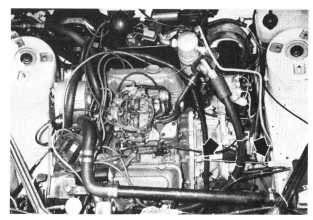

We soon discovered that the engine mounts allow the engine to move enough to let the alternator pulley touch the right spring tower during hard cornering. Consequently, the restraint cable (arrow) was added to eliminate the problem. In the static position, the cable is just barely slack to prevent engine vibration from being transmitted into the body panels. Aluminum plate at back of manifold blocks off the exhaust gas recirculation (EGR) system for more go and mileage.

This shot of the completed swap shows how everything, including air conditioning and power steering, can be installed as neatly as the stock setup. The only unsightly item is the upper radiator hose running all the way across the engine compartment. Although not shown here, a turbo V6 carb elbow and duct is used to connect to a remote air cleaner.

Although still fitted with the stock 4.1 aluminum intake manifold and Quadrajet carb, our Skylark now runs the quarter-mile in 14.97 seconds at 91.27 mph, a substantial improvement over the stock setup that makes this car an absolute ball to drive (it's a real sleeper!).

Swaps
Chrysler 440 in Plymouth Duster

By day, Anaheim, California's Blaine Anderson is systems engineer for Bell & Howell. By night, and on weekends, he's systems engineer on his dual-purpose, street/strip '70 Plymouth Duster. And his "system"—a big Chrysler "B" motor installed in a light A-body chassis—is both affordable and reliable. It is, in short, a combination perfectly suited for a dual-purpose vehicle.

When we say affordable, we mean just that. Blaine purchased the 3200-pound used car for a tad over three grand and has managed to make it race-ready for only another $3000 by doing most of the work himself. The results are 13.42-second, 112.29-mph ¼-mile blasts in street trim with street tires, hooked-up exhaust and 3.23 gears in the 8¾-inch '70 Chrysler pumpkin-style rearend. And having a pumpkin-style rear is really a treat, reports Blaine: Almost like a quick-change, the well-reared differential's street gears can be exchanged for a set of 4.57s. Combine that with open exhaust and 10.5-inch slicks and you have a 12-second machine.

These times seem even more impressive when you examine the relatively mild motor, built to run not only all day, but also all year. The 446-inch wedge motor (440 bored .030 over) is fitted with stock cast TRW '69-'70 350-horsepower passenger replacement pistons, giving a true 9.1:1 compression ratio with the '67 small 80cc combustion chamber high-performance heads, .030-inch-thick gasket and -.100 deck height. That means that "any pump gasoline is quite acceptable. The car never diesels." Thus, Blaine avoids the additive costs of ex-

otic mixtures. Additionally, the cast pistons do not expand when heated as much as forged slugs do, so they can be run with a tight .001 piston-to-wall clearance to obtain better sealing and ring control.

The reciprocating assembly didn't even have to be balanced, since all stock parts are used in the bottom end. The rods are stock 440 units, Magnafluxed and fitted with ⅜-inch-diameter Direct Connection high-strength steel bolts and nuts (part No. P4120068). Since stock pressed pins are used with the stock pistons, the rods couldn't be bushed. Since they couldn't be bushed, the center-to-center length couldn't be equalized, but Blaine reports that's not really necessary for this type of engine anyway. Speed-Pro supplied the stock-style ring set; the top single moly and cast middle rings are both gapped at .016, while the three-piece conventional oil ring is installed "as is." Anaheim's Precision Speed polished and indexed the '68 forged crank. They also squared, decked and honed the block.

Equally simple and reliable is the camshaft and valvetrain assembly. No high-buck roller or street mechanical in need of constant lash adjustments here! Blaine uses a Crower hydraulic grind with 284 degrees duration, .520-inch lift and 108-degree lobe centers, working through lifters, adjustable pushrods and 1.50:1 ratio rockers by the same manufacturer to actuate .100-inch longer than stock valves protected by chrom-moly lash caps. Ensuring timing accuracy are a Chrysler Direct Connection double-roller timing chain and cam button on the front snout. Crower dual valve springs with dampers offer 120 pounds of pressure on the seat and 350 open; they're kept on their seats by titanium retainers.

Pete Incaudo further improved the already desirable '67 cylinder heads. The intake ports were matched to the gasket, but were left relatively rough in order to better keep the fuel and air in suspension. By contrast, the exhausts were fully ported and polished to promote optimum flow of the spent

The .030-over 440 wedges neatly into engine compartment. Note motor plate, constructed of T6 aluminum alloy; water pump housing had to be machined ⅜-inch on back side to compensate for it. Chrome valve covers are available from Direct Connection.

No longer produced, Carter 1000-cfm Competition Series Thermo-Quad works great in dual-purpose street/strip, big-block/automatic trans application, thanks to its large total air-flow capacity combined with small primaries and vacuum secondaries. Their opening rate easily adjusts with a special tool inserted into air valve underneath protective lock screw (arrow). Metering rods pull out of the top, so disassembly is not required to change "jets."

mixture. The combustion chamber itself was also treated to a complete polish (to prevent sharp edges that could promote detonation), as well as being cc'd (to equalize the combustion chamber volume for all cylinders) and given full valve un-shrouding (to aid in better intake and exhaust flow). Speed-Pro bronze-wall valve guides were installed for durability. Also to aid durability, the rocker stands were machined for rocker blocks, which both stabilize and add longevity to the shaft-mounted rocker arms. The result is a reliable valvetrain system and heads that flow well for a stock-block, with equal cylinder-to-cylinder fuel distribution.

Of course, first the fuel has to get to the heads. That's the job of the induction system, which in this case is unique, yet (once again) reliable. The intake is a Holley single-plane Street Dominator, in keeping with Direct Connection's research, which indicates that manifold makes the best horsepower with a single 4-barrel and automatic trans in a bracket-racing application. Nothing unusual there. What is unique is the carburetor: a Carter 1000-cfm Competition Series Thermo-Quad. Newly rediscovered by bracket racers, it provides the air flow necessary for a hungry racing big-block, yet the vacuum secondaries perform well with an automatic on the street.

The spread-bore's smaller primaries also prevent bogging off the line with an automatic, as well as adding some measure of around-town fuel economy (if you can have economy with 1000 cfm). Unfortunately, no new 1000-cfm Thermo-Quads are being produced; so if you want one, you'll have to scour the swap meets.

Once delivered, the fuel has to be ignited, which is no problem thanks to a Stinger power module and coil working through a Chrysler distributor with 36 degrees total advance to fire Champion J11Y plugs gapped at .035. Once the fuel is fired, the spent mixture must be exhausted. That was a prob-

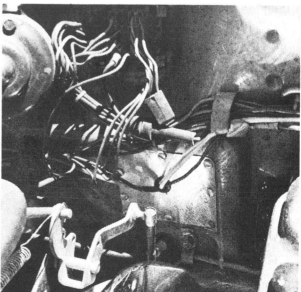

Throttle linkage and kickdown are stock GTX 440/4-barrel parts. Fuse block had to be relocated from stock position (now covered by plate) to clear linkage.

Swaps

Stinger supplied electronic ignition control module and coil, along with 7mm plug wire. So far, Blaine hasn't needed fatter 8mm wire, although he does use Stinger Hot Tips to retain wires positively on cap.

lem for a dual-purpose car, since nobody made a set of under-chassis headers suitable for connection to mufflers (only fenderwells were offered). Blaine had Ken Mooers at Positive Performance Headers (Orange, California) heliarc together a set that features 2-inch pipes and 3½-inch collectors. They are now available to the general public through the National Hemi Owners Association West Coast Region Parts Division (7010 Darby Ave., Reseda, CA 91335, 213/345-0314).

One more measure was needed to ensure reliability: oiling system mods. Paradoxically, the MoPar Wedge develops more than adequate oil pressure at normal operating rpm ranges; but at idle the pressure is sometimes lower than desired, and the oil blows right by the mains at too high a velocity to make the required 90-degree turn into the No. 4 main bearing oil feed hole. To correct this problem, a modification developed by Larry Atherton (formerly of A&W Performance) was utilized: A 45-degree fitting was installed in the main oil gallery leading from the oil pump, and a similar fitting was installed in the driver's side lifter gallery, just after the No. 1 cylinder lifter bores. The fittings are connected by a length of -6 braided aircraft stainless line that passes through a hole drilled in the block near the oil-pump-to-distributor drive. This ensured that the main bearing would get adequate oiling while at the same time continuing to deliver oil to the hydraulic lifters.

The rest of the oil system consists of a Chrysler oil pump with Milodon swinging pickup adapter and relief spring and Milodon 8-quart pan. With these mods, the system is able to deliver Valvoline racing oil with 35 pounds of pressure at hot idle and 55 pounds at 2000 rpm.

Interior is stock except for B&M Quick-Click shifter, fire extinguisher, and obligatory tach and oil-pressure gauge.

Trunk-mounted battery takes weight off front end and puts it over the right rear wheel where need for traction is greatest. MoPar makes it easy with kit No. P3690934; even you "other" guys could benefit from this one!

To gain additional clearance for large tires without flaring the fenders, leaf springs were relocated inboard. Blaine did it himself, cutting notch out of subframe and modifying it with new box to accept spring hanger. Direct Connection recently introduced a spring relocation kit that makes this mod much easier, although welding is still required; order part No. P4120665.

The resulting 450 dyno horsepower is transferred back to the rearend via a Thomson Transmissions (Fullerton, California) prepared, B&M Quick-Click-shifted, '70 Chrysler A727 Torqueflite automatic trans equipped with a 10¾-inch-diameter street Hemi-type torque converter.

The engine and trans slipped into place in the A-body easily. The rear trans mount and crossmember remain stock. Up front, motor plates had to be fabricated from ⅜-inch-thick T6 aluminum; they're tied to the frame by angle brackets.

To get the power to the ground, a Direct Connection 3000-pound-rate rear leaf spring package (P3690266 right, P3690265 left) works in combination with Sears 50/50 rear shocks that have ⅜-inch-diameter pistons. The front torsion bar is from a regular 340 Duster (rather than the 6-cylinder bar normally used by a race car), since Blaine feels that the smaller bar, although effective in promoting front-end lift and proper weight transfer at the drags, can't really handle the big-block's weight on the street.

Blaine's big-block bracket bomber has proved yet again that you don't need to be a millionaire to go racing—or to have a fast car. His secret "Plan B" is not really secret at all: You just put a big MoPar B-engine in a small A-car, stay away from super-exotic mods in favor of durable well-proven combinations, and do most of the work yourself. Old Dusters, Darts, Valiants and Demons are a dime a dozen, as are 440 blocks. But the same principles (if not the same engines and chassis) apply equally to Chevy's Vega or Chevy II/Nova, or Ford's Pinto and Maverick; so to "B" or not to "B" is entirely dependent on which marque you're biased toward.

Dual ½-inch-diameter fuel pickups are installed in back of tank to prevent fuel starvation under all conditions. Carter electric fuel pump is used near tank, backing up Carter front mechanical pump which operates off engine.

Note the high-efficiency exhaust system—2½-inch-o.d. pipe feeding into 2½-inch inlet and outlet Thrush Turbo mufflers. To ensure equal length tubes in this tight clearance chassis, one tube on passenger side must exit over and under frame.

Swaps
327 Chevy V8 in Chevy LUV

Mix one super-sharp air-conditioning repairman with a taste for mini-pickups that can tow his boat, and add lots of experience with speed, including a Camaro that's turned 12.97 @ 117 in the ¼-mile. That's a profile of Bruce Hall, and an understandable preface to the job he did on his '74 LUV pickup.

Since age 11, Bruce has been dreaming of a street sleeper that could turn on in a hurry. Quite naturally, a lifetime of rapid motoring experience has refined Bruce's ability in that area. Each succeeding machine has had a more pristine exterior, and each powerplant has been more of a fire-breather.

All this philosophy comes together in his brilliant red, stock-looking Chevy LUV. Although he has turned in pretty fast Javelin times, Bruce's Camaro laurels have recently capped the notion that he is a strong Chevy man. There's proof of that, too.

The LUV is a crisp package, but Bruce has equaled or bettered the cleanest of the clean. Best of all, from any angle it looks stock. The only possible giveaways are the white, flame-cut Tacoma steel wheels. But then, there are several good-looking LUV's running around with similar equipment in Bruce's Pico Rivera, Calif. neighborhood. The only other possible "red flag" on the red body is the exhaust tips, which are nicely flared outwards from

the rear bumper to each side. That might be a clue. Then again, maybe not. Hopefully, though, you won't run into this flame thrower at a stoplight with a clear road ahead.

But it's when you look under the LUV hood that your pulse begins to quicken. First you might get the notion that it's a 283 lurking there. How nice, you might think. Surely it's not the heavier 327. What about beefing the front springs with the heavier engine? What'll happen to the steering ratio? Well, hold on a moment. When you stop to think about it, you'll begin to find the first of many surprises.

Surprise number one is, of course, that Chevy's great looking little LUV doesn't have any coils. It's a farsighted design utilizing beefy lateral torsion bars. Evidently, the people at Chevrolet, a notoriously farsighted lot anyway, looked at the waves of boat-and-trailer-pulling, economy-minded, non-John Jacob Astor outdoorsmen who are turning their attention to mini-pickups. There's no getting around it, either—the LUV pickup is a lot of utility pleasure for the money. Especially when you can stuff heavier engines into it without noticeable front-end sag. For just a little stiffer ride with torsion bars, you get superior handling and relatively enormous weight-carrying ability. The 7.00x14 Firestone bias ply streeters on the slightly offset flame-cuts put the body nearly level at all points. No sag. Just a nice, stock-looking LUV.

Bruce wants to be able to tow his ski boat some 300 miles or so to the hinterland of the Colorado River recreational areas in the knowledge that there is ample torque on tap for off-road pulling power if needed in the desert terrain. He did not swap for the purpose of street hysterics—save for the occasional run through the lights at Irwindale Raceway. Basically, the idea was to stay low-key and neat. He has

Original '64 327 Chevy in its not-so-original home now displaces 370 cubes. The unit is used for heavy hauling in desert areas and features thicker radiator, fan, and 70-amp '66 GMC alternator. Note the dual hydraulic master cylinders and header design.

succeeded on both counts. And the proof of a swap is this: How hygenic is it? You'll have to hunt a bit before finding a cleaner swap than Bruce Hall's 327/LUV.

Strong Engine

The LUV's new engine started life in 1964 as a gleaming, aluminum valve-covered 327-cubic-inch V8, with its stock 4-inch bore and 3.25-inch stroke. Bruce let Hank the Crank take it from there. It was bored .125-inch and stroked another ¼-inch. Pistons are TRW, with Grant rings and stock rods. Floating pins were shotpeened and Hank the Crank balanced the bottom end. Total displacement of that "stock"-looking LUV is now 370 cubic inches of eager and well-fed, high-revving V8. To give you an idea of power-to-weight, the LUV originally weighed 2440 pounds. With fairly extensive engine work, the LUV now ·stands at 2990 pounds, although things like skid plate and heavier brackets were major contributors to the gain.

The heart of the 12.42@113 figures are in the cam and exhaust setups. Cam-wise, the Isky roller with Z-60 grind has upped max revs to 7900, which sounds good but in a truck has to be watched like a hawk. While a Monarch tach will give good readings to 10-grand, engine reliability becomes a crucial factor when lugging in the 3000-rpm range. As is well-known, roller bearings on the bottom end give outstanding freedom and become a major reason for allowable increases in rpm. However, lugging an engine equipped like Bruce's causes levels of heat buildup that can burn out rollers and/or dangerously magnify heat to the top of the pistons. Bruce went to the Isky roller to create the ultimate street sleeper—knowing all along what his hauling requirements would be, but determined to keep the rpm up at all times. You always give a little to get a little.

Isky dual valve springs on Crower rockers operate stock 327 valves. Head chambers are polished and

match-ported. With the split large roller bearings, rpm capability is truly fierce, especially running through a B&M 400 Turbohydro. Bruce decided to go with a smaller 13-inch torque converter. With the lower end he's got, to get what he was after the 13-inch converter seemed to be required.

The oil pump is a Chevrolet item. The L-88 Turbohydro is hooked up to a 4.88 rear axle, with Daytona Positraction. Steering is stock LUV.

A '57 Chevy rear axle assembly is not narrowed, and sticks the Firestones a little wider through the fenderwells. At first glance it might appear that Bruce slipped up by mounting the housing directly on the spring perches, causing the pinion shaft angle to produce a highly angular driveshaft. Some even suggested jokingly that he install shims under the spring perches.

In answer to this, Bruce reminded observers that mistake number one with many swappers was forgetting that a proper U-joint angle is needed for a particular axle assembly. With a '57 Chevy, especially one subjected to higher-than-stock torque loads, it becomes necessary to maintain a steady angle on the driveshaft so that the pressure at the Spicer U-joints will not spaghetti the yokes during off-the-line heroics.

The radio is 23-channel CB with 30-mile range. Tach is by Monarch and guards against lugging since V8 uses high-revving roller bearings.

The fan is from a '72 1-ton. Tips had 1¼ inches cut and were rebalanced. Carb is 650-cfm double-pumper Holley.

Swaps

Left front motor mount appears to support a missing part. LUV was at Champion for header installation, and the front exhaust port is not yet installed. Top mount piece is from '68 Camaro; bottom and pad are from stock '74 LUV.

With the LUV underpinnings, this became a bit of a problem. How do you maintain that angle with no room available? Well, first off, Bruce went to a '66 Olds, 8-inch front driveshaft yoke, in the belief that a weak point would be the point of connection between the Turbohydro and the front U-joint. There were two problems, here. One was the angularity problem, which Bruce solved by installing a U-bolt-shaped bracket between the rear trans mount and crossmember.

At first glance, this fix appears to lift the tranny much too high, shoving the front yoke right up against the driveshaft tunnel. Some people even advised Bruce to drill the rear crossmember and install the mount directly on top. Others opted for cutting the crossmember out entirely, and rewelding a drop-center crossmember, in order to get the trans down level.

Bruce, however, was determined to preserve driveline strength; therefore, he decided to go with the Olds yoke, which was identical to the original Chevy length, but beefier.

The second problem, after the Olds yoke was machined to fit, was in the raised driveshaft angle, which put the front U-joint within 1 inch of the tunnel. This turned out to be the least of his worries, however, and has produced no problems. With this approach, then, Bruce has been able to enjoy the best of all possible worlds. He can stand on it anytime he gets ready, without having to worry about an errant rear U-joint (normally the first to go) bouncing through heavy traffic at rush hour.

Other LUV Lovin'

Carburetion is by 650-cfm dual-feed double-pump Holley. A pulse-type electric fuel pump is mounted on the firewall. Bruce admitted that he might have mounted it "somewhere else"— but no one can quarrel with its accessibility.

Carb linkage utilizes the original LUV linkage run-

ning through new brackets. The idea was to have less friction on the cable, with as straight a pull as possible. It's a notion that certainly makes sense, in light of the Holley's performance potential atop the aluminum Weiand Hi-Rise manifold. With the LUV's standard 11-gallon gas tank, ethyl nets Bruce averages of around 14.8 mpg. Octane ratings are beginning to vary again, from brand to brand, sorry to say. Of course, when you're running double-pumper carbs, mileage is going to be down by definition. Still, the mpg figure is not all that unrespectable, considering what muscle lurks under the LUV's hood.

But it is in pursuit of the available horsepower that the installation really shines. The exhaust headers, for example, are a super-neat job, and the other half of the revving capability—the first part being the roller bearings. Champion Muffler had to make the headers by hand. Such quality fabrications are absolutely necessary for fast acceleration times. The Champion headers are sort of "far out," in that they

Harmonic balancer sits ¾ inch inside the frame and is stock. Clearance was a problem on all fronts, but steering remained intact, as did major components. Holes in the front engine-frame mount weren't intended.

Here, the headers are receiving a new exhaust system. Note skid plate under oil pan and large dust cover under starter ring—standard items.

had to be made in four pieces, two to a side. In the finished product, two tubes go inside the torsion bar, and two go outside the bar on each side. It was a very professional job. However, the headers were gas-welded, and as such may not be as strong as the heliarced items. Bruce reports no problems, but hopes that torque and vibration do not destroy what is an exceptional piece of work.

The alternator is a '66 GMC unit with max output of 70 amps, for towing into the aforementioned desert areas. The electricals are more than adequate, even with CB radio, with its 30-mile minimum capability. The radio is for locating lost campers and other emergency usage. To reiterate, Bruce, as the saying goes, "comes into the game ready to play."

Radiator cooling is no problem, with its mixture of 60 percent Prestone antifreeze and 40 percent water. Normal water temperature, in any outside air temperature, usually stays around 180 degrees F. Most of the credit for the sanity in this department goes to the six-pass core ("pass" referring to the number of tube rows, or radiator thickness). A two-pass core is standard LUV, but the thicker cooling capacity is not at all unwelcome. It provides the kind of margin that a perfectionist like Bruce expects. There is an oil cooler—of his own design and manufacture—mounted forward of the radiator, to handle extra requirements in that area. There is no air conditioning—another plus in the performance department; but who needs anything other than to know the meaning of the Spanish word, *cerveza*? A footnote on the engine cooling situation is the six-bladed fan from a '72 Chevy 1-ton truck. Bruce took off 1¼ inches from each tip for fit and then rebalanced the steel fan.

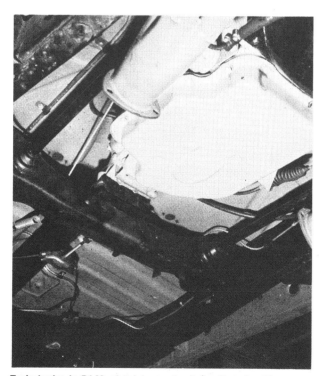

Turbohydro is B&M; clutches are beefed—otherwise it's stock. Cam setup requires smaller torque converter. Diameter of Bruce's is 13 inches. A '66 Impala trans mount fits to crossmember; LUV lateral torsion bars are a factor in the no-sag front end.

With tranny mount work, proper angle is maintained to preserve '57 Chevy U-joints and rearend. Shocks are Gabriel Hi-Jackers. Standard LUV gas tank of 11-gallon capacity is suspended inboard of rear axle to make room for the under-floor spare tire.

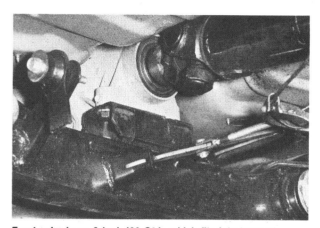

Front yoke is an 8-inch '66 Olds which fits into trans at original length, but is beefier. Driveshaft clears floor tunnel by at least 1 inch and is secure. Original muffler mount had to be cut.

Love that LUV

It's been many moons since a mini-truck swap has possessed the appeal of Bruce's LUV. That's an easy assessment to make after even one test ride. For even without the M & H Wrinkle-Walls with 12 pounds of pressure, the light tail-end gets down to business with none of the delay expected from such a combination. Shocks are from a '74 Plymouth Road Runner. They're Gabriel Hi-Jackers, adjusted for the firm setting—but the standard LUV springs are well-designed, and are strengthened with an extra leaf. In other words, when Bruce puts his foot into what's up front, it's what's in back that puts the power to the road in a hurry. People say, "LUV it!"

With a slight rolling start, a full-throttle punch will grab a knuckle full of rubber for the expected tire/track cremation; but just as abruptly it stops, and the LUV dances from side to side several times in very lady-like fashion, before heading straight and true for the balance of the sprint. Certainly, its already-demonstrated low e.t.'s are a fit companion to its excellent road manners.

All in all, here's one LUV swap that's very definitely for real.

Swaps
425 Olds V8 in Porsche 912

Duncan Brundrett has done one of those engine swaps that's so wild that when you first hear about it, you think, ''You've got to be kidding!'' But the more you know about it, the more you can dig it. He's gone and stuffed a Toronado V8 and its drive setup in the backseat of his '66 Porsche 912 (which right away sounds like a nightmare), but what he wound up with was a reliable street machine that not only outruns any Porsche on the road, but also handles better than stock, gets better gas mileage, and is quieter! And Duncan ought to know; he's the service manager of a Porsche-VW agency!

Actually, Duncan's history with engine swaps and hot rodding goes back a long way to the beginnings of the sport. Through the 1930s, he raced a modified roadster in the SCTA dry lakes meets, and midget racers on such famous old tracks as Gilmore Stadium, Atlantic Speedway, and Southern Speedway. Back in '33 his roadster topped 120 mph at Muroc with an early flathead, and many years later he was running a '55 T-bird that managed 126 mph at El Mirage. He's owned and built a lot of fine machinery in his 40-odd years as a car enthusiast, with much of the engineering touches and attention to detail coming from his years in the aerospace industry.

From modified roadsters at the lakes, Duncan shifted his attention to vehicles that went around corners better, and that's when he got heavily into the sports car field. Over the years, he's owned and restored several Mercedes gullwings, Jags, a Chevy V8-powered Ferrari coupe, and of course a number of different Porsches. Although he's wrapped up in late-model foreign cars, he still hasn't lost his love for nostalgic old American cars; his stable includes a beautiful 1908 Buick touring car and a venerable 1912 Hupmobile roadster.

Swap Rationale

How Duncan got into the Toronado-Porsche project is easy to understand. As the service manager at Bill Yates VW-Porsche in Capistrano Beach, California, he had looked up at the bottom of many a Porsche with the engine and trans removed, and he could see the possibilities for a swap.

Some measuring and figuring indicated that the Olds Toronado engine and front-wheel drive package would be perfect for the 912, because the engine is perfectly balanced over the axles and the total package isn't too long. The Toronado automatic could take plenty of punishment and still deliver super-smooth shifts, and Positraction was a standard feature of the car. The way the Olds engine sits over the drive setup was perfect because it would allow the engine to be placed semi-midships and still allow the driver and passenger the same legroom up front as the stock arrangement.

The Power Package

A stock engine/drive package from a '66 Toronado was selected and tried for fit after the old 4-banger was removed. A large section of the sheetmetal under the rear seat had to be removed, but it was taken out in such a way that it could be welded back in if Duncan ever decided to return the car to stock in the future.

Duncan liked the way the stock Porsche engine was mounted to the chassis, and he wanted to be able to change the engine/trans without a lot of hassles, so he elected to mount the Olds on the stock Porsche mounts. This was accomplished up front by welding extra steel plate to the Olds mount

Duncan's smiling because those innocent-looking pieces of luggage are what conceal the 425-cubic-inch V8.

Rugged, smooth, and powerful Olds V8 nestles right in where the rear seat used to be. It never overheats and it even has the smog equipment!

under the crank pulley, and at the rear by adding plates to extend the stock Olds mount out to the wide-stance Porsche rear mounts, which bolt up through rubber biscuits on the frame. The Porsche axles were cut, shortened 3 inches and rewelded, and plates were made up to mate the Porsche U-joints to the Olds axle flanges.

The suspension is all stock with disc brakes and torsion bars at all four corners, but Gabriel HiJacker air shocks were added at the rear to compensate for some of the extra weight. Bigger-than-stock snubbers were made up for the rear torsion bars, to keep the U-joints from working at an extreme angle on hard bumps.

Cooling the big Olds in the back seat was the only trouble spot foreseen, and Duncan met the challenge with a beautiful 2-radiator system. Just above the engine, at the back of the car, a 19x23-inch, four-tube radiator sits under the rear deck lid. Two Audi electric fans do the air-pushing if things get hot in heavy traffic, and sprint car builder Don Edmunds added four rows of 3-inch louvers to the rear deck.

A VW air grille, the only other body change, was added just below the front bumper to admit air to another radiator up front. Duncan bought this one from Dan Gurney's All-American Racers. Only 10x27x5 inches, it mounts in the original spare tire well, with 1½-inch copper pipe going back to the engine through the rocker panels. The low-pressure area of the front wheelwells has been drilled with large holes to allow hot air to escape after passing through the radiator.

The other changes necessary for the swap were those time-consuming little details common to every swap. The Olds Turbohydro was modified so that Duncan would have a reverse lock-out feature, and the shift rod was connected right to the Porsche floorshift through a crossbar mounted in heim bearings under the front engine mount. Seen many automatic '66 Porsches lately? A beautiful solution to the throttle linkage problem in this case turned out to be a 10-foot Bowden cable, Teflon coated inside.

Wanting the outside to look as stock as possible, Duncan found that the Olds could be coupled to a stock 911 Sport muffler and still be quieter than the original engine. With 425 inches in the back seat, this is one Porsche that doesn't have to rev like a Mixmaster to get anywhere.

Older, square-cornered luggage was purchased cheap, bolted together, and cut out from underneath to fit over the Olds engine in the back seat. Fiberglass insulation keeps noise and heat from the interior.

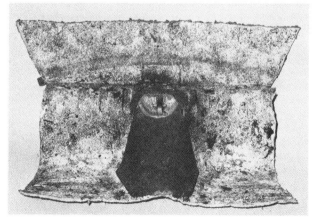

This is the section that was cut from the floor of the back seat area.

Swaps

The Toronado rear mount is welded to plates that hang from the stock Porsche rubber biscuits (arrow). Two electric fans above the engine pull air through the rear radiator.

From underneath, it's all engine and Toronado drive. Car gets 18 mpg with the 2.93 Olds automatic gears.

At the front of the engine/trans, the Olds mount was also adapted to fit the stock Porsche mounts, via a steel plate with spacer (arrow). A cross-shaft mounted in Heims couples Olds automatic to Porsche shift rod.

Here's another look, from inside the car, at the front mount. Water hoses run through door sills to radiator up front.

The Look of Innocence

Ah, yes, to top it all off Duncan needed something to conceal what he had done. The problem was how to make a back seat full of cubic inches look like it was stock. Duncan's answer was in keeping with the sneaky ingenuity displayed throughout the car. He shopped at swap meets and junk stores for old, square-cornered suitcases until he found enough of the right size. He bolted them together from the inside, cut the bottoms out, and lined the "camouflage" cases with foil-covered fiberglass insulation. Dropped in place over the engine, and with leather straps holding the dummy luggage in place, the car looks deceptively innocent, indeed.

We can assure you, though, that this car is no innocent. Although the insulation keeps you unaware of the heat and noise from the engine, there's no

The Toronado and Porsche axle shafts were both cut in half, trued and beveled on the ends, then welded together (arrow). Duncan hasn't had any drivetrain problems. Gabriel air shocks help handle the extra weight.

Torsion arms used are VW items. Steel spacers (arrow) were installed to limit rear axle travel to prevent U-joint damage on large bumps.

mistaking the punch of good ol' American horsepower on the road. With the engine now located almost midships (rather than hung off the back of the rear axle as the Porsche was), and the battery and extra radiator up front, the car has good weight distribution and better-than-stock handling. And with the Toronado drive's 2.93 gears, gas mileage is an incredible 18 mpg.

No one knows any better than Duncan how prone to expensive repairs these German sports cars are, and that's one reason he made the swap. Now he's got the most dependable, unbreakable Porsche on the road. Knowing Porsche owners to be a fiercely proud bunch, even when their beloved cars are being fixed in Duncan's service department, he just loves to put them on with his "stock ol' 912." Taking a ride in the hybrid, we can just imagine how their jaws drop when he massages the throttle slightly and the Olds quickly purrs up to 60 mph.

The front radiator is small but has a 4-inch core. Copper pipes go through door sills to the engine. After air has cooled the radiator it passes out vents cut in wheelwells.

Big crossflow radiator mounted above the engine works with the one up front and really does the job.

Short pipes were fabricated to hook exhausts directly to the stock Porsche muffler. The Olds engine is even quieter than the original.

Even if the car has been sitting for a month or two, starting is no problem with the big battery that Duncan installed in the trunk.

The only external change made on the Porsche was the addition of VW air grille up front.

With the better distribution of weight due to engine location, the handling was improved sufficiently that these 60-pound lead weights were removed from the stock front bumper.

Swaps
307 Chevy V8 in Chevy Vega

Even before the Vega was introduced to the public and had only been visualized in magazine artwork, there must have been someone out there who started thinking about stuffing a V8 in the little car to make it nasty instead of cute. And it wasn't too long before swappers around the country found that the V8 did fit and really produced a fine street machine. There are probably several thousand of these all-in-the family hybrids running around, now that there are several kits out on the market. We're featuring one here that was done somewhat differently, and we're including some pertinent parts interchanges and important little details that are always left out of the usual swap kit instruction sheet.

Engine swapper Bob Medina (Box 728, Lomita, CA 90717) performed the swap you see here for his younger brother, David, who wanted a nice high-performance car to drive, but also something small and economically reasonable, since he'd be using it to go back and forth to college. The solution turned out to be pretty simple, at least in the idea stage. Nineteen-year-old David already had a '71 Vega panel that he had started fixing up, but it just didn't have enough oats. He and Bob had tweaked over the aluminum 4-cylinder, but that just wasn't enough for spurting up the freeway ramps. Bob didn't want a radical rumper for an engine, so when they shopped around for a V8 they purchased a low-mileage '70 307 complete with 350 model Turbo Hydra-matic. It was a single-exhaust, 2-barrel type engine and would certainly be economical in a light car like the Vega, but it had enough displacement to easily "keep up with the traffic."

Tight Fit

Bob purchased a kit from Herbert Automotive (5467 Ballantine St., Sacramento, CA 95826), which included the engine and transmission mounts and headers, and began trial-fitting the pieces. Don't let anyone fool you about this swap; once it's in it looks like it grew there, but it is tight. The headers just barely clear and there are a number of those annoying small changes that have to be made that make a swap take a lot more time than you had figured. With the engine set down on the mounts, the room around the transmission could be estimated. Bob found that he had to add to the kit rear crossmember to lower the transmission 2 inches. Even so, the floor area around the bellhousing had to be hammered up about 1 inch.

The engine mounts and the headers must be in place on the car before attempting to drop the new V8 into place. A '69 or later oil pan, with slight re-working to clear the steering, will do the trick. Milodon offers a pan that is already reworked. No cutting is necessary at the firewall, but Bob found it necessary to go to the shorter '68 and earlier water pump up front for clearance. The lower pulley to use is Chevy part No. 3755820. The air-conditioning (heavy-duty) radiator was rebuilt with a four-tube core. The stock bottom outlet was switched to the top-left and then a new straight outlet was installed at the bottom.

Since the radiator is now thicker than stock, more right-hand mounting brackets are needed, since these are longer. Ribbed, flexible radiator hoses were purchased, with a 15½-inch piece (1½-inches diameter at both ends) working out best for the top hose, and a 13½-inch bottom hose (1¾ inches at one end and 1½ inches at the other end).

The engine mounts to use should be '68 or earlier, because the late "safety" mounts won't work. If an automatic transmission is used, as in this swap, then ½ inch must be trimmed off the right side of the bellhousing to clear the headers.

The suspension was left virtually stock with the exception that coil springs from the rear of a '63 Corvair van were added to the Vega front end to handle the extra weight. They're the same length as the stock Vega spring but stiffer due to thicker spring wire.

In this installation, the stock driveshaft was grafted to a turbo-type front yoke with a final length of 45¾ inches center-to-center on the U-joints. The stock Vega 2.93 rearend was retained for economy purposes, so a 22-tooth speedometer gear worked fine in the Turbo 350 transmission. The neutral safe-

ty switch should be swapped for part No. 1994153.

Electrics

The electrics of this swap are pretty straightforward, because the Vega engine already had an alternator to start with, so no changes had to be made to accommodate the new engine except a new alternator bracket. Even the stock Vega battery cables work. The stock throttle is too short for the new engine and won't reach full throttle, but a '70-'71 Chevelle throttle cable bolts in and works fine. Another small but time-consuming change is that the heater core must be reversed for the outlets to clear the V8's right cylinder head. This means cutting two new holes in the plastic heater core housing for the hose outlets. Now make a new alternator bracket (use a '64-'67 belt) and you're almost off and running.

Happy Result

In this particular swap, where economy was a consideration, a single-exhaust system was used after the headers and hooked up to the stock crossflow Vega muffler. Admittedly, there are easier swaps to do than this one, but in the end, the results of a swap must be considered successful if they accomplish what the owner set out to do.

In this case, the V8 Vega panel turned out to be just what David wanted, a performance car that was reliable, economical and didn't cost a small fortune to insure. Such a swap may interest you for the same reasons. But if you're like engine swapper Bob Medina (whose appetite was whetted by his brother's project) and you really want a street stormer, then the swap is still the same—you just drop in a high-perf small block instead of an economy motor, or add a few speed goodies. Bob is now hard at work on building his own V8 Vega, a coupe with a hot 350-incher that should really do the number!

Everything fits, but underneath there is a working-space problem. Oil pan has to be notched (arrow) to clear frame and tie rod.

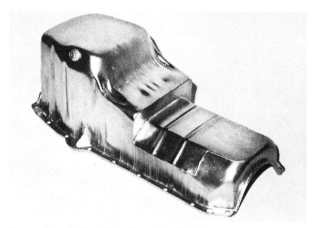

It wasn't available at the time Bob did this swap, but the Milodon oil pan people now have a special pan for the Vega/V8 swap which will clear the crossmember regardless of the type of motor mounts used.

Bob Medina built this V8 panel as a budget high-performance machine for his younger brother. In such a light vehicle, even this stock 307 and Turbo 350 have plenty of punch. Except for the tube headers, you'd think it was a factory installation.

Headers are the biggest bugaboo of the swap, and there's not much room for a dual exhaust system with the Vega's limited ground clearance. Since this was to be an "economy" swap, single exhaust system was made and hooked to stock Vega muffler.

Swaps

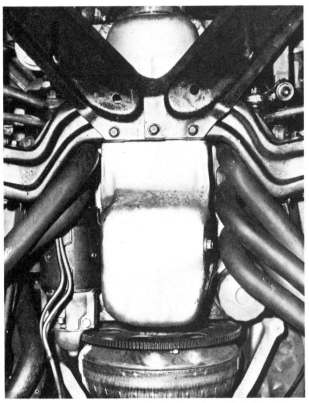

You can see here how tight the headers fit against the oil pan, the starter and the Vega's frame. The headers must be installed in the chassis before the engine goes in.

The stock Vega 2-speed automatic shifter can be used with Turbohydros, but you can't get into D1 with it. Chevrolet now has all the parts for a 3-speed Vega shifter.

To make the 2-speed shifter work with the 350 Turbo, the shifter arm must be removed and hammered flat (arrow) to provide a 3-inch throw.

The 350 Turbo uses a stock rubber mount. The Herbert tube rear crossmember was dropped 2 inches to save reworking the floor.

Stock-length battery cables work out okay. Oil cooler lines from the automatic transmission go through stock air-conditioning hose holes (arrow) to cooler.

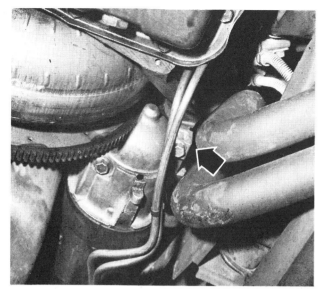

If you use the Herbert headers with a Turbo 350, you have to trim away some of the bellhousing (arrow) for clearance.

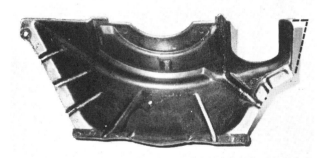

Part of the right side of the transmission bottom cover must be trimmed off also. A hacksaw does it.

A reworked Vega air-conditioning radiator will do the cooling chores. Whatever engine you use, you must use pre-'69 (short) water pump.

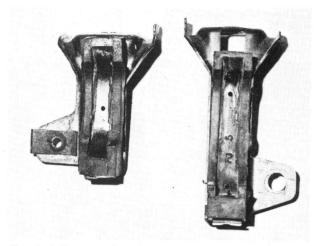

The stock Vega uses two short radiator mounting pads and two long ones. After the radiator has been reworked, you'll need to replace the short ones so all four are long.

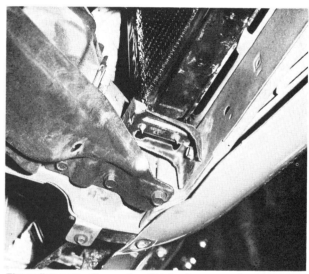

The radiator mounting pads will interchange easily, as they are each held by only one bolt. The longer pads, as shown, accommodate a thick or recored radiator.

The heater core must be reversed and two new hose outlet holes made. Arrows show original hole locations. Be sure you do this before the V8 is installed in the chassis.

Swaps

The stock alternator will work on '69-up heads with a fabricated bracket. Use '64-'67 belt.

A lift-kit was used on the stock Vega rear springs. For performance use, a Vega/V8 should be equipped with a stronger rearend, like the narrowed 12-bolt units available from Don Hardy and others.

By bolting your alternator in place on the engine and using the top adjustment bracket to align it, you can make up a cardboard pattern of the bracket you need. Make it from ⅜-inch plate and you won't need to space the alternator at all.

The Corvair van springs restore stock front-end height, but ground clearance is still reduced somewhat by the headers hanging down.

Comparison of the stock Vega front spring (right) with that from a Corvair van shows the Corvair unit is longer and thicker, yet it will interchange into the Vega chassis and restore proper front-end height with your new V8 engine in place.

A complete kit is available for the V8 swap from Doug Thorley, the header place. Besides the headers, the kit includes mounts, adapters, bolts, gaskets, and alternator mount.

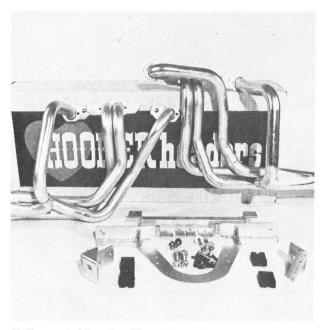

Unlike most of the other kits on the market, the Vega/V8 kit from Hooker Headers uses a front-mount system, á la Pro cars, with an unusual set of headers and mounts.

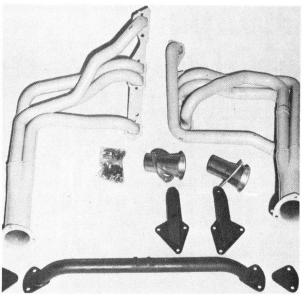

Ex-race car chassis builder and now street rod chassis builder John Buttera also markets a V8 kit for the Vega. Utilizing special Cragar headers, the kit features 3/16-inch plate in the front mounts, with a nice, round-tube rear crossmember.

The Vega is a cute little car, and with V8 power it can be strong on the street. His brother's delivery works so well that it has brought a flock of other Vega owners to Bob Medina's swap shop for similar V8 conversions—and no one has been disappointed with the results.

Swaps
350 Chevy V8 in Datsun 240Z

Bill replaced the Datsun six with a '70 350 cubic-inch Chevy LT-1. It's fully balanced, with shot-peened crank, forged pistons, Holley 780 cfm, and 11:1 compression.

The 370-hp Corvette engine mounts are used with the Datsun frame mounts. All that's needed is a 2½-inch riser between the two.

The Datsun Z series has been on the American scene for a number of years now, and its popularity is unquestioned; it sells so quickly you still have a difficult time finding a new one in some areas of the country. So far, owners have been quite satisfied with the 6-cylinder supplied by Nissan, and we've heard of very few engine swaps. Most Z owners seem content to dress up the exterior with custom paint, pinstriping, or rally stripes and let it go at that. But more adventuresome souls are beginning to appear in the ranks of Z owners, and Bill Robbins of Pacific Palisades, California, is one such soul.

A long-time car buff whose list of past acquisitions looks very much like the table of contents from a book on sports cars, Bill's previous car was a Cobra. When he acquired a cherry red 240Z, Bill looked for a way to endow the coupe with the power and handling of the Cobra. The Chevy-Datsun combination seemed to fit the bill, and you'll see why Bill's Z is just a little different from those of his friends.

Datsun alternator was retained to keep the electrical system stock. Everything fits so nicely you'd think that the swap was engineered in Japan instead of the U.S.

There's no overheating problem with this swap. A Harrison aluminum crossflow radiator with surge tank sees to that. Transmission oil cooler fits in front of radiator to accommodate the Powerglide.

Stock Datsun throttle and choke linkage was retained with only minor modifications. Datsun oil pressure sensing unit screws right into Chevy block, but watch it carefully for possible leaks. Tach, speedometer, water temp, and all other gauges hooked directly to the Chevy engine.

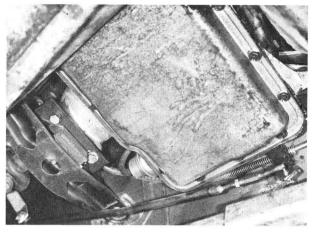

Powerglide trans was chosen over Turbo Hydra-matic because of the Powerglide's lighter weight and the fact that it fits into place as neatly as the engine. Datsun crossmember can be retained as shown, but shift linkage has to be modified.

Exhaust heat valve was moved from manifold and installed in exhaust pipe behind front tire.

The 240Z driveshaft was used by replacing the Datsun U-joint with one from Chevy. This required cutting and welding of the driveshaft, but connected to the 3.33 rearend, the swap gives the Z a top speed in excess of 165 mph.

Rerouted exhaust system required circular cutout on each side behind front wheelwells. Chrome-plated pipes were fabricated for this swap.

Swaps
350 GM Diesel V8 in El Camino

Sometimes we don't have to go looking for tech stories; they come looking for us. Such was the case with the turbocharged Olds diesel engine installation in the '64 Chevrolet El Camino shown here, which just happens to belong to photo editor Eric "Rick" Rickman. Longtime readers will remember Rick as being part of the HOT ROD Magazine staff from the early '50s until the end of 1970, so he's no newcomer to the world of high-performance and engine swaps.

With over 180,000 miles on the clock, the original 327-cubic-inch engine in the El Camino had gone through just about all the rebuilds and use that any engine can reasonably be expected to endure; but the truck was basically sound, so Rick began considering the engine swap alternatives. The goal was to find something reliable, responsive, and, above all, economical to operate. The solution came in the form of a '78 350-cubic-inch Oldsmobile diesel V8 engine, which is offered optionally in several GM cars. This engine would produce the reliability and economy, but the responsiveness left a bit to be desired, which is where Roto-Master (13402 Wyandotte St., North Hollywood, CA 91605) entered the picture. Roto-Master installed a prototype turbocharger system which was to serve as a basis for a turbo kit for the Olds diesel. That kit will soon be available to fit the stock Olds diesel V8 installations in both passenger cars and pickups.

The accompanying photos detail the turbo installation, exhaust system fabrication and the complete engine swap into the El Camino. To simplify the swap, an Olds 350 Turbo Hydra-matic transmission was also used. Subsequent trips have proved the combination to be a respectable performer while virtually doubling the fuel mileage of the original 327.

The turbo diesel added about 140 pounds to the total vehicle weight, including the dual batteries and larger radiator. The majority of this weight increase (120 pounds) was on the front end, but air conditioning front spring spacers were all that was required to restore the original ride height to the El Camino. Boost is held to a maximum of five psi, which seems to be more than adequate. Rick reports that it takes some care to keep the El Camino from climbing above the double-nickel while cruising (see accompanying chart).

The only problems confronting anyone who contemplates a similar swap are the need for a heavy-duty dual-battery starting circuit to supply the required cranking power as used on the Olds diesel-equipped stockers; a large and efficient radiator to dissipate the increased heat output of the diesel (Rick's El Camino uses a specially constructed 16x23.5-inch radiator with *five* rows of tubes); and a thorough cleaning of the fuel tank and lines, plus the addition of a diesel fuel filter.

After studying the accompanying photos, we think you'll agree that ex-HOT ROD staffers don't just fade away; they get even sharper, even if they do need a "boost" for climbing hills these days!

STEADY-STATE MILEAGE
(Turbo Diesel)

Speed Range	Mileage	Observed Boost
65/70 mph	22.94	2 psi
60/65 mph	25.26	1 psi
55/60 mph	26.26	No boost indicated

The above figures were observed while cruising near sea level, with ambient temperatures of 78-80 degrees F. Final axle ratio was 2.78:1, with a turbo A/R ratio of .81:1.

The '64 El Camino engine compartment housed the original 327 V8, which was delivering an average of only 12 mpg. Stock vehicle weight was 3700 pounds, with 2040 of that on the front.

Intake manifold modification consisted of machining an opening at the rear of the stock crossover manifold and heliarcing a short length of aluminum tube in the opening to connect the turbo compressor. A machined cap covers the stock air cleaner opening at the top of the crossover. The small tube in the cap is for connecting the intake manifold boost gauge.

The completed turbo-diesel swap reflects the compactness of the Roto-Master system. Note the dual Trojan LM-74 used to spin the diesel on cold mornings. Batteries are connected in parallel (12V with double amperage) to crank the 20:1 compression engine. Note, too, the diesel fuel filter on the right inner fender. Not apparent is the massive five-row radiator from U.S. Radiator Company in Los Angeles.

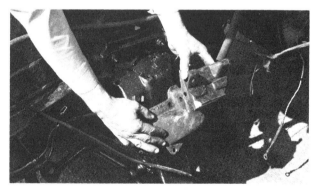

Exhaust system modifications were made by John Fort at Roto-Master. Exhaust was routed up and slightly forward to clear the firewall-mounted heater on the right side of the engine compartment. John fabricated the new system from Tube Turns, cast-steel 3/16-inch wall elbows, from Kaywood Steel Products company in Cudahy, California. The entire turbo unit is supported by the cast-steel piping. With the turbo mounted directly over the rear of the engine, the turbo oil return was provided by drilling and tapping the intake manifold at the right rear corner (not visible in photo).

Stock Olds motor mounts were bolted to the front two mounting bosses on each side of the block. Although the Chevy frame mount accepts the Olds mounts, it's too far forward. The stock frame mounts were cut apart, retaining only that part that bolts to the engine mounts. The altered mount was then attached to the engine mounts and welded to the frame.

Swaps

Engine installation was engineered by Mike Capanna, son of old-time hot rodder Tony Capanna, at the Wilcap shop (2930 Sepulveda Blvd., Torrance, CA 90505).

The only alteration to the stock frame during the installation was the dimpling of the front crossmember about ¾ inch to clear the starter. Olds uses an oversized high-torque starter to overcome the diesel's 20:1 compression, which requires a 100-rpm spin on a cold start.

Since a diesel engine has no intake manifold vacuum, the Olds vacuum pump is used to power the brake booster and transmission modulator. Transmission is controlled by a vacuum valve mounted on the fuel injector pump throttle shaft.

Flex line to the top of the turbo is an oil line from the cam oil gallery at the front of the engine. Note oil pressure line running off the back of the turbo oil fitting to a dash-mounted pressure gauge. The large paper-element air cleaner is from Ak Miller Enterprises (9236 Bermudez St., Pico Rivera, CA 90660).

The diesel fuel injector pump uses a bypass system which necessitated the installation of a return fuel line made up from 6-foot lengths of steel brake line. The fuel tank had an elbow vent fitting soldered in the upper right corner to accept the return line via a short length of fuel hose.

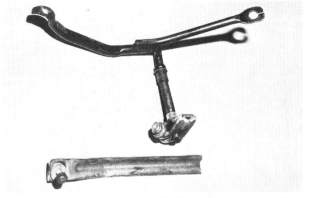

Throttle linkage hookup is simplified by using the stock Olds throttle cable and the stock Chevy pedal assembly. The lever arm in the engine compartment is cut off, and the lower end is retained to keep the clamp which secures the pivot shaft in the firewall mounting. A short length of steel rod is welded to the upper end of the throttle pedal shaft. The rod has a flattened end with a hole and slot to accept the inner end of the Olds throttle cable. Length of the added arm must be worked out to give proper full-throttle travel at the injector pump.

Diesel fuel must be absolutely clean and free from water. This Racor 500 filter has a removable paper filter cartridge in the top and a sintered metal element in a glass bowl at the bottom. Fuel is pumped by an electric pump at the tank, through the filter to the mechanical pump on the engine. The electric pump is almost a must to prime the fuel system if the engine ever runs out of fuel.

The El Camino originally had a Muncie 4-speed, but a Turbo 350 was installed with the diesel V8. A cable shifter was installed by switching the lever off the transmission shifting shaft and fabricating an aluminum spacer to properly position the cable bracket on the transmission pan rail.

A complete 2½-inch-diameter turbo exhaust system was designed and built by Champion Muffler (14426 E. Whittier Blvd., Whittier, CA 90605). The muffler is a low-restriction Walker turbo unit.

Everything fits just like stock. Note the stock mounting flanges on the frame for the transmission support. The Olds exhaust crossover fit perfectly. Everything was a bolt-up. Even the driveline slipped into place with no alterations.

Console-mounted Stewart-Warner gauges are intake and exhaust manifold pressures (boost and back pressure), with a pyrometer in the middle to read exhaust gas temperature as it enters the turbocharger.

Swaps
350 Chevy V8 in XJ Jaguar

W hy would anyone wish to install a Chevy V8 engine in a Jaguar? A good question; let's let Gary Mundorf explain the logic of this swap as he does so eloquently in the introduction to his installation kit:

"There are those purists who can afford the almost unlimited mechanical upkeep of the Jaguar, and I don't want to offend them. Hopefully, they will respect those of us who choose not to commit the $1000-$5000 a year that it takes to maintain the purists' position. I too have driven the Jaguar. It is incomparably agile and plush. The easy handling and secure road feel are the result of 40 years of European road racing development. However, comfort and style have never suffered. The body styles have always been distinctive, sleek, and sedate. The Jaguar's indomitable powerplant was the factor that tied it all together.

"I believe we are in an age where automotive complexity is threatening the survival of the species itself. It's time to become practical and time to pursue simplicity.

"Installation of a 350 Chevrolet V8 immediately changes one's perspective regarding ownership and upkeep of the Jaguar. You are now able to have your car serviced by any independent service facility, or perform maintenance services yourself. Chevrolet parts availability is unparalleled due to the tremendous dealer network backed by independent parts jobbers, distributors, and independent garages."

Since Jaguar engines are heavy, you will notice that after installing a Chevy in an XJ-6 the front end will be 180 pounds lighter. In the case of the XJ-12 the weight loss will be 200 pounds even with a larger radiator. Weight reduction is a plus in the Jaguar, according to Gary, because the Jaguar normally plows, eats tires and brake pads, and has front suspension ailments, all due to the weight of the massive engine. Handling improvements are immediately noticeable; this improvement is amazing considering the Jaguar handles so well in the first place.

The XJ-6 has a displacement of 4.2 liters (256 cubic inches); the swap will reduce weight and increase displacement, (a difference of 94 cubic inches), plus increase gas mileage from 10-12 mpg to 17-19 mpg with a 2 barrel carb on the V8. The XJ-12 engine displaces 326 cubic inches yet is rated at greater horsepower than the Chevy 350. Unfortunately the additional horsepower is only available at high rpm's, which is murder on gas mileage. You really have to put your foot into the carb to get the high horsepower performance advantage. The Chevy 350's torque curve comes in at a much lower and more usable rpm range.

Gary's kits feature a minimum amount of welding; in the XJ-6 kit the only welding is in the exhaust system. The XJ-12 kit requires no welding at all. Gary also recommends the use of an aftermarket water temperature sensor and gauge as Jaguar instruments are much too temperamental to be trusted.

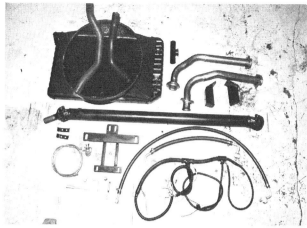

The Mundorf kit supplies everything you will need for the swap, including air conditioning plumbing if you so desire. A wire loom provides direct Chevrolet to Jaguar plug-in electrics. The oversize radiator has automatic trans cooler connections.

The Chevrolet engine nestles comfortably in the Jaguar engine compartment with plenty of clearance all around. Gary details his engines completely before installation.

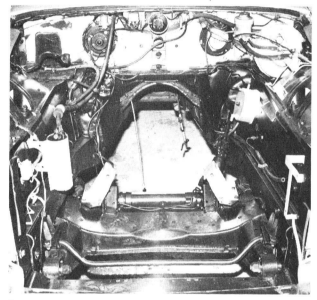

Gary cleans and completely details the Jaguar engine compartment before doing an installation. Note the new kit motor mounts bolt in place in the original mount locations.

Small U-shaped strapiron saddles with insulators are provided to support the oversize crossflow radiator. Saddles are installed on both upper and lower radiator framing.

Jaguar steering has an odd U-joint which provides excellent clearance for the V8 engine. The only welding required in an XJ-6 installation is to reroute one pipe of the dual exhaust

The stock Jaguar air conditioning condenser is installed in stock position in front of the newly installed radiator. Radiator-supporting framework (across top) is completely removable in a Jaguar, providing easy access to engine space.

Swaps

The coolant filler neck is provided by inserting a short tube with a neckpiece (furnished in kit) into the center of the molded one-piece upper radiator hose, also supplied in the kit.

View from below (right side) of engine reveals mount attachment. Note excellent exhaust and starter clearance. Stock Chevy mounts attach to boxed-steel kit mounts.

The kit's fabricated rear transmission mount bolts into place utilizing the existing Jaguar mounting locations. A stock Chevrolet rear transmission rubber mount is also used.

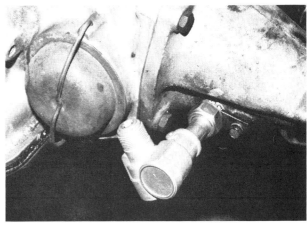

An angle drive speedometer cable adapter is supplied in the kit. Specify your rearend ratio since the adapter matches the speedometer to rearend ratio for correct speed readings.

A small bracket (arrow), provided in the kit, is bolted to the existing bracket on the Quadrajet carb to support the Jaguar throttle cable. The clevis at the end of the Jaguar cable (circle) is flattened and slipped over the carb throttle arm pin. The clevis is secured by a circlip installed between the faces of the flattened clevis and into the groove in the tip of the throttle lever pin for pull-type linkage.

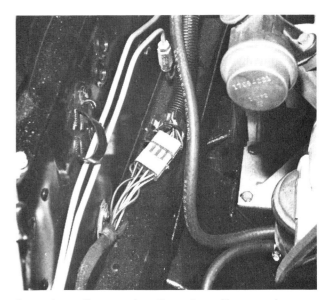

Jaguar has gotten away from the early positive ground electrical system. Late Jags use a 12V negative ground system. A kit-supplied wire loom plugs into the Jaguar electrical system.

There is more than adequate room for the later Chevy V8 with the HEI ignition system; both under-hood and firewall clearance are excellent. Note use of stock Chevrolet cable throttle system with the later engine. The cable pushes the throttle open, and the spring returns the throttle to idle.

The finished job appears factory stock. Note the coolant recovery system attached at filler neck, and that the crossflow radiator has no upper tank reservoir. Remember that all smog equipment pertinent to the year of the engine must be retained.

Swaps
350 Chevy V8 in SE Mercedes

What do you do when the engine in your '73 280SE Mercedes finally gives up the ghost at just over 120,000 miles? It seems Mercedes dealers don't like to rebuild this particular model engine and always call for a new replacement at a cost in the neighborhood of $7000. But car owner Tom Berry decided he could put together a new Chevrolet 350 engine, 400 Turbo Hydra-matic, plus turbocharger for about $4000. All things considered, it was a much better deal. The Mercedes is famed for its Teutonic engineering and longevity; however, parts and service still remain in that rarefied high-priced neighborhood. As an example, a set of eight plug wires go for a neat $175.

The 4.5 liter 280SE engine translated to 274.59 cubic inches, which was delivering only 11 mpg around town. The new 350 Chevy is getting 14 mpg around town and 20 mpg on the road, plus the car is now 150 pounds lighter on the front end.

This swap was so easy that Tom and his partner, Rod Nefke, decided to make a kit available, or they will do custom installations on request; the kit is only for the 280SE and SEL series cars.

The hardest part of this swap was solving the crankcase crossmember interference problem. A bit of research revealed that a '66 Chevy oil pan had the sump in front. With this pan the engine could be installed, with very minor pan alteration, to clear the crossmember. A Chevrolet driveshaft is used by ma-chining a small adapter disc to adapt the Chevy U-joint bolt pattern to the Mercedes pinion shaft companion flange. This adapter is included in the kit.

Since the 400 Turbo Hydra-matic has the same shift pattern as the Mercedes automatic, no alterations had to be made in this area. The Mercedes shift cable connects directly to the 400 shift lever.

There is no welding involved in this installation, other than a trip to your local muffler shop after installation to have the exhaust system hooked up. Since this car is a '73, it has no catalytic converter in the system, so the engine, whatever the year, need only be equipped with whatever smog devices that were required in '73, and can use regular (leaded) gas.

To avoid plumbing hassles, and ensure proper line pressure, Tom made up a special bracket to mount the Mercedes power steering pump on the Chevy engine. You could probably use the Chevy pump if the engine is so equipped. This model Mercedes uses a fuel injection system, which requires unusually high fuel line pressure. Tom took a shortcut here by retaining the Mercedes pump and installing a Holley pressure regulator at the carb. We would recommend that a standard electric pump be substituted for the high-pressure pump back at the tank for safety reasons.

The Mercedes has an electric tach which can be connected directly to the Chevy ignition. Use the Mercedes water temp sender in the Chevy block, and the dash gauge will read correctly. Oil pressure is obtained via a copper tube connected to the Chevy oil pressure connection.

Keep in mind that, although the swap is basically very easy, the oil pan replacement might present problems. All in all, however, the swap is a dream with good mileage, inexpensive upkeep (compared with the Mercedes), and Mercedes good looks and long life.

As much of the original Mercedes as possible was retained. Here we see the radiator, air conditioner condenser, and auxiliary electric cooling, all stock Mercedes. There is also a transmission and crankcase oil cooling system that can be connected to the Chevy engine's lubricating system.

The stock Mercedes power steering pump (arrow) was retained by fabricating a bracket to mount it on the Chevy block. The Mercedes air conditioning system was plumbed to the Delco air conditioning compressor, and works perfectly.

The key to this swap is the use of a '66 Chevy front-sump oil pan. The pan had to be altered slightly for additional clearance at the crossmember. The steering linkage is located behind the front crossmember.

Swaps

Apparently Mercedes designed the SE for several engines. Notice the long slots in the side rails, allowing the rear crossmember an almost infinite variety of locations. For the Chevy and 400 hydro combination, the crossmember is located to the rear. The exhaust system is stock Mercedes up to the headpipes.

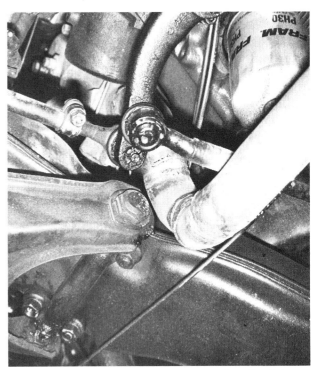

Here is where you will need a good muffler shop. Ram's-horn Chevy manifolds are used, and the exhaust headpipe is fabricated to pass between the crossmember and steering. Tricky!

Firewall clearance is minimal, but not any worse than many stock installations. There's plenty of room for an HEI distributor. Clearance around the transmission in the floor tunnel is about 1½ inches.

This close-up of the left side of the engine reveals the location of the Mercedes power steering pump and left front motor mount. The mount is a length of 3/16-inch steel plate. Prototype mount is two pieces of steel welded together; this was done while locating proper engine height. Finished mounts are one piece.

Underside view of the right side mount reveals the use of a stock Chevy motor mount on the engine block. The lower end of the fabricated steel plate mount has a foot resting on the crossmembers forward flange. Longer, grade 8 or better bolts are substituted to secure the mount foot and suspension A-arm pivot shaft.

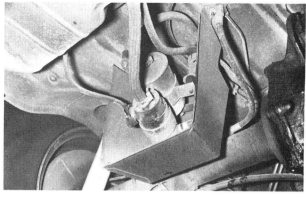

This is the stock Mercedes high-pressure fuel pump, located just ahead of the rear axle. We suggest you use a standard automotive electric fuel pump, as the high-pressure feature isn't needed and might prove dangerous.

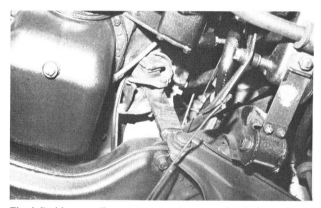

The left-side mounting system can be seen clearly here. The mount has a tubular crosspiece at the upper end to accept the long motor mount bolt. Remember to use grade 8 bolts at vital points.

It was much easier to use a Chevy driveshaft with the 400 Turbo Hydra-matic, so a small adapter was machined to mate the Chevy U-joint to the Mercedes pinion shaft companion flange. The driveshaft may have to be cut to length.

The throttle connection is straightforward. The Mercedes firewall throttle arm wasn't quite long enough to provide adequate travel, so Tom made up a slightly longer arm with several holes at the tip to fine-tune the throttle travel.

Swaps
283 Chevy V8 in Porsche

Although this swap is not for the faint of heart, it can be accomplished in ⅓ the time and at 1/17 the cost of stock-parts replacement, that is, if you opted for a new Turbo Carrera engine at about $25,000 instead of a fresh 283 Chevy V8 for around $1500. Of course, you also need Rod Simpson's kit, which in basic form is another $1540, and a host of Chevrolet, Porsche, Jaguar, Lucas, Dayco, Hedman, and Gates bits and pieces, but you'll still wind up with a 911, 912, or 914 Porsche which is easier on fuel, quicker in elapsed times and top speed in the ¼-mile, and a heck of a lot more reliable than the original car, to say nothing of a lower maintenance cost.

Once looked at in awe, and then perhaps only in a specialty car show, Chevy/Porsche swaps are Rod's stock-in-trade. But while a swapper's credo has always been "anything will fit in anything," Rod cautions that using anything bigger than a 283 will destroy expensive transaxles, clutches, and other Porsche components. You could, of course, cram a rat motor in that rear engine compartment from a physical standpoint, but why? The 283 is a reasonable, far less expensive substitute for the stock Porsche flat-motor.

And even while delivering a high mpg figure, it'll squash you back in the seat while doing it. Expect 12-second ¼-mile times and 25 mpg if the 283 is used with an Edelbrock Streetmaster intake manifold crowned with a 650 cfm Holley, an Ingle mileage cam, and a Z28 distributor running vacuum advance.

Rod's instructions are so complete they include factory part numbers for the alternate stock parts not included in the kit, as well as color photographs of one such swap in step-by-step form. But if you think the whole project is easy, be aware that Rod invites all the users of his kits to telephone him before beginning each major step.

Cooling is not the problem one would expect with a rear-mounted water-pumper, but it does take time to set it up properly. A Vette crossflow radiator, front-mounted, is recommended together with a 180-square-inch air intake opening cut into the Porsche's front sheetmetal and a larger, 200-square-inch air outlet through the front wheelwells (the kit includes templates for these). Coolant is routed through high-pressure hoses that run up and over the suspension in the front wheelwells, then on back through the hollow rocker panels, and finally to the engine compartment.

While the stock Porsche transaxle is retained, the original starter just doesn't have the beans to spin that Chevy to life, so a reworked GM starter is used. Rod uses the internals of a Buick V8 starter with a Buick marine drive and case. While the starter from a Turbo motor *could* whirl the 283, they go for a cool $627. So, the converted GM is the only way to go.

While there is a small total-car weight increase of about 100 pounds after the Chevy is installed, the balance of the car is scarcely affected. About 50 pounds of the increase goes on the front wheels through the added radiator and the dual-fan Jaguar shroud. To check handling, Rod has turned the famed Riverside Raceway course in a 283-powered 911 in 1 minute and 34 seconds. Substituting aluminum heads for the cast iron jobs trimmed 1 second off this time. With the Porsche 4.43:1 rearend ratio and using 6500 rpm as the shift point, the mph is 31 in 1st, 60 in 2nd, 90 in 3rd, 120 in 4th, and 148 at an easy 6500 rpm in o.d. 5th. That's really getting with the program, considering it's a docile powerplant instead of a sharply-honed, race-type flat-motor, and also considering the 25 mpg the combo will deliver.

So, as we say, the conversion is not easy but with care not too difficult, and while it'll relieve your purse of some of its bulk, it's much cheaper than going all-out Porsche. It's really a case of having your cake and eating it too, and that's what a performance swap like this is all about.

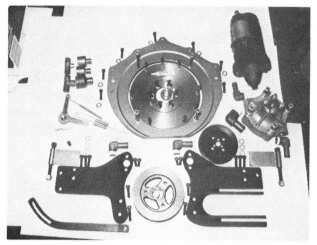

The Rod Simpson Hybrid Chevy/Porsche kit includes everything of a specialty nature needed to plant the V8 where the rear-mounted flat-motor used to live. Additional parts are factory stock from such sources as GM, Porsche, Jaguar, and others; a listing with part numbers is included in the kit's instructions. Among trick pieces shown are special water pump, clutch pressure plate, transaxle adapter, and converted Buick starter.

An alternate 283 with plate mounts needed for the 911 conversion. Here, the remote water pump is on the opposite side, and the alternator is yet to be installed.

Ready for its Porsche, this freshened and mildly reworked 283 is set up with the strut-type mounts needed for the 914s. The strut (arrow) bolts to the stock Chevy mount location on the engine to the Porsche chassis mount pad at the base. Special alternator bracket puts this necessary component down low, and a remote water pump is needed for body panel clearance.

Swaps

Once the engine is fitted with its accessories and various adapters (there's little room to add these after it's in place), it will slide in here from underneath the car; then the car will be lowered over it.

This is a 911 conversion as seen from the rear with body panels yet to be installed. Now you can see why the water pump must be remotely located.

Once everything is in place, there's fairly generous accessibility to the plugs and even the distributor. Hedman makes a special set of headers for this engine swap. Rod claims there's even room for an air conditioning unit.

Rod's kit includes bellcrank and linkage to connect the Porsche throttle assembly to the Chevy's carburetor.

Kit buyers are fortunate that Rod has effectively solved the water hose routing problem. Lines are ¾-inch i.d., necessitating enough pressure to collapse a thermostat, so one is not used; yet cooling on these conversions is no problem.

The heavy-duty Dayco hose is routed over rear suspension in the wheelwell, then through the hollow rocker panel where it is both protected and out of sight.

A Vette cross-flow radiator, shrouded to catch all the air it can from the opening cut in the front sheetmetal, can be successfully used, together with twin electric motor-driven fans from a Jaguar.

Up and over the front suspension runs the hose, and finally goes to the front-mounted radiator.

If you plan some real hard usage, Rod has this optional, custom radiator.

Kit-supplied templates are used for openings that have to be cut, as this air intake in the lower front body panel.

Swaps
231 Pontiac V6 in Datsun 4x4

As might be expected, it wasn't long after the advent of the mini-truck that owners of these vehicles began to cast envious eyes at their four-wheel drive big brothers, and wish that they too could go brush-busting in their minis. Seeing a huge potential market, Spencer Low, owner of Low Manufacturing and Dist. Co., got busy and designed a 4x4 conversion kit for the minis.

It came as no great surprise that as soon as a customer converted his mini to four-wheel drive he began to look for more power to better utilize the 4x4 potential. As Spencer puts it, "The minis aren't under-horsed, they are under-torqued." Both the Datsun and Toyota engines don't begin to develop their maximum torque until they reach 3200-3300 rpm. At this rpm with stock gearing you would be going much too fast for the slow-going required to negotiate really rough stuff. GM's little V6 engines begin to develop torque at 1500-1600 rpm, down where you need it, and torque continues to build to about 4000 rpm, which makes this swap a natural.

Suddenly Spencer was in the engine swapping business to complement the four-wheel drive conversions. Before the factories got wise, they built a lot of two-wheel drive Datsuns, Toyotas, and LUVs. Low will make the swap in any of these minis, or sell you a kit to do it yourself. Be advised, however; although there is little welding involved, there is a great deal of cutting torch work in removing crossmembers and the like before the V6 can be installed. Low charges about $350 to hang your engine in your vehicle, which doesn't include making it run; it is for installation only; you make the hookups. However, as the price goes up you can wind up with a complete drive-it-away job, where Low provides the engine and trans of your choice, from 350 Turbohydro or Muncie 4-speed to a Borg-Warner 4-speed with overdrive. This includes your choice of shifter too—stock, B&M, or Hurst. This also includes a special oversize radiator, and all drive line modifications necessary. Low can provide a complete, drive-it-away conversion.

The stock mini-truck rearend and geartrain are strong enough to handle the larger engine's power. In fact, Spencer recommends you go to a slightly higher gear ratio in the differential; 3.89:1 is about right. Datsun short bed and King Cab models came with this ratio in '80. In '78/'79, and prior to that, back to about '71, Datsun used 4.37:1 rearend gearing.

Almost any of the small V6 engines can be used in this swap; it is important that the engine have a close fitting exhaust manifold on the left side to avoid conflict with the steering. Low has a special manifold where left side clearance is no problem. Low will do engine swaps or conversion to 4x4 in any of the mini-trucks, this includes, body lift kits, installation of rollbars, winches, or anything you desire.

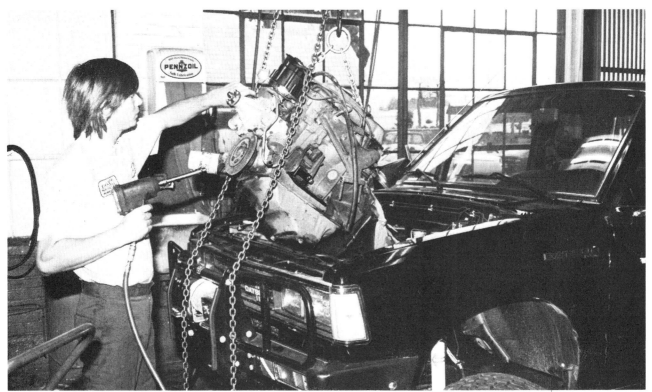

Front to rear dimensions of the '80 Datsun engine compartment are minimal. The water pump is being removed for added clearance. This is a 231 cubic inch Pontiac V6 engine.

Removing the water pump provides space to jockey the engine into position. Front-to-rear location is determined by the relationship of the rear crossmember and transmission mount.

Install the water pump temporarily before installing the radiator; fan clearances have been known to vary from model to model. The Datsun usually has adequate room for a stock fan.

Eyeball engineering comes into play here. The engine can be properly located by lining up the carb air filter bolt with a pair of dimples in the firewall. Other installations will require centering the crank pulley between the frame rails.

This is a Low custom radiator; it is wider and thicker than stock. Relocated hose fittings are enlarged to 1½ inches. The 90-degree fitting at the lower right is designed to clear the engine oil filter.

Swaps

The LUV installation has insufficient water pump clearance. Remove the pump and burn 1 inch off the hardened shaft; later, clean things up on the grinder.

These are the kit mounts, which are designed to bolt directly to the Datsun frame motor mounts. The V6 mounts are slightly ahead of the Datsun frame mount locations, and so require offset.

The upper end of the mount is designed to accept a stock GM safety block mount. The spacer between the ears prevents bending when the long motor mount bolt is drawn up tight.

Steering clearance can be a problem; choose an engine with a close-fitting manifold if possible. Low has a custom unit for this problem. Note the spacer in the steering U-joint; this is necessary as the body has been raised on the chassis for the four-wheel drive kit.

The Pontiac V6 starter is on the right side. Looking forward on the right side, you can see where the Datsun front crossmember must be burned off to provide starter clearance.

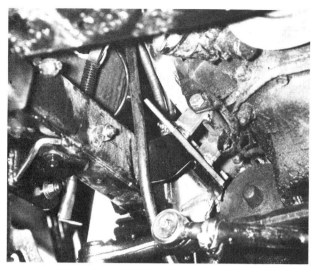

Looking aft on the right side, the minimal starter clearance is revealed along with the new motor mount bolted to the existing Datsun frame mount, providing good, solid mounting.

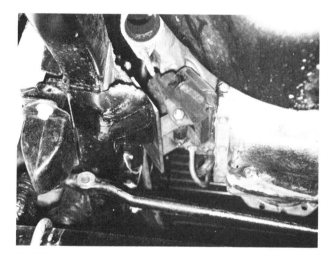

Looking forward on the left side, you can see the mount and the point at which the Datsun crossmember was removed. The crossmember not only interfered with the starter, but it would not pass under the crankcase.

Looking aft on the left side, here is where the V6 mount attached to the Datsun mount offset. Bolt-in brackets are sturdy and easy to install.

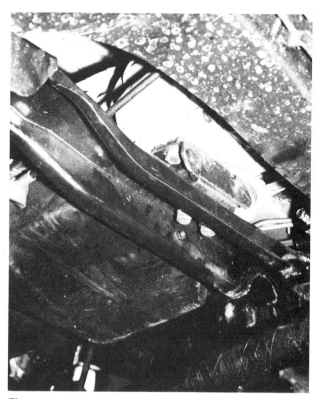

The rear crossmember remains in the stock location, but must have transmission mounting holes drilled to ½ inch for larger bolts. The transmission mounting determines fore and aft engine location when using the small automatic or 4-speed manual transmission. Note the cuts in crossmember to clear driveshaft.

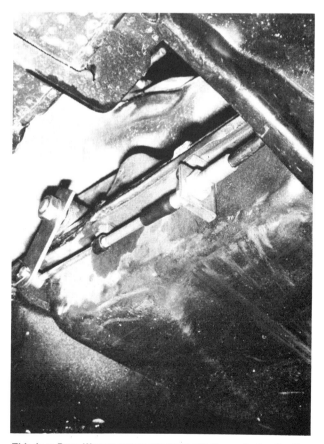

This is a Borg-Warner automatic transmission out of a Pontiac Sunbird. A B&M Quick-Click cable-controlled shifter is used.

Swaps

In this 4x4 conversion, torsion bars have been removed along with the entire front crossmember torsion arm supports. Torsion bars are retained in the two-wheel drive swap, and the front crossmember is notched to clear the starter, then boxed to restore strength.

Here, a measurement is being taken between the transmission U-joint yoke and the transfer case yoke for a short shaft. A two-wheel drive installation has a single driveshaft from transmission to differential.

Be it a two or four-wheel drive conversion, Low provides the necessary shafts, yokes, and U-joints to connect everything properly.

In the 4x4 conversion, the B&M Quick-Click shifter is mounted on the center console with the transfer case shifter on the floor. The carpet will cover the base of the shifter: a neat installation.

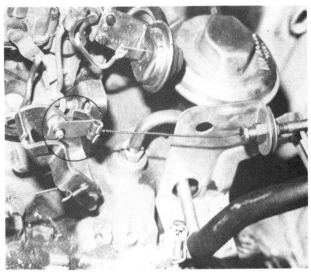

Datsun has a small motorcycle cable-type tip on the throttle cable. Low provides a small metal clip that attaches to the carb throttle arm pin and accepts the Datsun cable tip.

To simplify the electrics, Low provides a bracket to mount the Datsun alternator on the V6 engine. All that remains is to make the starter and ignition connections using the Datsun wire leads from the four-cylinder engine.

In some installations, the steering linkage will come up against the crankcase in hard right or left turns. To correct this, Low removes the pitman arm and reverses the ball joint, correcting the taper with a reamer. This allows the steering link to be installed below the pitman arm for added clearance.

When installing V6s in '72½-'79 Datsuns, it will be necessary to remove a short section of the firewall flange where it passes over the top of the bellhousing. It can be snipped and bent up or burned off as in this picture.

This is a V6 LUV installation. It is virtually identical to the Datsun installation except for the upper radiator hose connection and the GM-to-GM stock throttle hookup.

Swaps
350 GM Diesel in XJ Jaguar

While diesels require cheaper fuel and get better mileage, a "diesel-ized" Jaguar XJ would have to roll up about a million miles before it became cost-effective, that is, if you're only looking at it from a fuel economy standpoint. But when you consider that a tune-up on a Jag 6-cylinder will run the owner around $85 ($175 on a 12-cylinder) and that a valve job for a Six will run $600-$900 ($1200-*$3000* on the Twelve) and compare that to the fact that diesels don't need tune-ups and valve jobs run a fraction of the above, such a swap no longer seems so absurd.

Jaguars have everything that a superb, roadable, handsome car needs in terms of comfort, styling, quality, and so forth, but the engines . . . . Oh, they're fine for the mild weather, short trips, and the by-ways of Europe, but on America's long interstates, where daily commutes of 100 miles are not rare, and where local weather conditions can vary from -20 degrees to over 100 degrees over the course of a year, the English engines just don't stand the gaff.

Interjag offers a kit for installing the GM diesel in 6 or 12-cylinder XJs. In fact, it makes the finely-engineered parts for the Mundorf 350 Chevy V8/Jag conversion, and uses some of them on its own diesel setup. But many parts are peculiar to the diesel installation, which makes the diesel kit about twice the price of the Chevy, or about $2500 to $3000 not counting the engine and transmission work.

Transmission work you say? Yes, unfortunately. The English seem to have a fetish for making things complicated, and while the Jags of '77 and up use a Turbohydro 400, it won't match the GM bellhousing, diesel, or gas version. Also, the 400 has been English-modified to purposely slip (for a smoother shift), so you're better off opting for the standard US 400 Turbo. (But a word here to stock-trans Jag owners: If you don't like the slipping shifts, just replace your valve body with a domestic one.)

Installation more or less follows the Chevy/Jaguar swap on page 148, but there are a few differences where the diesel is concerned. The fit between the oil filter and the frame is especially tight; the exhaust system is a real headache; and the starter/steering box clearance can be measured with a thin feeler gauge. But these problems are solved for you with the Interjag kit, which also includes a wiring loom that plugs into the Jag circuitry so you have no electrical hassles. A switch to a Chevy truck diesel pan (if your engine is the Cadillac or Olds/Buick version) will open up steering and crossmember clearance. The kit's instructions, of course, detail all the problem areas and answer them for you. Or, Interjag will do the entire swap, so you needn't even get your hands dirty.

What you wind up with is high English quality in looks and general feel, but good old American engineering under the hood.

The GM diesel is a tight squeeze under the Jaguar's bonnet, but improved mpg and the low, low maintenance cost makes the swap worth exploring. Jaguar quality in all but its engine area will make the converted Jag last, and last, and last.

The stock Jaguar has an external engine cooler, which the GM diesel can plug right into. Trans oil cooling is routed through a line (arrow) to a cooler within Interjag's special radiator in this swap. A special shroud is included in the kit, and the diesel's fan is kept.

The starter, steering box, and exhaust headpipe area is really snug. This is a prototype installation with a quick-and-dirty header, but the kit pipe looks factory-made.

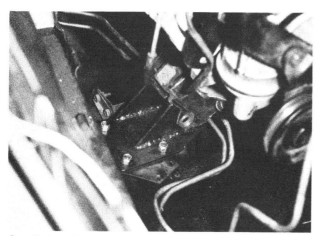

Supplied engine stands bolt to the Jaguar frame mounts and to the stock diesel insulators.

Interjag's kit includes this rather massive trans crossmember that bolts to the original Jag mount pads, and uses the diesel's rubber insulator.

The Jag's fuel plumbing is almost totally discarded. The Jaguar fuel pump at the tank is retained, and supplies fuel first to the AC filter on the inner wheelwell then to the water separator, and then to injectors.

Twin batteries mount in the trunk. Interjag solves the electrical hassle with a special loom that plugs into the Jag's wiring, allowing use of all-stock Jaguar instrumentation. The glow plug system is controlled from the ignition switch.

BARRACUDA WITH BIG MOPAR

1. As soon as Eric Rickman snapped the engine-going-in scene, he walked up, looked everything over, and issued forth a typical Rickmanesque comment: "No way."

2. But there was a way. All we needed were mounts, man, mounts. This was a typical bucks-down, non-trick operation, so the game was to get the powerplant/transmission squared away, make cardboard templates and have Don Long weld them up. Right away the street-Hemi-TorqueFlite had to be spaced forward 1½ inches from stock 273 placement with a small steel plate.

3. & 4. These are the mounts, gang — to be used with 273 biscuits normally, Hemi if you're going to race a lot. Don Long made these from 4130 steel, prompting one Chrysler engineer to comment: "They're probably the strongest thing on the car." If power, steering column/gear assembly must be exchanged for manual (PN 2880986).

5. Left-hand manifold is 383 Dart/Barracuda (PN 2899002) with 3-inch section added. Right header is 383 too (PN 2836900), but stock. Custom, tube-steel headers are strongly recommended.

6. Radiator was raised approximately 1 inch, stock 273 hoses used but in reverse; 273 fan just clears. High-performance Guardian oil filter is safety measure.

7. Unlikely enough, 440 almost fits better than 383. The 273 oil pressure sending unit must be installed to suit wiring. Additional weight of the new engine can be successfully carried by production Formula "S" heavy-duty suspension only. Working on-and-off piece-meal fashion dragged the job out far too long but the experience was still satisfying in that the engine went in virtually as is, normal pan (with windage tray), production crossmember and all. Since no cutting or welding was required (except for the exhaust) it wasn't really a major operation but then, we wouldn't exactly call it minor either.

The deal is always the same: a few minor modifications and your car — yea, your entire personality — is swept to the top of the heap. The catchword is "minor." Arlen Vanke put a 440 Magnum into this '67 Barracuda, see, and — pow! — the power of Dr. Frankenstein was unleashed upon unsuspecting 435 'Vettes before their vacuum-operated secondaries could come in. Plymouth was pretty interested in the 440/Barracuda combination not only because of the plastic cars but 427 Camaros were coming out from every rock and the hottest car they had was the Hemi which, for some reason, was relegated to a special class along with other nuclear weapons unsuitable for conventional warfare. Oh, yes, there was the 383 'Cuda but its severely restricted manifolding, which breathes about like one of the "baddies" Roy Rogers used to lasso off a moving horse, put it somewhat at a disadvantage. Anyhow, the way the public relations people saw it, we could duplicate the swap ourselves at home with simple hand-tools and the resulting story would possibly create the demand for the factory to do it. We had Arlen's step-by-step instructions, didn't we? Oh, you bet.

—Eric Dahlquist